THEORY AND PRACTICE OF EDUCATION
Third Edition

Meriel Downey is former Deputy Dean and Head of B.Ed at Goldsmiths' College. She is the author of *Moral Education* (with A.V. Kelly) and *Interpersonal Judgements in Education*.

Professor A.V. Kelly is Dean of the School of Education, Goldsmiths' College. He has written and edited numerous books on education and the curriculum, including *The Curriculum, theory and practice, The Primary Curriculum* and *The Primary Curriculum in Action* (all with Geva Blenkin), *Microcomputers in the Curriculum, Knowledge and Curriculum Planning* and *Early Childhood Education*. His most recent book is *The Curriculum, theory and practice 3/e*

THEORY AND PRACTICE OF EDUCATION

Third Edition

Meriel Downey and A.V. Kelly

P·C·P
Paul Chapman
Publishing Ltd

71509

370.1
DOW

British Library Cataloguing in Publication Data
Downey, Meriel
    Theory and practice of education. – 3rd ed.
    1. Education
    I. Title   II. Kelly, A.V.
    370'.1   LB1025.2

    ISBN 1 85396 094 2

Typeset by Gedset Limited, Cheltenham
Printed and bound by Athenaeum Press, Newcastle upon Tyne

E F 4 3

CONTENTS

vi

Foreword

The publication in 1975 of the first edition of this book was prompted by a conviction that an integrated and practically relevant approach to the study of educational issues was needed and the belief that little of the literature then available in the field of education theory was meeting that need. The response to that book from practitioners of education, both serving and student teachers, was such as to suggest both that we had been right to identify that need and that we had succeeded in beginning the process of meeting it. This encouraged us to offer a second, revised and extended edition in 1979, and the response to that was equally satisfying. This continuing interest has now emboldened us to offer a third edition.

Some of the revisions we have made here have been suggested by our own criticisms of the earlier editions; some by the comments of many interested colleagues and students. They reflect in the main the continuously developing nature of educational theory and practice, and the changes which will be apparent in this third edition are primarily the result of our attempts to keep pace with that. Again, we would stress that what is offered here is intended merely to help teachers and students to identify the issues and to suggest how they might explore them further. It is not our purpose to provide a substitute for reading and examining educational research and publications at first hand.

At one level, then, the concern has been to update discussions of all the issues we address ourselves to by including reference to recent developments in research and publications. Beyond that, however, two particular general themes have been built into these discussions more explicitly than hitherto — those of race and gender in education. The chapter on the curriculum has been extensively revised, indeed much of it has been rewritten, to take account of the rapid and dramatic events of the last several years in that field, in particular the increase of political intervention in curriculum planning and the massive output of documentation on curriculum from official sources. And a new concluding chapter has been added which explores and attempts to define the kind of educational theory and research which teachers are most likely to find of value as they attempt to respond to the increased demands created by these external pressures and, conversely, the kind which is more likely to inhibit their work by adding to these pressures.

We hope, then, that this third edition will prove as useful and helpful to teachers and students of education in the last half of the 1980s as its two forbears seem to have been during the last ten years. And we hope that those who have received the first two editions of the book so generously, and by doing so supported us in what we were attempting to do through them both for education theory and for the practice of education, will agree with our assessment of the changes of emphasis which are now needed and will welcome this third edition with equal generosity.

Meriel Downey
Vic Kelly

October 1985

Introduction

Although the picture is a good deal more cheering than it was, the theoretical basis of the practice of education is still far from satisfactory, The gulf between theory and practice continues to yawn so that discussions of educational issues can still be divided into those that are academic to the point of almost total irrelevance and those that, in their determination to be practical, lose sight of the need for a proper rigour and the right kind of academic basis. The academicism of the former has been rejected by many practising teachers so that, since there can be no practice in any sphere without principles of some kind, they have come to rely on little that is more substantial than folk-lore, intuition or even passing whims and fancies. On the other hand, the absence of any kind of intellectual base for the other kind of debate has prevented the emergence of a satisfactory form of educational theory and has led to an undue reliance on other more clearly established bodies of knowledge — in particular those of philosophy, psychology and sociology.

Decisions of educational policy, therefore, some of them of a far-reaching kind, have been made either under the urgings of some ideological view promulgated by whatever political faction happens to be in power, as has been the case with the comprehensivization of secondary education, or on the basis of evidence culled from some other field of knowledge which can have only a partial contribution to make to any educational issue, as was the case with the establishment of selective forms of secondary education. At the same time, the decisions made by the individual teacher in relation to the education of his or her own pupils are still too often made on the basis of a less than adequate appreciation of their significance and implications or of alternative approaches that might be more productive.

The fundamental problem is that no one has ever been quite clear what education theory is and, until recently, no one has been sufficiently convinced of its importance to endeavour to find out.

The term 'theory' seems to have at least three different meanings. In the first place, it is most commonly used to refer to an explanation of a group of related scientific phenomena, as when we speak of the theory of radiation. In this kind of context, it denotes a set of interconnected hypotheses that have been framed in order to describe and explain a particular series of natural phenomena. The word 'theory' is also used, however, to refer to a body of doctrines, a collection not of descriptions but of prescriptions intended not to explain but to guide action. It is in this sense that the word is used when we speak of such things as Marxist theory, where the concern is to offer a coherent body of opinion, a 'philosophy'. Finally, we find the term used in an intermediate sense, in which it does no more than pick out a related body of problems, as when we speak of the theory of knowledge. Here we are neither referring to an explanatory system nor to any particular set of views; we are merely indicating the relatedness of certain kinds of problem.

Much of the difficulty that has surrounded education theory arises from the fact that no one has been clear into which of these categories to put it, or, indeed, whether it fits into any of them. Some have seen it as being a kind of scientific theory, an attempt to frame hypotheses to explain certain phenomena. They have been attracted, therefore, to the scientific versions of psychology or sociology, to behaviourism and/or to positivism, and the result of this has been that their view of educational problems has been one-sided and inadequate and their practice consequently misguided. A scientific theory is concerned, as we saw, to describe and explain; it may even be used as a basis for prediction, although in the case of the human sciences this is fraught with particular difficulties; but alone it can never provide guides for action; practical decisions must be made also in the light of other considerations. Any view of education, therefore, that excludes such considerations because it is taken from the standpoint of any one of these disciplines will be a warped and dangerous view, as the history of the development of the educational system in Britain and of the curriculum both there and elsewhere will reveal.

Others have, therefore, taken the view that education theory involves the generation of bodies of doctrine, collections of more or less coherent prescriptions as to what teachers and schools ought to be doing. This approach has led to the production of a great deal of what has rightly been castigated as 'mush' or 'beautiful thoughts' and has done more than anything else to bring educational theory into disrepute. As a result, it has in recent years been rejected entirely in favour of a more rigorous and differentiated study of the 'foundation' or 'contributory' disciplines of education, in particular philosophy, psychology, and sociology. Unfortunately, this seems to have been an over-reaction, a rejection of the baby with the bath water. For one merit that the prescriptive approach did have was that it injected into discussions of education a sense of purpose, an awareness that education is a practical activity, essentially concerned with issues of value, and some ideas about what teachers and schools ought to be doing, of a kind that can never come from the sciences of psychology or sociology or from the analytical processes of the philosopher. This element is vital if education theory is to have full relevance for educational practice.

In fact, it seems that education theory must have elements in it of all the three kinds of theory that we delineated. It denotes a range of problems, those practical problems that teachers and others concerned with the practice of education need to give thought to and to make decisions about; it needs to offer some set or sets of views that may help us to decide on the directions in which these decisions are to take us; and it must also contain a proper and rigorous scientific basis to ensure that these decisions are theoretically sound and consistent with whatever evidence is available.

If this is what education theory is or ought to be, two things seem to be required to ensure that it offers the teacher the support he or she needs. In the first place, it must start and end with the problems that the practice of education throws up; it must be firmly rooted in the school and the classroom and must have a direct practical relevance to all aspects of the teacher's work. Without this, it is the study of something else and not of education, which is after all a practical activity, or it is a study of education from the outside. Secondly, if it is to deal adequately with issues of this kind its approach must not lean too heavily on other disciplines or bodies of theory which have been devised for other purposes and are concerned to consider different questions. We have already commented on the disastrous consequences of basing educational decisions only on psychological or sociological considerations. We must add our conviction that it is not enough that the study of education should draw on all relevant disciplines separately. A much more concerted approach than that is needed. It is not what each individual discipline or subject has to contribute to any particular issue that is interesting, important, and useful; it is the combined effect of them that is needed, along with something more, a full account of and allowance for the purposes and principles of our educational activities.

Lastly, both of these objectives must be achieved without loss of rigour. We must not return to the days of 'mush' or 'beautiful thoughts' unless it be to sort out the mush and find a sound basis for the beautiful thoughts. We are now entering a further stage in the development of educational theory when it can stand in its own right as a rigorous body of theoretical knowledge that all teachers can respect and profit from in the practice of their profession.

It is towards that end that this book has been written. We hope that it will link theory to practice and bring a coherence to the theory itself in a way that will not only help students of education to pass their examinations but will also improve their professionalism as teachers. We hope too that it will prove of value to practising teachers and will lead to a better understanding of some of the highly complex professional tasks they must undertake.

We have tried to focus, therefore, on those aspects of education theory that are directly relevant to the practice of the teacher in the classroom. All areas of education theory should have such relevance for the work of the schools but, since some selection had to be made, we felt it appropriate here to concentrate on those areas which are of immediate import for the individual teacher.

We have begun with an examination of that interchange that occurs in every classroom between the teacher and the pupils and among the pupils themselves, since the teacher's understanding of the educational process must begin with an appreciation of that interaction that is its base. We have then considered, as a particularly important aspect of this interaction, how the judgements that teachers make of their pupils and the attitudes they have towards them can determine the progress those pupils will make in their education. We go on to discuss in more detail some of the most significant of these judgements and attitudes — the views the teacher holds about the nature of intelligence and the kinds of ability he or she values, his or her approach to the problem of motivating pupils, the multiple impact of language differences, the methods of control that he or she favours, and his or her attitudes to questions of freedom and authority and relationships generally, examining in particular the implications of these for the personal, social and moral education of children. We have then looked at some of the questions that need to be asked about the curriculum, since the current trend towards an increased individualization of educational provision places responsibility for many decisions in this area on the individual teacher, while current governmental policies are leading away from this kind of individualization and towards an increase of external, and even centralized, control and thus towards a reduction in the scope of action available both to schools and to teachers in this crucial area. The tension created by this dispute over where curriculum decisions can most effectively be taken is thus a major focus of this chapter. The debate over the curriculum raises in turn questions about the notion of equality of opportunity in education, about the significant failure to achieve this and, in particular, about the role of the curriculum both as the source of inequalities and as a potential solution to this problem. It is to these issues that we turn next. Finally, we have returned to the issue of the relation of theory to practice in education and we have devoted some attention to the questions of why so much research in education, along with the theoretical perspectives it has generated, has in the past been largely ignored by teachers and what kinds of new approach to research must be explored and adopted if teachers are to take it seriously and if it is to have any kind of proper influence on the development of educational practice. This discussion, then, which is the subject of our final chapter, brings us full circle back to the central ambition outlined in this Introduction — the desire to assist towards the achievement of a more productive relationship between the theory and practice of education.

If we have failed to attain our objectives, we hope that this will be attributed to our own inadequacies rather than to any fundamental weakness in the view of education theory from which we start, since it remains our conviction that unless something is done to establish the study of education along the lines we have indicated, both the theory and the practice of education will continue to be held back from their proper development.

CHAPTER 1

CLASSROOM INTERACTION

Education, as most teachers, parents, and pupils will agree, is essentially a social process. When children come to school, they do not simply learn a given body of knowledge which they carry away in neat packages as though they had been shopping. Rather they learn from other people, both teachers and peers, by sharing their knowledge and experience, by seeing the world through their eyes and by developing an understanding of what others consider important and worthwhile. Their learning is not only cognitive but also social, emotional and moral. In other words, children are not only developing their intellectual abilities by mastering concepts and retaining facts relating to various curriculum areas, but are at the same time learning to communicate with others, to form judgements of them and eventually to develop autonomy both intellectually and morally. Almost all learning situations provided in school are then essentially social in nature, apart from the occasions when pupils, usually older ones, withdraw on their own to the library for private study to consolidate what they have learned in the company of others. The ways in which teachers and pupils interact and the factors which influence this interaction will be of prime importance if we are to try to understand the social context of education.

This chapter sets out first of all to describe the origins and the development of techniques of interaction studies. We shall then go on to analyse some of the factors affecting teacher-pupil interaction and to consider the effect of teaching style on pupil behaviour. Studies of pupil interaction, the use of language by pupils and teachers, and the implications for curriculum development of classroom interaction will be discussed. Many of these issues will be developed in greater detail in later chapters in the book.

Methods of studying classroom interaction

Interaction studies have their roots in social psychology and were initiated by American researchers. Lewin, Lippitt, and White (1939) first drew attention to the importance of group dynamics and leadership patterns for the way in which children work together and behave, depending on whether the group leader adopted an authoritarian, democratic, or laissez-faire style. Their studies however were essentially laboratory-type observations, where adult leaders were trained to exercise particular leadership styles with groups of children working in an extra-curricular setting. Anderson and Brewer (1945) showed that with a democratic or socially integrative teacher, children were relaxed and friendly, worked well together, and showed an interest in what they were doing. Children working with an authoritarian or dominative teacher were likely to be over-submissive, yet aggressive and uncooperative when left on their own. Studies of this nature abounded in American research during the 1950s and early 1960s, while at the same time, in this country and in the USA, psychologists were developing sociometric techniques, based on the work of Moreno (1934), in order to map patterns of interaction between pupils. The procedure is in fact so straightforward that it has been used by many class teachers to help them group children at the beginning of the year in a way that the pupils themselves find acceptable. All that is needed is for the teacher to ask his pupils relatively simple questions, for example, to say whom they would like to sit next to, work with on a group basis, or choose as a partner for PE. From this information, friendship patterns within the class emerge; isolates who are not chosen by anybody are identified; highly popular children and closely knit cliques are recognized.

However, interaction studies of a more systematic kind were not developed until Flanders (1970) introduced his Interaction Analysis Categories (FIAC), designed primarily for examining teacher-pupil interaction by coding and classifying classroom talk. Flanders devised a series of ten categories into which public classroom talk could be classified: seven categories for teachers, two for pupils, and one residual. An independent observer listening to classroom talk then records and codes what is being said over a given period of time, say, forty minutes. Eventually the score for any one teacher can be worked out arithmetically and compared with scores gained by other teachers, as a measure of what proportion of their teaching time is spent talking. Such studies soon revealed that what is now known as the law of two-thirds operates in most classrooms where class teaching is the principal method used. Two-thirds of classroom time in typical American schools was usually spent talking, and two-thirds of this talk was done by teachers. Wragg (1973), using a similar technique, found that the same held good for British classrooms. And although it might be expected that the proportion of talk would be reduced in less formal, more open classrooms, where pupils are encouraged to talk more among themselves, Walker and Adelman (1976) found that teacher talk still dominates to a similar degree, although it is of a less public nature. Indeed the later ORACLE studies carried out by Galton and others (1975-1980) show that even in primary classrooms where an individualized learning approach is adopted, teachers still spend much of their time telling individual pupils what to do and asking closed factual questions.

The sort of systematic observation schedule introduced and developed by Flanders has clear advantages over earlier methods of studying teacher style. Firstly, it was planned specifically for classroom analysis, unlike the earlier studies which were based upon techniques drawn from social psychology and developed within a laboratory setting. Secondly, it pioneered the way for studies of different teaching styles such as those carried out by Ashton (1975) and Bennett (1976) and also gave impetus to studies of language in the classroom, of which there were very few before the 1970s. Nevertheless, although this kind of analysis can provide systematic data on certain aspects of classroom interaction, for instance by showing the overall differences between ways of teaching, it has its limitations. It does not show enough detail about teacher-pupil interaction to explain why teachers differ from one another or why their behaviour varies according to the particular group of children they are teaching.

Galton et al. (1980) used systematic observation techniques to study teacher and pupil behaviour in primary classrooms. Whereas researchers using Flanders' Interaction Analysis Category (FIAC) system had paid little attention to classroom organization or curriculum planning, Galton's team aimed to remedy some of the weaknesses of earlier research of this kind. Not only were observational data gathered on the behaviour of teachers and pupils, but trained observers also obtained information about classroom organization and curriculum activities during visits to schools. They were thus able to examine organizational and curriculum variables alongside classroom interaction. This kind of analysis was intended to identify different pupil and teacher behaviour relating to achievement over a range of curriculum activities and with different types of classroom management.

There still remains however the problem of the disturbing and possibly distorting effect of an observer in the classroom, however inconspicuous he or she tries to be. The ORACLE studies were carried out in fifty-eight primary classes, each of which was visited for six teaching sessions (of approximately one hour each) in each term of the year — that is, eighteen sessions in all. We need to ask whether such a schedule of visits where a relative stranger is introduced into the classroom is really an ideal method of observing behaviours 'as they really are'. A further problem is that it is very difficult, if not impossible, for the observer to understand the hidden culture of the classroom with its subtle nuances in language, nonverbal communication and rituals unique to any one group.

Other research techniques have been developed which do not rely on prespecified schedules, but which allow categories and concepts to emerge over a period of time during the research. Techniques of participant observation, hitherto not used in the classroom, have during the past decade or so become recognized as far more productive and accurate, while at the same time imposing fewer restrictions on the observer. More flexible teaching methods and open classrooms have made such a development possible in that both teacher and pupils feel less inhibited by a researcher, when they are already used to working informally and very often welcome visiting speakers to contribute to their work. And many researchers, like Lacey (1970), who taught in the school in which he gathered the material for his study of Hightown Grammar, have some teaching built into their research programme. After a two-month period of finding his way around, getting to know the teachers and the structure of the school, Lacey spent a further sixteen months in the school, during which he taught twelve periods per week and observed for a further twelve. Similarly, Hargreaves (1967) spent a whole year at Lumley Secondary School, teaching all the fourth-year boys, on whom the study was focused, at some stage, as well as observing the same boys being taught by other teachers. Both took part extensively in extra-curricular activities. Woods (1976) spent a year in a mixed rural secondary school, as participant observer, in order to collect data for his study of survival strategies used by teachers. Such methods avoid the use of prepared observation schedules since these fail to allow for the unexpected. On the contrary, observers are free to record any unit of teacher or pupil behaviour that they find relevant to their investigations, but unless the observer is intimately acquainted with the particular teachers and pupils he is studying, much of the significance of their behaviour is likely to be misunderstood or to prove completely baffling. Walker and Adelman (1976) show how classroom talk (or indeed conversation of any kind) is full of hidden meanings, and jokes are shared only by those among whom they have arisen. A stranger walking into a classroom and hearing the following snippet of conversation would surely wonder what was going on:

Teacher: Wilson, we'll have to put you away if you don't change your ways and do your homework. Is that all you've done?

Wilson: Strawberries, strawberries. (Laughter from class)

Apparently the teacher had once commented that some boys' work was like strawberries, 'good as far as it goes, but it doesn't last nearly long enough'. This remark had in time become part of the culture of that particular classroom. Such personal meanings are not readily accessible to those outside the immediate experience of the group. To understand the richness of such associations, the researcher has himself to become, at least for a time, a member of that group. No amount of analysis in the Flanders style would uncover such hidden meanings.

Most researchers concerned with classroom interaction studies insist now on the importance of long-term participant observation studies. Furlong (1976), in a case study of how pupils judge their teachers, acted as participant observer in a class of fifteen-year-olds for two terms in a school where he had taught for three years. It was this context that prompted him to develop the concept of an 'interaction set', a more flexible tool than 'friendship group' that can be used to explain how and when pupils interact to control classroom activity. Short-term observations would not have allowed time for the nature of this particular kind of group perspective to become apparent.

Walker and Adelman (1976), as we have already seen, use long-term observation and have developed valuable techniques of recording data, using both film and audio recordings as well as taking extensive notes as they watch whatever is going on in classrooms. In 1973 they initiated the Ford Teaching Project, designed to monitor the practices of forty teachers in fourteen East Anglian schools who were attempting to use enquiry/discovery methods. Similar techniques were employed in their SAFARI project, which set out to examine the effects of four major curriculum innovations: Nuffield Secondary Science; the Humanities Curriculum Project; Geography for the Young School Leaver; and Project Technology. Because Walker and Adelman are interested not only in teacher-pupil interaction, but also in teachers' interaction with heads of departments, heads, advisers, and so on, they are extending their methods to include case histories and life histories of individual teachers. Classroom interaction, they claim, is affected not only by what goes on inside the four walls, but also by outside influences impinging upon the teacher's interpretation of what is significant and upon his relationships with others who less often enter his teaching arena.

We see that, although observation techniques have become more sophisticated, there is still no foolproof method which eliminates the effects of the observer's presence and presents findings objectively. Participant observation studies which have the advantage of greater flexibility in the absence of a prespecified schedule, inevitably allow a high degree of subjective judgement.

Teacher-pupil interaction

Interaction between teachers and pupils depends not only on a deliberate policy adopted by the teacher to encourage pupils to communicate with them and with their peers, but also upon factors implicit in the situation which impinge upon social behaviour. Some of the most important forces influencing the nature of interaction are the physical setting: rules, rituals and routine of the classroom; interpersonal judgements and mode of communication, both verbal and nonverbal. We shall therefore consider here ways in which some of these factors can affect classroom interaction, leaving a discussion of language until later, since it is important enough to warrant a separate section.

Until fairly recently, studies of interaction had curiously ignored the nature of the physical setting in which interaction takes place. However, if we examine the spatial context more closely, we shall appreciate how the use of space within the school and the classroom affects social behaviour. The location of the school itself can have a significant impact on the formation of friendship groups and cliques. The vexed problem of splitsite buildings affects not only the way in which pupils interact as they have to make a rushed change from one building to another, but also the way in which teachers have contact with one another. It is not unusual for some teachers to be quite unacquainted with colleagues working mainly in another building. One administrative solution to the problem of time-wasting movement brought about by constant switches from one building to another has been to allocate teachers and pupils mainly to one site. But this often results in an unhappy rift between younger and older pupils, not to mention apparent stratification of teachers into upper and lower school staff. However, individual teachers seldom have any control over such major physical considerations; it is the physical layout of their own classroom that they can plan themselves up to a point.

Traditional classrooms provided for chalk and talk teaching methods, with a class of children sitting in straight rows facing the teacher and a blackboard. The teacher's authority was symbolized by his or her position behind a desk, often raised onto a dais. In this way the teacher was not only physically separated from his pupils, often indeed regarding his desk as a protective barrier, but was psychologically remote from them. Such a physical context was highly appropriate for didactic teaching methods where the teacher talked most of the time, on average two-thirds of it, as Flanders showed. Adams and Biddle (1970), using videotape recordings from a large number of classrooms, showed that teachers interact most of all in this kind of setting with pupils sitting in a V-shaped wedge down the middle of the room, paying less attention to those at the sides and at the back. Pupils are clearly aware of this, as most teachers know who have witnessed the rush for places in the back row by those who wish to escape notice. Most infant and junior schools have long since dispensed with the formally arranged classroom in favour of one where furniture is easily moved about and can be arranged to meet the needs of particular activities, which in turn encourage different kinds of interaction among children. Of the fifty-eight classrooms in the Galton study only four contained pupils sitting in rows facing the teacher, while in the rest, children sat in groups. However, although this method of seating aims to encourage cooperation and collaborative learning, most pupils observed in the study were engaged in individual work and most teachers spent their time in private exchanges with children, thus leading to a very unbalanced kind of interaction. Experiments with open-plan classrooms and school buildings allow added flexibility, though it has been noted that most children feel more secure when they have a home base and a specific place in which to keep their belongings. Secondary schools have been rather tardy in breaking away from formally arranged seating, but many curriculum projects in operation nowadays require a far greater degree of flexibility and hence a greater proportion of pupil interaction than class teaching. The Humanities Curriculum Project, designed to develop in pupils of fourteen to sixteen the ability to think critically about controversial issues, uses discussion as its main learning technique. Clearly pupils cannot discuss seriously unless the physical setting allows them to watch other members of the group as they are talking. Seating arrangements must allow for this and not inhibit the give-and-take of argument between pupils by a setting where remarks can only be addressed to the teacher. Indeed, the teacher, as neutral chairman, cannot be in a position which suggests to group members that he knows the answer to problems under discussion.

It is interesting to note that, in most studies of mixed classrooms, teachers interact far more with boys than with girls. Stanworth (1980) reports that at all ages boys receive a disproportionate share of the teacher's time and attention regardless of the sex of the teacher. Spender (1980) shows that boys tend to dominate classroom talk, to call out and to interrupt more than girls, while Clarricoates (1978) points out that boys in primary classrooms demand teacher attention by creating a disturbance if their interests are not met. One result of constantly reprimanding boys who misbehave is, according to Sarah (1980), to reinforce boys' assertiveness and to contribute towards the feeling that they are the dominant and superior sex, but an obvious consequence is that girls tend to receive less teacher attention.

We know from the work of Argyle (1969) the importance of the function of nonverbal communication in interaction. Gestures, facial expression, bodily posture, eye-contact all play an important part in conveying meanings implicitly to others. A teacher who sits behind a table or a desk so that children who want to speak to him have to form a queue, is implying by his very position a different sort of interaction with his class from one who walks around and sits down with an individual or a group to discuss their work. Tone of voice too can suggest enthusiasm and general interest or, on the other hand, impatience and exasperation, without any change in the actual words used.

To some extent we all, teachers or not, use nonverbal means of projecting a particular self-image to others, or, as Goffman (1959) puts it, we present a personal front to others. Teachers, sometimes deliberately, but occasionally without being aware of it, play upon external features to convey to their pupils the sort of personality they would like pupils to think they have. Dress, hairstyle, mode of speech, and posture can all help to project a particular self-image which can encourage or inhibit interaction with pupils. Delamont (1976a) showed how pupils' judgements about their teachers can be affected by the personal front they project. Of two teachers she observed in the same school, one dressed severely in tweed suits, seldom sat down in class unless she was marking books, and hardly ever indulged in casual converation with her pupils. The other teacher dressed fashionably in styles the girls themselves might have chosen, carried her books in a shopping basket rather than a brief-case, sat in a relaxed fashion on pupils' desks, and chatted informally with them. Most pupils felt more at ease with the second teacher but all agreed that the other was very efficient and made them work hard and behave properly. It is jnteresting however that pupils do not always appreciate teachers who try to adopt a casual image. Many of them prefer to maintain a minimum of social distance and regard it as an encroachment on their privacy if teachers dress or speak in their style.

Interpersonal judgement, as we shall see in the next chapter, is one form of social interaction and as such is an integral part of classroom dynamics. The process of forming judgements of others is essentially interactive rather than reactive in nature. When we perceive others and judge their behaviour, the judgement we make in turn affects the way they behave towards us. Thus, as we know from the ample evidence drawn from research on self-fulfilling prophecies, unfavourable judgements made by teachers of pupils are coupled with low expectations of attainment. In response to this, pupils often do achieve little, partly because their motivation is depressed and partly because the teacher offers little to stretch their abilities (Downey, 1977).

Judgements made of an individual by others of significance to him play an important part in the development of the self. G. H. Mead (1934) sees the self as a social product arising from the experience of a child interacting with significant others, as he terms them, namely parents, peers, teachers, and so on. The self, in his view, develops as a result of the interpretations a child makes of how others perceive, judge, and evaluate him. Thus the self or self-concept is influenced initially by the child's parents, but since its development is continuous, it is affected too by his teachers and peers when he comes to school. Teachers can either reinforce the view a child has of himself, be it a positive or negative one, or help to reverse a child's negative self-concept or boost his self-esteem by creating in him a more positive view of himself and his abilities.

Concern about the negative effects of teacher expectations upon pupil performance, motivation, behaviour in class has been widespread over the past two decades, particularly since the publication of the rather dubious findings of Rosenthal and Jacobson (1968). However, later evidence has substantiated the claims they made (Downey, 1977) and most teachers are at least aware of the influence they can have over their pupils in this respect. But as we mentioned earlier, since interpersonal judgement is a two-way and therefore essentially an interaction process, we should expect to find that pupils' judgements of their teachers affect them in some degree. So far there is little systematic evidence to show the nature of this influence clearly, but what little there is suggests that most pupils have similar expectations of their teachers. In Taylor's study (1962), pupils were required to indicate their notion of a good teacher by rating him on control, personal qualities, and teaching skills. Nash (1974) used Kelly's personal construct theory to investigate pupils' attitudes towards their teachers, in order to discover primary school children's concept of an ideal teacher. More recently Furlong (1976), using participant observation techniques and talking casually to a class of fifteen-year-olds, investigated their expectations of a good teacher. All these studies, despite their varying methodology and the different age groups under scrutiny, suggested that most pupils have a similar, fairly stereotyped concept of the ideal teacher. He is one who can keep a class in order, make them work hard, explains clearly, provides a clear structure for them, and who is fair in dealing with them. It seems strange at a time when students and pupils are demanding more responsibility that the concept of an ideal teacher that emerges from these studies is of one who allows little freedom of choice. Pupils seem to want guidance and to be made to behave well and to work hard. It is when a teacher does not live up to these expectations that pupils tend to misbehave, as Furlong's study showed. But some degree of negotiation inevitably goes on in a classroom. Although pupils like teachers to be strict, there has to be mutual agreement about what counts as being strict, as Werthman (1963) showed in the study of delinquent adolescents in school. Through this process of negotiation, to which we shall return later on, acceptable norms of behaviour are worked out between the teacher and his class, though clearly, since they are arrived at by mutual consent, the norms will vary according to the particular class and the particular teacher.

Interaction in most classrooms is supported by some kind of routine or ritual which provides a structure or framework for the pupils and gives support to teachers. In fact, Woods (1976) regards ritual and routine as part of a teacher's survival kit. However, the regularity of routine imposes a structure on school life which both pupils and teachers come to accept. Among the most common routines are of course school assemblies, registration, handing in homework, and queuing up for lunch. Teachers who regularly begin their lessons with some sort of formal greeting can usually be sure of a response even though behaviour may deteriorate later. School rules too provide a structure for teachers and pupils and, provided they are rationally based, most pupils will accept them without undue infringement. Rules within any one classroom are negotiable but, once they have been agreed upon, become an essential part of classroom interaction, so that children who see others breaking them are often duly indignant. Rules of this kind must hold for teachers and pupils alike. For instance, if children are not permitted to wear outdoor coats in class, they can see no good reason why teachers should have the privilege of doing so. Rules and classroom ritual are essentially unwritten. They belong to the hidden curriculum and are apparent only to those who participate and as such are a part of classroom interaction accessible only to an observer who spends a long period of time as a participant.

Teaching styles and pupil behaviour

Our discussion of aspects of classroom interaction, such as the physical layout adopted by the teacher, his personal image, interpersonal judgements made by teachers and pupils of one another, suggests that there is a wide discretionary area where teachers are free to adopt their own style, regardless of the type of school in which they teach or the age group of children with whom they are concerned. As we have already seen, early studies of variation in teaching styles were rooted in leadership studies carried out by social psychologists. However, since the mid 1960s those concerned with the theory of education, as well as practising teachers, have tended to use pairs of terms to distinguish pedagogical styles such as 'progressive/traditional', 'child-centred/teacher-centred', 'formal/informal', 'discovery-learning/instruction'. Teachers consider themselves progressive if they work in an unstreamed situation, use discovery methods rather than instruction, encourage collaborative or individualized learning rather than relying mainly on class teaching. Interest and even controversy have centred around the relative advantages and disadvantages of different teaching styles for pupils' progress and behaviour in class. Teachers employing informal methods have claimed that their pupils are more cooperative, more interested in their work, are better behaved, and even make greater progress. Some early research comparing streamed with unstreamed classes at the primary level indicated an improvement in the social adjustment of pupils even though there was no significant difference in scholastic performance (Kelly, 1978).

Flanders (1970) was one of the first to attempt a systematic analysis of factors which affect classroom interaction by examining the degree and nature of verbal exchange in American classrooms. Flanders initiated an eight-year research programme involving the development of interaction analysis as a tool for quantifying patterns of teacher influence upon pupils. One hundred and forty-seven teachers representing all age levels took part in the study. Overall findings, as we saw earlier, produced the rule of two-thirds: about two-thirds of the time spent in the average classroom is taken up by somebody talking. Although these are findings for the average classroom studied, Flanders' hypothesis that the more indirect the teacher's influence, the more favourable were pupils' attitudes towards school, was supported by a comparison of differences in interaction scores. Teachers who spoke for only about 50% of the time and who were less directive when they were speaking produced in their pupils more constructive attitudes towards classroom activities, hence their interaction was of a more positive nature. In this country Wragg's study (1973) of classroom talk suggests that positive interaction, indicated by the proportion of pupil talk, tends to diminish as children progress throughout secondary school. The amount of pupil talk in the classes he studied fell from 32% in the first year to 23% in the fifth year. Unexpectedly, pupils also talked less in the sixth form than in their earlier school careers. A greater degree of pupil participation might have been expected since most sixth-form pupils are taught in smaller groups.

Notions of freedom and control are central to problems of teaching style, and findings suggest that a teacher's personal style is revealed by the proportion of time he spends talking and the nature of the language he uses. Before we look more closely at teachers' use of language in the classroom, let us explore a little more some of the studies of teaching style.

Ashton and others (1975) in a national survey of 1513 primary school-teachers found that, although they readily saw themselves as either progressive or traditional, there was a great deal of consensus between them over basic issues. They all gave high priority to the basic skills of literacy, numeracy and oracy, and agreed that children should be brought up as acceptable members of their community and to conform to its conventions. It seems then as though their overall aims were the same although they claimed to exercise different methods of achieving these aims.

Drawing on a sample of 871 primary schools in Lancashire and Cumbria, Bennett (1976) analysed different teaching styles and attempted to assess the effects of these on pupils' progress. The two major questions he set out to explore were, firstly, whether different teaching styles resulted in disparate pupil progress and, secondly, whether different types of pupil performed better under certain styles of teaching. From responses given to questionnaires by all third- and fourth-year teachers in the schools studied, twelve teacher types, ranging from the informal to the highly formal, were distinguished by a process of cluster analysis. Informal teachers were those who favoured integration of subject content and allowed pupils choice and responsibility for pursuing their own tasks. They allowed children to sit where they wanted, to move about the classroom, and to talk to one another while they were working. Formal teachers preferred to teach subjects separately and chose class teaching as their main approach. They did not allow pupils to choose their own seats, nor were talking or walking about the classroom permitted. These examples are of course extreme types; mixed styles, as a closer analysis of Bennett's findings reveals, vary in the extent to which they approach a high degree of formality or informality. Although the overall findings suggest that pupil progress in the basic skills is promoted more by formal and mixed styles of teaching than by very informal ones, informal teachers were on the whole antipathetic to formal methods. They claimed that formal teaching styles fail to encourage responsibility and self-discipline, that they do not allow pupils to think for themselves or develop to their full potential. Moreover, such methods, in their view, do not make sufficient demands on teachers. These views seem to suggest that the sort of classroom interaction they favour is one where children can enjoy what they are doing, feel socially at ease, and can exercise their imagination and initiative. However, informal and unstructured classroom environments where direct teacher control is less evident do not appear to suit all children. Anxious and nervous children seem to be unable to cope with the responsibility of self-directed activity and waste a good deal of time in aimless wandering about, gossiping, fidgeting, and gazing out of the window, and they furthermore spend less time interacting with their peers, unless in a contentious manner.

Bennett's findings provide little evidence of a general movement towards informality in the primary school, at any rate at the upper age level. Only about 17% of the teachers in the overall sample were in fact teaching in the informal manner described by Plowden, while the majority used mixed styles. The more recent government survey (1978) of 542 primary schools visited by HMIs between 1975 and 1977 shows a trend towards greater formality with about 75% of teachers in the sample using mainly didactic methods, compared with only 5% teaching by discovery techniques.

Galton et al. (1980) identified four main teacher types in their sample: individual monitors, class enquirers, group instructors and style changers. Individual monitors, forming 22% of the sample, engage in little group or class teaching but adopt a high degree of individualized work. In spite of this, their teaching is largely didactic. Class enquirers, 15% of the sample, spend most of their time on class teaching but, contrary to expectation, tend to be less didactic than the former group since they use a greater proportion of open questions leading to a higher level of cognitive functioning in their pupils. Group instructors constitute only 12% of the sample and come closest to adopting the group strategy suggested by Plowden (1967). However the style of these teachers too tends to be largely didactic with emphasis on conveying information to pupils. The fourth group consists of three types of style changers: those who change their style in response to pupil reaction; those whose pupils rotate from one curriculum activity to another throughout the day and finally those who make regular changes between class and individualized instruction.

Of particular interest in this survey is the small proportion of teachers who adopt group strategies for learning. Most teachers seem to use grouping purely as a managerial device. Such findings indicate that so-called informal or progressive teaching methods are practised far less in primary schools than critics of the movement would have us believe.

Bound up with issues of teaching style and classroom interaction are also a teacher's view of education, his aims and objectives, and his concept of an ideal pupil. In fact all these factors are interdependent and must be considered as mutually influential. As early as 1952, Becker introduced the concept of an ideal pupil, showing how teachers classify children according to their notion of what constitutes such a model. Becker's data, drawn from interviews with sixty teachers in Chicago schools, showed that, for most of them, the ideal pupil was one who was cooperative and obedient, enabling them to do their jobs effectively with the minimum of conflict or stress. Such pupils behave well in class, do their homework assiduously, and arrive punctually. However this ideal exists only with teachers whose aims are primarily cognitive and who employ mainly didactic methods. Pupils who try to be independent, to initiate and direct their own learning, and who attempt to collaborate with their peers are likely to fall short of the ideal held by a traditional teacher. They disrupt the smooth running of the class by wanting to assume independence and by asking awkward questions for which the teacher's well-planned lesson content is not prepared.

Self-styled progressive teachers, as we have seen, have different overall aims and hence are likely to hold a different ideal pupil concept. They emphasize the importance of social and emotional development and stress the value of self-expression, creativity, and the enjoyment of school. Docile pupils who sit waiting to be told what to do will hardly meet their ideal.

So far we have discussed the effects of teaching style upon pupil behaviour, but since we are concerned with interaction processes, it would seem surely that there must be some indication of the effect of pupil styles upon teacher behaviour. The research by Galton *et al* (1980) also identified four main pupil types: attention seekers, intermittent and solitary workers and quick collaborators. Attention seekers interact more with their teachers than with their peers since they constantly seek out the teachers to ask about their work. Intermittent workers on the other hand avoid teacher attention and, as the term suggests, work only when the teacher is supervising them. Not surprisingly these are found mostly with individual monitors, since there is plenty of opportunity for them to escape notice while the teacher is occupied with other children.

Solitary workers and quick collaborators interact little with teachers or peers; instead the solitary workers prefer not to have their privacy disturbed. They interact with the teacher as members of their group rather than as individuals. Quick collaborators also prefer to work alone but will cooperate with others when told to do so, even though discussion with a partner is then minimal.

This study shows little evidence that teaching style changes according to pupil type, rather that pupils adapt to new teachers and new styles. However, Klein (1971) had shown experimentally that student behaviour can affect teaching style, by training a student audience to alter its behaviour towards a lecturer, according to a prearranged plan. When students were highly attentive, the lecturer was lively and relaxed, but when they became bored and restless, the lecturer showed signs of impatience and exasperation. Lacey (1970) and Hargreaves (1967) both showed the force of friendship groups among secondary school pupils in establishing and maintaining classroom norms. A troublesome pupil in an A stream is regarded as a deviant not only by teachers but also by pupils. Thus group behaviour of this kind supports the teachers' standards, aims, and teaching style. But when a whole group of pupils adopts what the teacher regards as deviant behaviour, as Hargreaves showed among his lower stream pupils, the teacher is forced to change his tactics and negotiate with them, in order to survive.

Furlong (1976) introduces the notion of an 'interaction set' to show how a set of pupils, whether they normally belong to the same friendship group or not, can band together to act against the teacher and force him to relax his routine or refrain from punitive measures, if they all perceive and interpret the situation in the same way. Members of an interaction set can, for instance, interpret a teacher's behaviour as unfair and, by obstinate refusal to attend to his wishes, press him to act differently. As we saw earlier, Furlong's study of fifteen-year-old girls showed that, provided teachers lived up the *their* ideal concept of an efficient teacher, they caused few behavioural problems. It is only when the teachers deviate, by not being strict or directive enough, that trouble arises. Teachers using the Humanities Curriculum Project and attempting to take on the role of neutral chairman have often encountered difficulty because by the nature of their role they have to remain silent when pupils expect them to take the lead.

Pupil-pupil interaction

It would be impossible to discuss any aspects of classroom interaction without some mention of how pupils interact among themselves; thus our discussion so far has inevitably touched on pupils' classroom behaviour, even though this was not the focal point of the discussion. But let us now look at some specific studies of pupils in class. If teachers accept that group work is an important educational device, as most if not all those concerned with younger children do, as well as a good many of their secondary school colleagues, they need to look carefully at methods of grouping within their classes (Kelly, 1978). The methods and rationale behind them will naturally influence the kind of classroom interaction that ensues.

There seem to be three main approaches in schools: grouping by ability, by friendship, and by interest. Although grouping by ability within the class negates the principle of nonstreaming within the school, there are still those teachers, as Barker-Lunn (1970) and Ferri (1972) showed, who do attempt to create relatively homogeneous groups within an unstreamed class. They claim that children progress better when they work with peers of roughly the same ability and that, at any time, pupils can be moved to another group fairly easily. However, as we are well aware, groups of pupils soon become labelled as bright or dull and the danger is that friendship patterns will be established only within those groups and not between them. In addition, those in the 'top' group will regard themselves as superior to the 'duds'. Lacey (1970) showed that friendships made in the first year when boys were unstreamed tended to be broken in the second year as a result of streaming.

The second approach adopted by many teachers is that of friendship grouping. As we saw earlier, there is a simple sociometric device adapted from Moreno's techniques that enables teachers to discover from their pupils whom they regard as their friends and to allow them to work together. Friendship clearly is an important factor in school, especially in its bearing on children's behaviour. But as most teachers realize, friendship patterns among younger children are not very stable, and a group working together amicably one week will be at odds the next because of some apparently trivial disagreement that looms large in the children's minds. Probably the best known studies of friendship groups among older pupils are those by Hargreaves (1967) and Lacey (1970). Both studies took place in streamed boys' schools and revealed how far academic segregation can lead to polarized subcultures within the school. Cliques of 'goodies' adopting pro-school norms were to be found in A streams, while those adopting anti-school attitudes collected in the lower streams. Antagonism between these cliques soon built up and, even in physical activities, when year groups of boys were not segregated, the barriers between the groups were not broken down. Friendship groups seem to be partly determined by sex. Observation of pupils in mixed secondary schools (Mahony, 1983) shows a striking physical barrier between boys and girls, who never choose to sit together in class.

There are however some children who do not find it easy to make friends and seem isolated in class. These are usually individuals who are extremely shy and withdrawn and very often display some deep-seated anxiety problem. Children with low self-esteem are often those who find it difficult to make friends, as Coopersmith (1967) showed. They do not feel confident that others will accept them, are doubtful about their own opinions and judgements, and are unlikely to take much part in discussion or to engage in activities with others. They prefer to remain listeners or onlookers. On the other hand there are some insecure children who try to buy friendship by some kind of bribery, such as offering sweets or the use of expensive equipment or even acting the fool in class, as Lacey showed in his example of the unfortunate Priestley.

Interaction that is understood only in terms of friendship groups leaves some interesting features unexplained. It assumes that membership of a friendship group is constant and that nonmembers never participate in group activities. It assumes too that, in order to remain a member, an individual must succumb to group pressure and abide by the norms set out by majority consensus. However, there are occasions when an individual feels morally obliged to disagree with his friends and to act independently. This is after all what moral autonomy implies and what we hope all pupils will eventually learn to achieve. On the other hand, there are also occasions when pupils who are otherwise regarded as outsiders decide to go along with a group adopting its behaviour patterns. Long-term observation of what actually happens in classrooms shows that pupil interaction does not necessarily involve all friends of any one group and may include some who are not usually friendly. In other words, who interacts with whom depends very much upon prevailing circumstances. Furlong's notion of an interaction set (1976) is a useful explanatory tool here. Individuals are not forced by group pressures to act with others but can give tacit support, if they so choose, by their mere demeanour, for instance by smiling, nodding approval, and so on. Furlong cites occasions where the same rather troublesome pupil is at one time supported by her friends when she has defied the teacher but later is ignored by them when they choose to work alongside normally hard-working pupils. The interaction set has thus changed according to the way in which pupils interpret the situation and decide to act.

To resume our discussion of methods of grouping practised by teachers, the third main approach is to group pupils by interest. This presupposes that some sort of interest-based or enquiry-based teaching is going on and in this context it clearly makes sense for pupils who share common interests to work together. It follows that working groups of this kind will be flexible. A set of children working together for drama, for example, will not necessarily share the same interests in an environmental studies project. And if we consider one of the important social aims of grouping pupils within a class we should surely hope that they would not always work with the same people but should have the opportunity to cooperate and collaborate with others of different talents, personality, temperament, and background. Social experience is thus broadened and the flexibility ensured by changing groups should help to prevent rigid prejudices being built up within an insulated in-group.

Several curriculum projects, designed for use by secondary school pupils, rely on group discussion and group activities — the Humanities Curriculum Project, McPhail's Lifeline Moral Education project, Bruner's MACOS project, to mention but a few. And, for these to have real educative value, it is essential that pupils do learn with one another, above all to develop the skills of conversation and discussion so that they address their remarks to one another rather than to the teacher as an authority figure.

Language and classroom interaction

Most people in a society such as ours share certain cultural assumptions about the relationship between teaching, learning, and talking. We not only expect teachers to talk to pupils much of the time but also assume that pupils show what they have learned by answering teachers' questions. Pupils themselves expect teachers to talk and such expectations are difficult to shed. One of the most disconcerting aspects of the changing role of the teacher required by some of the moral education projects, for example, is that the onus is on the pupils to initiate and maintain discussion. A teacher who sits silently waiting for pupils to begin is regarded with great suspicion by them.

However, typical classroom talk that most participants expect is not the sort that would generally be accepted in most situations outside school. Cross-questioning, interrogation, and correction which would cause consternation, bewilderment, or indignation in everyday life are the general order of life in the classroom. Much school discourse is characterized by its threefold structure: the teacher asks a question, the pupil replies, then the teacher evaluates his answer. Since the questions are not genuine ones, asked by somebody seeking information, this model indicates one kind of teacher control. Verbal exchange takes the form of a pseudo-dialogue, as Stubbs (1975) terms it, where pupils are kept in their place by the sort of talk that is expected of them. Indeed, intending teachers are usually encouraged by their supervisors to get pupils to talk more, and often a high proportion of class participation is taken as a criterion of successful teaching for those on practice during their professional training. However, since the assumption that teaching and learning necessarily involve talking is very culture-specific, teachers are likely to encounter difficulties when working with children from different cultural backgrounds. Dumont and Wax (1972), for example, showed that European teachers working with Cherokee Indians found themselves entirely at a loss, since learning for these children was not equated with talking in class. In their culture, speech is minimal in the learning process which relies far more on observation and participation. Even young children regard it as rather odd to be asked questions to which they know the teacher already has the answer.

Analysis and observation show that the kind of language used in any social exchange is situation-specific. Only in certain social situations is the monitoring of speech such as we have described permissible. This suggests a context where specific role relations hold between speakers. A policeman can cross-question a motorist for example; a judge can interrogate the defendant in court. But normally, we do not cross-question in this way or ask questions to which we already know the answers, unless we wish to catch people out by way of jokes or riddles. The very way in which a teacher talks to his pupils imposes on them his definition of the situation and the form of social relationship he considers appropriate. Many pupils learn to participate in a form of interaction in which authority and knowledge are linked. Because of the nature of the teacher's authority, in terms of his control of both knowledge and behaviour, the interaction is inevitably unbalanced to the advantage of the teacher, whose status is indicated by the kind of language he uses. Thus, to demonstrate intelligence or ability pupils have to learn to answer his questions in a fitting manner. By learning to give the teacher what he wants in terms of answers, they are being socialized into a world where knowledge is possessed by those in authority. Holt (1964), Barnes (1971, 1976), and Rosen (1967) are among the most vociferous in their criticism of teachers' use of questions to determine what counts as valid knowledge in school.

We have already noted that a substantial proportion of teacher talk is directed towards classroom control. Direct instructions or commands more obviously show the teacher's authority position. But although these can be veiled when they are couched in indirect terms, it is still clear what the role relationship between teacher and pupil is intended to be. Any pupil who is told that it is not a good idea for him to sit at the back knows quite well that he has to move or else he's in trouble. There is no question of his disagreeing. There are very few situations outside school where the nature of social interaction is indicated so clearly as it is when pupils have to ask permission to speak or when what they say can be corrected. The assumption that such intervention in the language a pupil uses is permissible indicates very clearly who is in control.

In addition to these more direct ways in which control is exerted by a specific use of language, there are more indirect means which warrant attention. Pupils are easily humiliated into obedience by the use of sarcasm or wit directed against them. Woods (1975) suggested that teachers sometimes deliberately set out to embarrass their pupils in order to establish and maintain power, to punish them, or even to take revenge on them. Showing pupils up by sarcastic remarks in front of others, especially younger children, can arouse resentment which often smoulders for a long time because of the personal smart, until the object of ridicule can retaliate.

Humour and jokes in the classroom, as opposed to wit or sarcasm, are more usually shared by teachers and pupils and can often serve to enhance a sense of comradeship and well-being. Walker and Adelman (1976) and Walker and Goodson (1977) show how hidden jokes and bizarre meanings, accessible only to those who have shared common experiences, can reveal important aspects of classroom life. Humour may indicate social solidarity within a group and can also help teachers to put pupils at their ease. Walker and Goodson draw a distinction between the kind of humour used in formal and informal classrooms. In the latter, when joking relationships between pupils are generated, the humour is that of equals, whereas in formal classrooms it is easy for teachers to joke at the expense of pupils and for these to use jokes to challenge a teacher's authority. The use of language in this way proves interesting and informative to an experienced observer, provided he is well enough acquainted with the participants to recognize its subtleties.

Any kind of social intercourse involves some sort of give-and-take arrangement where everyone's needs and wishes are satisfied as far as is comfortable. In school, where the interaction is inevitably unbalanced because of the nature of the relations between pupils and teacher, teachers will often admit to certain survival strategies to help them cope with classes of reluctant pupils. Negotiation, for example, involves not only coming to a tacit agreement about what is acceptable behaviour in class, but also deliberate appeals, promises, or even threats and bribes. Teachers who arrange activities so that the more obviously academic part, such as writing, recording, working of examples, comes early in the day, hope that the promise of something more relaxing later will serve to keep pupils down to work with the minimum of disruption. Woods (1976) suggests that apologies and praise also play a part in classroom negotiation. A teacher will apologize perhaps for talking too long, explaining that it had to be done in order to progress to something more interesting. Or he will praise pupils, perhaps even flattering them a little, for having worked hard at a difficult task.

Reliance on rules, ritual, and routine is also part of a teacher's survival kit, since most pupils come to accept what occurs regularly as part of the school day. A teacher who has to struggle hard to maintain control in class can relax rather more on routine occasions such as assembly or registration.

During his participant observation study, lasting a year in a mixed rural secondary school, Woods noticed that in addition to negotiating with pupils and relying on routine, some teachers indulged in various forms of fraternization with pupils, as a means of surviving and maintaining some measure of control. Younger teachers attempted to identify with pupils in their dress, manner, and speech, often joking with them to show general bonhomie. Even flirtatious behaviour was not unknown. Others became friendly with pupils outside the classroom by genuine shared interests in television, sport, and various aspects of popular culture.

But whatever techniques the teacher may adopt to maintain control and ease personal relationships in the classroom, most pupils tend to have a similar model of the ideal teacher, as Furlong's study of a group of West Indian fifteen-year-old girls clearly showed. These girls, all reluctant pupils but by no means devoid of ability, wanted their teachers to offer them a rigidly defined and structured syllabus so that they knew exactly what had to be mastered. They preferred material to be given to them, rejecting enquiry methods, and welcomed constant feedback from the teacher about their progress. In their eyes, the teacher who could supply all this was acceptable, even if he had to be strict. Mary Fuller's study in a London comprehensive school (1981) showed a group of black girls to be strongly committed to achievement, even though their attitudes were not pro-school. They valued school for utilitarian ends and respected only those teachers who could help them gain success in public examinations. Werthman too (1963) had shown how a teacher could survive even with delinquent adolescents if he were prepared to make them work hard and could demonstrate that he was fair in dealing with them.

Classroom interaction and curriculum development

Since pupils over the whole age range, as far as the studies available suggest, seem to prefer teachers who provide them with a firm, structured framework, and who adopt didactic methods, it will be interesting to see how pupils respond to more open styles of teaching. Many curriculum developments during the past decade or so require a change in the role of both pupil and teacher, placing more responsibility on pupils for their own participation and learning. An obvious example illustrating the different demands upon pupils and teachers is the Humanities Curriculum Project, where the teacher is required to act as neutral chairman. Enquiry and discussion methods replace direct teaching, so that pupils can no longer rely on their teacher to provide them with information or help them to arrive at a solution in their discussion of controversial issues. Instead, he provides them with materials relevant to a particular issue, but his main responsibility lies in creating conditions and opportunities which encourage pupils to develop their own understanding of values relating to human behaviour and experience. Using the evidence supplied by the materials in the learning pack, pupils must learn to judge, appraise, and assess critically what is relevant to the topic in hand. Furthermore, they must learn to tolerate an outcome that probably does not produce consensus. All this is difficult for pupils to learn, especially if they have been used to being fed with teacher-selected information. The kind of interaction in this situation is essentially that of equals, in the sense that everyone has a right to contribute and to criticize other people's views. There is no appeal to authority, nor must the teacher intervene to assert his own viewpoint. Subsequent evaluation of the project (Walker and Adelman, 1976) revealed that both pupils and teachers found their new roles difficult to accept. Pupils found the procedure unnerving in that they were expected to put forward their own views, yet received no teacher guidance or approval to tell them whether they were right or not. The monitoring procedures developed in the Ford Teaching Project showed that when a speaker, teacher or pupil, intended an action or remark to have a particular meaning, that meaning was frequently misinterpreted. The triangulation technique, which will be discussed further in a later chapter, is intended to help those engaged in enquiry/discovery methods to understand other people's behaviour and to help teachers in particular to see themselves through their pupils' eyes. SAFARI, 'Success and Failure and Recent Innovation', a three-year project, was set up in order to investigate the impact of curriculum projects on teacher-pupil interaction, precisely because some developments had run into difficulties on account of changing role relationships. In fact some teachers, because of the difficulties encountered in the nature of their new role, had been found to adapt materials to suit their original didactic methods. Galton (1976), for example, showed that up to 25% of his sample of a hundred teachers using Nuffield Science schemes never asked pupils to plan and work out their own experiments but, rather, resorted to instructing them.

In a discussion of Bruner's 'Man, A Course of Study' (MACOS), Edwards (1983) points out some of the difficulties encountered in a project which sets out to encourage pupils to 'research, speculate, analyse and discuss, rather than passively assimilate a body of facts or concepts' (p284). A framework which facilitates and encourages open-ended dialogue is essential and requires a reappraisal of traditional assumptions about pedagogy and the nature of knowledge. In discussions with first-year pupils there was clear evidence that the children enjoyed working within a framework that was speculative and hypothetical and where they were able to articulate and share ideas with their teachers. Teachers in turn had learnt to assume the role of co-learner rather than remain information givers.

If part of curriculum development is seen as a joint enterprise between teachers and pupils, a model of classroom interaction that allows for openness, flexibility and collaboration is essential. Education can then be a cooperative and truly interactive process.

Summary and conclusions

In this first chapter we have attempted to explain the nature of classroom interaction, and have shown how methods of examining social intercourse in school have developed with changing views of education. Studies of teacher-pupil interaction as revealed by the physical layout of the classroom, interpersonal judgements, nonverbal communication, and general rules and rituals have been discussed. We have seen how teaching styles are both influenced by pupil behaviour and themselves evoke particular kinds of behaviour among pupils.

We have shown how groups of pupils contribute towards the general give-and-take of classroom life by examining methods of grouping adopted by teachers and ways in which pupils band together in specific situations.

Use of language in the classroom, as we shall see again later on, is an important indicator of the type of role relationships developed between teacher and pupils. The discussion of the function of language in social control is particularly interesting when more subtle linguistic techniques such as jokes and humour are considered.

Finally, we have briefly commented on the relationship between curriculum innovation and classroom interaction, an issue to be developed further in a later chapter.

CHAPTER 2

JUDGEMENTS OF CHILDREN

The nature of judgements

In recent years the importance of social influences on children's learning and development, in fact upon their total educational experience, has, as we saw in Chapter 1, been recognized. If their school experience is to be a worthwhile one, they must be regarded as persons in their own right, with their own individual interests, abilities, and personal characteristics, as people who are capable of making choices and decisions. Yet all too often children are labelled and categorized by their teachers as if they were not unique individuals worthy of respect and consideration.

One aim of this chapter is to promote further thought about the nature and effects of judgements that teachers make. We shall examine the implications of such judgements within the social and institutional context of the school and shall suggest how pupils' motivation, achievement, and self-image might be affected by such judgements. The personality make-up of those making judgements is explored and some practical issues such as record-keeping and report-writing are discussed.

Judging others or forming impressions of them is an integral part of all social interaction; forming judgements of children is an inevitable part of any teacher's task. And whereas in everyday life the judgements we make of others help us to get along with them, to communicate with and to understand them, they do not necessarily have long-lasting effects. However, what a teacher says about a pupil, either in informal staff-room conversation or on a more formal written record, may shape that pupil's future more than a teacher can ever imagine. It is particularly urgent then that teachers be aware of the effects their judgements may have on pupils and gain some understanding of how their opinions might be influenced by external factors as well as by their own personality make-up. They can then try to ensure that the judgements they make are as fair, unbiased, and objective as possible. But as soon as we begin to talk of objectivity, we run into difficulties, because the human being making the judgement is not a measuring instrument to be calibrated and read with any degree of accuracy. Hamlyn (1972) contrasts the objective statement with the subjective, the idiosyncratic, or the prejudiced, implying that judgements made about others purely on grounds of personal whim or preference are inevitably distorted. However, the impressions teachers form of their pupils as individuals and the judgements they make of their abilities and progress are inescapably subjective up to a point. The view a teacher has of a pupil is *his* view, since he can only see people through his own eyes. The important thing, therefore, is that teachers learn to make their judgements as fair and as just as they can, by making only those inferences about a child's behaviour for which there is direct evidence.

In addition to being fair, objective, helpful, and educationally relevant, the judgements teachers make of others must also be morally acceptable. Teachers must, in other words, not confuse judgements of performance and achievement with those about the pupil's worth as a person. A child is not better or worse as a person because he can read well or fails to learn to read, or because he is deemed capable or otherwise of obtaining O levels. Yet because our society is achievement-oriented, intelligence, often equated with academic success, is highly valued, and, although as a concept it is morally neutral, it might mistakenly become associated with moral acceptability.

If, in making judgements of children, teachers are to avoid this confusion, it is highly important for them to remember that respect for persons is an essential part of education, part of the teacher-pupil relationship. The notion of respect for persons involves treating children as individuals, recognizing and valuing their personal characteristics. It follows then that to see them simply as members of a category could result in overlooking these individual characteristics. For a child to develop and function as a person, he needs to be treated as one. He needs to be able to develop the kind of self-concept that allows him to regard himself as of value. To treat children as persons in their own right, who are able to develop this kind of self-image, involves regarding them as responsible for their own actions and therefore having some control over what they do. To see children as passive entities whose destiny is shaped by influences beyond their control is to lose sight of their power to be autonomous. Children who are regarded as doomed failures because of their lower working-class background, for instance, are not being accorded due respect because, firstly, they are being placed in a category where all members supposedly share common characteristics and, secondly, they are not considered to have any control over their own future. If many of them are not *seen* to be able to determine their own career and in the school context are given less encouragement to do so, many will inevitably fail, thus conforming to the working-class pattern, reinforcing the stereotype and confirming the self-fulfilling prophecy.

Included in the concept of developing personal autonomy is the notion of coming to terms with constraints imposed upon one's freedom, including one's own limitations. To be allowed to try, but then to fail, helps children to learn what their strengths and weaknesses are. It would be foolish to assume that all children could be equally successful at all things; part of developing as a person is to realize where one can succeed, but also, to acknowledge that there are standards of excellence one might not reach and nevertheless to value others' achievements. For a teacher to prevent a child from attempting something in which he thinks the child will fail is to omit to treat him as an autonomous being or to show him respect as an individual. However, children do need some guidance from adults as to what they might be able to achieve; they need to know what the tasks involve that they hope to tackle, and need to be encouraged to estimate their own abilities realistically. It would surely be just as misguided to let children think they could achieve what for them would be impossible as to prevent them from ever trying because of some preconceived notion of their abilities held by the teacher. The sad cases of children who for many years aspire to be doctors or teachers when they cannot cope very adequately even with the basic skills of literacy and numeracy act as a reminder that one of the most important reasons for assessment and judgement by teachers is to help children to gain a realistic picture of their own capabilities and to make the most of them, while at the same time accepting their limitations. Recognizing and accepting one's own limitations is not incompatible with acknowledging standards of excellence in areas where one is not highly competent; if comparison between individuals is avoided, especially where it implies differential worth of persons, then it should be possible to achieve this idea in practice.

However, since children have to learn to develop as persons and to recognize their own weaknesses as well as strengths, uninformed or uncritical respect is insufficient and misguided, as it would involve regarding everything a child did as acceptable and would offer them no standards on which to base their own developing moral principles or standards of excellence in any area of achievement.

With this proviso, treating children as individuals is essential to help them develop as persons or to develop a consciousness of self. G. H. Mead's concept of the self (1934) offers a view of personality development which is essentially active, reflexive, and dynamic. In Mead's view, the individual ceases to be at the mercy of other people or external circumstances which cause him merely to *respond*. Because of an ability to reflect upon, interpret and judge his own actions he becomes independent. However, he does not learn to do this in a vacuum. He learns to reflect upon himself by living in a social world with other people who have significance and meaning for him. The views of others, especially 'significant others' (specific people who are close to him and whose views and actions matter to him) help to influence the development of the self by a process of interaction. It follows that if such significant others, such as parents, teachers, peers, hold a view of a human being as a typical occupant of a role or status rather than a unique individual, he will fail to develop individual qualities as he too will see himself as a mere typification. Berger and Luckman (1967) in their discussion of how we experience others in everyday life talk of 'typificatory schemes' which affect our interaction with other people and which help us to make judgements of them. A *typificatory scheme* is based on our past experience of others in certain situations where specific cues lead us to interpret their behaviour in a certain way. For instance, we perceive someone who approaches us with a stern look, an unsmiling expression, who remains impassive to our first approach, as unfriendly. This is our typification of him. But in face-to-face situations, the interaction can advance so that his change of facial expression, the tone of his voice, even his posture can present us with contradictory evidence that forces us to modify our initial typification and to begin to see him as a person rather than an anonymous type. If typifications are not modified, then anonymity and type casting are inevitable, implying that we perceive others merely as members of a category, occupying a particular status. They are seen not to have an individuality but share the same characteristics as everybody else in the same category. To see our pupils in this way is to fail to respect them as persons and to make judgements of them which cannot fail to be so general as to be unfair, rigid, and possibly damaging to their self-respect.

Categorization of pupils by teachers

A brief review of some of the recent literature on educability will enable us to examine some of the assumptions that teachers make about the relationship between educability and social class, ability, race, and gender. We can then consider the implications of some of these assumptions for pupils' school achievement and behaviour in class and ask why teachers' assumptions or typifications have the effects that they do.

From the early 1950s onwards, extensive research has been carried out both in this country and in the USA to show how working-class children are at a disadvantage compared with middle-class children in school achievement and educational opportunity. Much of this early work set out to show the extent of these differential opportunities. In fact substantial evidence of working-class failure was attributed to poor home backgrounds, lack of parental interest, and insufficient encouragement at home. Preschool programmes were set up in the USA in the early 1960s to compensate for inferior home backgrounds, in the hope that 'disadvantaged' children would catch up before they came to school.

In this country, following the recommendations of the Plowden Committee (1967) for a policy of positive discrimination, certain areas were designated as Educational Priority Areas. Primary schools within them were granted a more favourable allocation of finance and resources and teachers offered additional salary allowances, in order to reduce the high proportion of staff changes suffered by such schools at the time. Educators were already beginning to ask whether schools themselves had contributed towards the failure of the children who were now being offered special help. And if part of the responsibility did rest with the schools, how in fact had they helped children to fail? Holt (1964) had already produced his highly personal account of why children fail, and from the late 1960s on we find a series of investigations both in this country and in the USA which aim to answer this question. Fuchs, for example (1968), in the USA carried out a small-scale study of probationary teachers in New York slum schools, in an attempt to show how teachers (perhaps inadvertently) help children to fail. A detailed account of one young teacher's experiences in a slum school illustrates the point. The teacher began her work in the school by trying to examine her own methods critically, and attributed children's failure to her own lack of experience and expertise. But very soon she was persuaded (reluctantly) by more experienced teachers that the cause of failure lay not with her, but in the inferior home backgrounds from which the children came. Children were thus being typified as failures right at the beginning of their school career because of their home background. As Fuchs says: 'the slum school system's tacit belief that social conditions outside the school make such failures inevitable *does* make such failures inevitable'. Furthermore, children are tracked (or streamed, in our terminology) right from the beginning, thus receiving labels which will follow them right through their school career and will result in differential teaching which serves only to widen the gap even more between those judged as able, indifferent, or poor at the age of six.

Rist (1970), aware of the dearth of studies attempting to explain exactly how the school helps to reinforce the class structure of society, reports results of an observational study of one class of ghetto children from the time they entered kindergarten to halfway through their third year of schooling. As soon as they entered school, they were placed by their teacher in reading groups which reflected the social class composition within the whole group. These groups remained stable over the two and a half years of study and the teacher's differential behaviour towards each group was noticeable. Thus she had made initial presuppositions about the children on the basis of how she perceived their social background. These typifications were to have clear consequences for their socialization into the school system. Rist suggests the following stages in this process of differentiation and its consequences. First of all, the teacher has an ideal type of pupil in mind who possesses those characteristics necessary for success. Since the criteria could not be based on any kind of school attainment (as the children had only just entered school) the characteristics were related to social class. Thus early in their school career a subjective evaluation was being made as to the presence or absence of these desired characteristics and children were grouped accordingly. From then on, groups were treated differently according to whether they were seen as fast or slow learners. Markedly less attention and encouragement were offered to the slow group who in any case were not expected to succeed. Patterns of interaction between the teacher and children thus became rigid; later on in their school career the whole process would repeat itself but this time based on supposed evidence of success or failure — actual performance in reading.

British studies too revealed a similar tendency on the part of teachers to correlate educability with social class. Part of the NFER project initiated in 1958 to study children's reading progress was concerned with teachers' attitudes towards children's home background, their expectations of children, and their assessments of children's reading ability and their actual performance on a standardized reading test (Goodacre, 1968). Teachers' subjective assessments, based on their records of book level reached by each child, suggested that children from middle- and upper working-class areas had a noticeably higher reading ability than those in lower working-class areas. Middle-class pupils were rated highest. However, when tested on a standardized reading test (NFER's *National survey 7+ Reading Attainment Test*) this marked difference was not apparent. Lower working-class children were still inferior to the other two groups but there was no marked difference between middle-class and upper working-class children. It is possible then that teachers' assessments reflect the standards they themselves apply to pupils from different social environments. All working-class children are expected to perform less well than middle-class children and so they do, it seems. Are they held back because they are expected to be slow? Or because teachers simply do not give them more advanced reading material?

The studies referred to so far show how teachers categorize children according to what they know, or think they know, about their social background. Yet another important basis upon which teachers form their typifications of pupils is the school stream in which they are placed. In fact, stream and social class are often confounded or even taken to be parallel. Keddie (1971) shows how the 'knowledge' teachers have of children, or the way in which they judge their ability, is based on the stream in which they are placed as well as the social class from which they come. The ideal pupil is one who is seen to be easiest to teach, who is like the teacher, and who accepts what the teacher offers unquestioningly. He presents no problems in class, works quietly and independently, doing what the teacher wants. He belongs to an A stream and stems from a middle-class background. The less than ideal or problematic pupil is the one who questions what the teacher offers, demands to know the point of the activity, and in fact is generally seen as unlike the teacher. As a participant observer in a large comprehensive school, Keddie studied the progress of a Humanities Course designed to be taught as an undifferentiated programme across the whole ability range to a fourth-year group, and eventually to be examined by mode 3 of the CSE and O level. She tries to show how, in fact, although the avowed aims of the course are to develop autonomy and independence, to allow children to work at their own speed and to learn to think for themselves, in practice it seems to be designed for an ideal pupil who already exists — the A stream pupil, who because of his middle-class background already possesses the desired characteristics. Thus these docile pupils accept a new subject with a different label (Humanities, Socialization) which they readily take over from the teachers. The problem pupils are the C streamers who accept it less readily and want to recognize the content as History, Biology, and so on, with which they are more familiar.

One of the points of particular interest in the study is the way context affects teachers' typifications. Keddie sees teachers at the planning stage as acting within an *educationist context,* basing their ideas on what they deem theoretically desirable. In this context they hold ability and social class separate, condemning streaming and differentiation by ability because they are socially divisive. But in the other context in which they work, with a practical orientation, the *teacher context,* these ideals tend to be forgotten. Ability and social class are confused. Treatment of pupils is different according to their stream. For example, teachers admit to preparing different material according to the stream they are going to teach even though the programme was designed to be taught right across the ability range. They even admit to insufficient preparation for the C streamers on the assumption that these pupils won't notice and won't ask questions. They are prepared to answer questions asked by A stream pupils which they would gloss over with C streamers as trivial, irrelevant, or disruptive. Different kinds of behaviour and application are accepted and even expected, according to stream.

Further evidence showing how teachers typify pupils according to stream is found in the work of Hargreaves (1967) and Lacey (1970), both of whom based their observations on secondary schools in which they worked. In studying social relationships between teachers and boys in four fourth-year streams in a secondary modern school, Hargreaves shows the gradual deterioration of relationships and segregation which seems to follow upon streaming. Pupils are judged as different in ability at the beginning of their secondary school career and are streamed accordingly. Interestingly enough, although teachers perceive the separate streams as homogeneous in ability, they are in fact, according to IQ scores, less homogeneous than when they were first grouped in this way (for example, in the second year the D stream contained no boys with IQs above the median, whereas by the fourth year there were six). But this differentiation, now embedded in the organization of the school, has repercussions for other aspects of the pupils' behaviour. Because they come to see themselves as different (this self-image is obviously reinforced by teachers' attitudes towards different streams), their relationships deteriorate so that there is marked hostility between the A and D stream pupils. As Hargreaves comments, academic and delinquescent subcultures develop, one subculture perceiving the other as a negative reference group, so that hostility and lack of communication between the two groups becomes marked. Teachers too have grown to expect little of their D stream pupils who adapt to these lower expectations with lowered aspirations and diminished interest in the school. Not only do teachers expect less of the D stream pupils academically, but they also expect them to behave badly and accordingly discriminate against them, for example, even where school holiday trips are concerned. Little wonder then that their hostile attitude grows. Hargreaves is at pains to point out that it would be dangerous to generalize these findings to other secondary schools and this caution must be respected. But certainly the possible implications must not be overlooked.

Lacey's study takes place within a selective school where boys are segregated on the basis of first-year examination results into four streams before the beginning of their second year. Just as in Hargreaves' study, we see how the initial process of differentiation on the part of the teachers has repercussions for the boys' behaviour. Pupils in separate streams see themselves as progressively different, as is seen from a study of changing friendship patterns. Their interest in and attitudes towards school, their acceptance of school values, as well as participation in extra-curricular activities, takes on a different character according to whether they have been placed in a high or low stream. Lacey refers to this differentiation among pupils as polarization. He describes it as 'a process of subculture formation in which the school-dominated normative culture is opposed by an alternative culture ... the antigroup culture' whose members reject school values, indulge in antisocial activites, and so on.

Again it would be unwise to assume that streaming in all secondary schools would have similar repercussions as at Hightown Grammar described by Lacey. However, these two field studies serve to draw our attention to some of the undesirable repercussions that can follow where teachers are tempted to typify children and when the ensuing categories become part of the structure of the school. Progressive retardation of those placed in lower streams leads to the following sequence of processes. Firstly, we find reduced teacher expectations of low stream pupils, with less demanding academic tasks set for them. Then pupils' own level of aspiration is lowered because of lack of academic challenge and adequate or appropriate incentives and, finally, a sense of present and future failure follows, leading to an even more reduced level of aspiration, motivation, and performance.

If differentiation in the form of streaming were removed, would these undesired consequences also be alleviated? Would the removal of formal institutionalized categories that are established within the school also result in the absence or reduction of unfair typifications made by teachers?

There is in fact some evidence to suggest that where mixed-ability classes have been in operation in the lower part of the secondary school, pupils who might otherwise have been placed in a lower stream and never given the chance have been allowed to join a 'top set' and to follow a CSE or GCE course in their fourth and fifth years (Kelly, 1978). Such pupils do not seem to have suffered from the disadvantage of low teacher expectations as they might have done in a rigidly streamed school. However, although mixed-ability grouping became more widely practised in secondary schools during the 1970s, there was still evidence of differentiation with the growth of the options system. Ideally, to be given a choice of subject in addition to some kind of core curriculum in the fourth and fifth years suggests offering pupils freedom of choice, but again all too often pupils are guided, persuaded or even coerced into courses teachers deem them capable of; those considered bright are directed, albeit subtly, into high-status courses leading to O level, while those thought to be capable of less are placed in CSE and non-examination groups.

As we have already seen, where streaming does not take place, even in classes of younger children (Goodacre, 1968), there is a tendency to typify according to perceived social class and consequently to assume a correlation between social class and ability, even where it does not manifestly exist. Some of Barker-Lunn's findings (1970) show that teachers can in effect stream within their classes, very often with an assumed social class relationship, even when the school is formally unstreamed. Even in the reception class, it is not unknown for five-year-olds to be grouped by ability, under the guise of being in different teams, or designated by different colours or names, and so on. It is interesting to consider race as a further basis on which typifications are formed. It has long been recognized that immigrant children, new to British schools from their countries of origin, unfamiliar with the English language, the organization of British schools and methods of teaching, as well as the way of British life in general, are likely to be at a disadvantage in school achievement in comparison with native children. This disadvantage should in fact apply only to first-generation immigrants whose difficulties might be predominantly linguistic. Yet should second- and third-generation children of immigrant parents experience similar problems when they have grown up in the same neighbourhood as their British peers, learning the same language, be it a Cockney or a Liverpool dialect? Coard's early study (1971) posited that their educational disadvantage lies not so much in their actual ability or the actual language they use as in their *perceived* ability. Teachers, Coard suggested, in his highly impassioned monograph, typify them as being low in ability, speaking a language inappropriate for school learning, and it is thus the teachers themselves who help them to fail. Coard quoted figures obtained from the ILEA in that year, showing that a disproportionate number of West Indian children were placed in ESN schools: 28% of all pupils in their ESN schools were immigrants, compared with only 15% in ordinary ILEA schools. Further analysis of these figures was indeed alarming, since it revealed that 75% of all immigrants in ESN schools were West Indian even though West Indians formed only half the immigrant population in ordinary schools. Since ESN schools are designed to enable less able children to cope with their low abilities and to make the best of them, Coard was forced to ask whether all these West Indian children needed to be socialized to a low scholastic achievement in this way or whether they had been wrongly placed because they were inappropriately judged by their teachers.

Low achievement of West Indian children was for a long time attributed to low self-esteem and insecure self-identity, brought about by low teacher expectations and negative teacher attitudes (Coard, 1971; Milner, 1975). Theories which explained low achievement in these terms put schools under pressure to provide special curricular projects designed to enhance pupils' self-image, for example, Black Studies or Caribbean history. Owen Cole (1981) claimed that teaching children about their own cultures could contribute towards the development of self-esteem by reassuring them that their heritage is to be valued. Maureen Stone (1981) however is highly scornful of such projects, suggesting that such measures in themselves might even have contributed towards low achievement, stressing as they do vague affective goals of self-expression and self-fulfilment. Her own research suggests that regardless of teachers' attitudes black pupils are becoming increasingly self-confident. In her view teachers play little part in developing the self-concept of black pupils simply because they do not count as 'significant others'. They should rather try to understand these pupils in terms of the development of their own culture, including language, dialect, music, religion.

Mary Fuller's study (1981) of black girls in a London comprehensive school revealed a high degree of self-confidence and a very positive self-image. These girls expressed their anger and frustration at sexist and racist attitudes in the form of high commitment to achievement. They thus saw themselves in control of their own future and regarded academic qualifications as a *public* statement of the self-worth which they knew they already had. They used school purely for utilitarian purposes, while still showing anti-school and anti-teacher behaviour in class.

Maureen Stone's research (1981) suggests a mutual antipathy between teachers and black pupils, even though some individual teachers may be appreciated. She claims that teachers who stress affective goals, self-fulfilment and happiness are doing a disservice to West Indian children who themselves feel the need to acquire skills and knowledge. She therefore advocates formal teaching with an emphasis on the acquisition of mastery of basic intellectual skills. In this way, she argues, teachers would be giving due respect to their black pupils. While this view, espoused, according to Maureen Stone, by many black teachers, would meet present-day demands for standards and accountability, it is unlikely to be sympathetically accepted by teachers who embrace a more child-centred philosophy. Thus, while it is questionable whether teachers' judgements do lead to the development of a poor self-image, it can still be argued that their views of black children can lead to their placement in lower streams.

The relationship between educability and gender is a complex one. The extensive literature on gender and schooling produced during the last decade points to teachers' stereotyped attitudes towards boys and girls. These attitudes can affect their self-image and achievement with the result that girls learn to see themselves as inferior to boys. Stanworth (1980) claims that when teachers do hold stereotyped views on boys and girls they may heighten any differences that already pertain. Evidence clearly exists (Dweck, 1980; Clarricoates, 1978) that boys claim more teacher time in class, while girls tend to see themselves as less important in the eyes of the teacher. They become passive and participate less in discussions and other class activities. Spender (1980) asserts that it is normal for teachers to ignore girls for long periods of time and instead to devote time to boys who dominate classroom talk and create a disruption if their interests are not met.

In terms of curricular provision, claims for male superiority in some subject areas have deep roots. Newsom (1948; Newsom Report, 1963), writing on the education of girls, made strong claims for differential provision on the grounds that girls would become housewives and mothers and therefore should devote time to domestic and practical rather than theoretical subjects. CSE and GCE candidate lists (DES 1980a) show marked differences in choice of subjects, with very small percentages of boys entered for domestic subjects and very few girls for technical papers. The traditional distinctions in the sciences likewise show far fewer girls taking physics and chemistry than biology. How far these differences are to be attributed to teacher influence is difficult to determine, but we need to ask why so many girls opt out of mathematics, physics, design and technology because they have learned to regard these as boys' subjects.

Categorization of pupils by specialist agencies

Teachers are however not the only adults who might be responsible for labelling children by the judgements they make of them. Every school has officially sponsored links with certain members of the community whose concern it is to support the general welfare of children, even though they do not all work directly in the school. These include educational psychologists, school counsellors and youth employment officers.

Children are generally referred to a psychologist when teachers or counsellors feel they can no longer cope with severe behaviour problems or marked difficulties in learning. One of the tasks frequently presented to the psychologist is to diagnose the learning difficulties of supposed under-achievers and of children thought to be in need of special education. There are several stages in this procedure which entail selecting and therefore labelling children as different from their peers. First of all, at the stage when a teacher makes his recommendation to the head to call in expert advice, he has to pick out the child as a special case, thus creating a category. It is not unknown for teachers to be reluctant to ask for expert help or even to avoid doing so altogether because they do not wish to label a child in such a way. Secondly, the child is likely to see himself as stigmatized in some way if so selected — supported often by the taunts of his peers. And thirdly, many parents see a referral as carrying a stigma, especially if a recommendation is made that their child be transferred to a special school. This does not imply that such services are unhelpful or unnecessary; it does however reveal the difficulties of judgement with which such selection is fraught. A child who might benefit considerably from psychological help or special educational treatment could suffer either because his parents refuse it on the grounds of being stigmatized or because of the attitudes of parents and peers towards him once he is receiving special treatment.

The Warnock Committee (DES, 1978b) expressed concern about the effects of labelling and categorization and recommended the abolition of statutory categorization of handicapped pupils, since this process tended to enhance the differences between them and their nonhandicapped peers. The Committee recommended the use of the more flexible term 'children with learning difficulties'. Children in need of special educational provision would be selected on the basis of a detailed profile of their needs prepared by a multiprofessional team. Such a profile would ideally contain details of the child's personal and family background together with information about the schemes of work followed, books used, results of diagnostic tests and examples of work. Naturally the quality of this record would depend on the skills of the teachers who compile it so that, here too, fairness of judgement is paramount.

Similar problems are likely to arise in referring children to a school counsellor.

Counselling has long been subsumed under the general pastoral care duties of teachers, who have given advice to pupils of all ages when occasion demands. Class teachers in primary schools constantly act as counsellors to their pupils and are called upon more and more to offer advice to young mothers. But as pressures put upon older pupils by an increasingly complex and multifarious society increased during the 1960s and 1970s, a need was felt, especially in larger secondary schools, for specialists with experience in teaching to be appointed to act as counsellors. A counselling system has long been firmly established in large schools in the USA in response to the need expressed by parents and teachers. Many teachers were reluctant to see a similar counselling system introduced into schools in this country, partly because they consider themselves capable of doing the job alongside their teaching, and partly because they feel threatened by the presence of somebody who has access to more information about their pupils than they have.

Most counsellors would ideally like to work in collaboration with teachers so that information about pupils could be collected and pooled, thus minimizing the risk of drawing on partial or biased information which would lead to a stereotyped and limited view of the pupils concerned.

There are three main sources of information upon which counsellors can draw: direct observation of pupils during the counselling session; what pupils say about themselves; and objective records of their school performance. Each of these can be coloured by judgements made of the pupil. As we saw earlier, any one person perceives others and forms impressions of them through his own eyes. His judgement is coloured by his past experience and initially he must necessarily form typifications of those consulting him in order to have a rough idea of what kind of person he is dealing with. The very nature of direct counsellor-pupil interaction is limited, since the counsellor sees the pupil usually only during the interview session and can witness only a very small sample of behaviour under rather special conditions. Furthermore, what a child says about himself is likely to reflect the self-image built up by interaction with others. As we know from the work of Mead (1934), one's concept of self is influenced by the view of 'significant others'; and if these views have been negative or deprecatory, the pupil will have a poor self-image. Supposedly objective records of a pupil's school performance can again be coloured by a teacher's attitude towards that pupil and merely offer the counsellor labels of little use.

Gill (1967), one of the organizers of the counselling course for experienced teachers at Keele University, saw the development of a pupil's self-concept as one of the important aims of counselling. He suggested that, through counselling, individuals are helped to understand themselves, to clarify their self-image, and also to define questions they are asking of themselves about personal, educational, and vocational matters. The assumption made is that the individual is of supreme worth in and for himself. But pupils have to be convinced of this and to be shown how to use their personal qualities – a difficult task when their opinions of themselves are low. It is important to accept that counselling does not entail personality change (no counsellor is professionally equipped to do this), but involves helping pupils to find effective ways of using the aptitudes, abilities, and personal qualities they already have (Hamblin, 1974). One of the first stages in helping pupils to realize the value of their own qualities is to show them their own strengths and weaknesses and teach them to accept these as a basis for development. Thus the process of reversing any negative stereotype can begin and the shared task of counsellor, teacher, and pupil can be seen as building up self-respect in pupils who have previously learned to see themselves in a negative way through the eyes of others.

Many teachers, however, have misgivings as to the role of the counsellor, fearing that he might take over some of the responsibility that they jealously regard as their own. Further doubts about the effects of counselling are voiced by Cicourel and Kitsuse as early as 1968, writing on counselling in high schools in the USA. They are concerned with the way in which adolescents come into contact with counsellors and how pupils are selected for such contacts. They see the school system as 'an institutionalized differentiator of adolescent careers'. Included among the adolescents' problems created by the organizational structure of the school are issues related to pupils' academic work, their behaviour, especially breaches of rules, and their emotional problems. Any one pupil may of course be seen by teachers to present one or more of these problems, although the pupil himself would not necessarily be conscious of them as problems. This then is one of the crucial issues: are problems created for pupils by the presence of a counsellor whose job is to deal with them? The problems which may have been transitory can become highlighted and exacerbated when attention is drawn to them, especially with pupils who are inclined to seek attention. To be singled out for official attention on the grounds of strange or bizarre behaviour can easily reinforce the kind of behaviour under scrutiny. Furthermore, as Cicourel and Kitsuse point out, the labelling of a pupil as a trouble-maker or a truant, in providing the occasion for singling him out for special treatment, may mean that he is more closely supervised and punished for minor misdemeanors which would go unnoticed in other pupils.

The provision of off-site units to cope with disruptive secondary pupils in urban areas was welcomed with relief by harassed teachers who could no longer cope with highly disturbed and disturbing pupils in their own large classes. Pupils are withdrawn from school for short periods ranging from six weeks to one or two terms. They are given special help on an individual or small-group basis with a far greater share of teacher time and a greater degree of freedom and flexibility to pursue their own interests or express their emotions and frustrations. However, although this system has its merits, we still need to ask whether in the long run singling out pupils for special treatment is going to exacerbate their problems by creating for them a stigma in the eyes of their peers and helping to develop a negative self-image. The uncomplimentary term 'sin-bin' which is frequently applied to such units suggests the negative way in which pupils regard them.

The ideal pupil concept

In considering ways in which teachers' judgements of their pupils are formed, it should prove interesting to ask whether teachers have a preconceived notion of an ideal pupil. If they do, then several consequences are likely. Firstly, their aims might be towards producing ideal pupils according to the model they hold. Secondly, it would follow that any pupil not conforming to the model is perceived as less than ideal in some way and therefore judged less favourably. Thirdly, teachers might see their own success reflected in the ideal pupil and conversely their failure reflected in anyone less than ideal. Several important questions can be pursued in this connection. Do all teachers have an ideal pupil in mind before they begin their teaching career? If so, what influences have helped to create this ideal? Do they set out to produce ideal pupils? Or do they claim to recognize and identify them in practice and in retrospect? Does a teacher's ideal pupil vary according to the educational aims he considers most important? Becker's concept of the ideal pupil (1952) as one who is bright and easy to teach and belongs usually to a middle-class background has already been discussed in Chapter 1. But a teacher's ideal rests not only on his view of a child's background. The ideals held by teachers vary according to their educational aims, to those of the school in which they work, and ultimately to their view of man.

Teachers who adopt a process model of curriculum planning and work in the ways outlined by Blenkin and Kelly (1981) place emphasis on active learning, where pupils learn by discovery and enquiry, with the minimum of teacher direction. Ideal pupils then in such classrooms are those who are capable of organizing their own work and of raising problems for which the teacher has no ready solution. Children thus learn how to recognize and solve their own problems with their peers and teachers as co-learners — a far cry from those who are content to sit passively, waiting to be told what to do and how to do it.

And if teachers embracing different kinds of educational aim do have different notions of an ideal pupil, we need to ask how these ideals affect pupils themselves, namely their achievement, their self-concept, and their relationships with others. Neville Bennett (1976), in his highly controversial study of the relationship between teaching styles and pupil achievement, points out that teachers aim to engender different outcomes in their pupils. Formal teachers tend to lay greater emphasis on promoting a high level of academic attainment and the acquisition of skills in number and reading, whereas informal teachers value social and emotional development, stressing the importance of self-expression, creativity, and the enjoyment of school. If these are their avowed aims, how do they affect teachers' concepts of the ideal pupil? And how are children who do not conform to this ideal judged by their teachers? Although there is no hard evidence, it seems a reasonable hypothesis that pupils' self-images might be affected indirectly. One subsidiary finding that emerged in the now classic study by Getzels and Jackson (1962) of intelligence and creativity revealed that many teachers in their sample drawn from a highly selective school viewed divergent thinkers with suspicion. They preferred pupils who gave the answers they knew teachers expected to those who asked what were considered awkward, critical, or impudent questions. The unconventional behaviour and interests of divergers led teachers to regard them as disruptive in class, so that on the whole convergers, who are more conventional and tend not to ask unusual or awkward questions, provided the ideal pupil concept. The same teachers rated divergent thinkers as only average in ability within that school, despite the fact that their school performance compared favourably with that of convergers who were preferred in class. Similar results were obtained by Torrance (1964) and Hasan and Butcher (1966) who replicated the Getzels and Jackson study, using a sample of Scottish schoolchildren. Again teachers rated their divergent pupils as less likeable. Children who tend to see unusual problems that others might have missed or even a teacher not anticipated are likely to be disconcerting, especially to the teacher's self-image. Thus again we see that pupils who conform to a teacher's ideal tend to support his self-image. Divergent pupils may then tend to find themselves in an anti-teacher or anti-school position. Is it likely that they too, like the academic failures reported by Hargreaves and Lacey, will begin to form a delinquescent subculture?

The suggestion by Haddon and Lytton (1968, 1971) that divergent pupils are more popular and better liked by teachers and peers in informal schools than formal schools brings us back to the vexed issues of differences in aims, expected outcomes, and ideal pupils in two quite different educational climates.

Interpersonal perception

Our discussion so far has shown how typifications made of pupils become embedded in the social context of the school and are developed and confirmed by social interaction. However, a further important set of influences which affect the way an individual judges others are revealed to us by psychological studies of person perception.

Interpersonal perception can be described as the forming of judgements by people about others, especially those judgements which concern us as social beings. Such judgements are concerned with the ways in which people react and respond to others in thought, feeling, and action. Whereas people tend to form snap impressions of others, taking an immediate dislike to another on first sight, for example, in a rather intuitive manner, most of the judgements we make are by inference, both from available evidence and from general principles we hold about human behaviour. It is partly because interpersonal perception is largely inferential that such factors within an individual can have such a distorting effect on his final judgement.

But before we examine this process at work in the classroom, it is useful to look at some of the features of perception in general. The way in which we perceive other people is necessarily different from our perception of objects, in that person perception is a two-way process. Merely by perceiving another and interpreting his behaviour, we have an effect on the very behaviour we are observing which in turn affects our interpretation of it, whereas objects do not change when we perceive them. Object perception is a one-way process. Yet in spite of the fact that people change and usually have more emotional significance for us than objects, there is no fundamental difference between object and person perception since in both cases we use cues available to us and make inferences on the basis of such cues.

When we meet another person for the first time, as for instance when a teacher confronts a new class of children at the beginning of the school year, we have certain cues immediately available to us — physical cues such as physique, dress, hair colour, and style. These are static features in that they do not change under our scrutiny, and although they are of little actual value in helping to form accurate judgements, they nevertheless are used. When Secord (1958) presented subjects with still photographs of people and asked them to describe the personalities of those represented in the photographs, most subjects did so readily and without apparent difficulty, producing surprisingly uniform descriptions. There do seem to be facial stereotypes which can help produce a distorted judgement based on no further evidence. Swarthy complexions tend to be disliked and unpleasant characteristics attributed to their owners. The kind of stereotype liked or disliked will of course depend on the context and even on fashion and current approval. It is sad to note in this connection Coard's observation that his black pupils drew themselves as white. Both Negro and white pupils refused to see their teacher as black (although he was) because black skin apparently in the social context in which he was working was disliked and had unpleasant connotations. Stereotypes exist about physique, suggesting that fat people are conceived as happy, fun-loving, and thin people as anxious (Strongman and Hart, 1968). Further stereotypes are held about voice, accent and dialect, and about clothes and hairstyle (Gibbins, 1969). If teachers are equally susceptible to such stereotypes as the subjects tested in the laboratory, inferences they make about their pupils are likely to be wildly inaccurate and unfair. Dynamic cues such as facial expression, posture, movement, gestures, rate of speech and intonation offer a similar array available to the teacher on first meeting his class. But although these offer some kind of information helping to create a first impression, they are highly unreliable if further evidence is not available.

Luchins (1959) confirms that first impressions tend to be long lasting but are not the most accurate. Experiments showed that the first of two conflicting descriptions of a boy determined the final impression but that the second description tended to be ignored. It is to some extent reassuring that the rigidity of first impressions can be reduced by warning the person making the judgement of its dangers. If teachers are made aware of the misleading nature of first impressions, they can be on their guard and ready to accept further evidence. However, first impressions can easily be created by others' prior judgements. In a now classic experiment Kelley (1950) informed one group of students that a speaker was a cold person, another group that he was a warm person, thus creating prior expectations (or a mental set) for them. This mental set duly had its effects in that those expecting the speaker to be cold and distant saw him as such and participated less in discussion than did the other group. Moreover their impression of him was rigidly held and was not altered by subsequent evidence. There are clearly many occasions when teachers are exposed to a mental set of this kind created by others, such as in staff-room gossip where teachers prepare a new colleague for trouble-makers (Hargreaves, 1972) or from reports and record cards made available to him. Impressions offered by others are particularly undesirable when we remember that children do in fact behave differently according to the way in which teachers treat them (Nash, 1973). To be influenced by another teacher's impressions would mean that the newcomer picked out and interpreted cues from a child's behaviour that conformed to a prior judgement with the result that similar teacher-pupil interaction would be perpetuated.

Kelley's study suggested that within a cluster of characteristics detected in a person there is a central feature which is likely to affect one's whole picture of him; a person described as warm was seen as generally acceptable and likeable, for example. Asch (1946) had already identified such a central dimension and found in fact that whereas terms like warm and cold do seem to colour one's whole picture of a person being judged, others like polite or blunt are less central in that they have little effect on other dimensions. This halo effect, as it has been called, seems to be a consistent feature of the way in which most people make judgements of others. Since most people expect their ideas about others to be consistent, they expect those they rate highly on a valued trait to possess other positive traits to a similar degree.

If this is a general feature of person perception, then its implications for teachers is obvious. A teacher who sets high store by neatness, tidiness, well-spokenness, politeness might well perceive a child possessing these characteristics as more assiduous, interested, and highly motivated than one devoid of them. Such children tend to be found on the top table in the infant classroom long before streaming is admitted to be happening. Jackson (1964) suggested that well-spoken, neatly dressed children tended to be found in A streams of junior schools. Is this because they conform to the teacher's image of an A stream stereotype or because more intelligent children *are* neatly dressed and so on? Related to the halo effect is the tendency to base one's judgements on a logical error, that is, to suppose that the possession of one characteristic automatically implies another. Such traditional beliefs as 'all redheads are hot tempered' probably originated in this way. This kind of error can be perpetuated by accidental reinforcement. The case of one redhead who is in fact hot-tempered confirms the view previously held, so that from then on one notices redheads who have this characteristic, but not those devoid of it. Such impressions can also be confirmed by particular authority sources. Many falsely held assumptions surely stem from one's parents whose word in early childhood is not doubted.

Just as in object perception, the way we judge other people can be affected by our needs and values. Several laboratory experiments have shown that where subjects value high status, they see those holding positions of high status as more powerful, more influential than those of lower status, even in the absence of any objective evidence (Thibaut and Riecken, 1955). Similarly we tend to judge favourably those who fulfil our needs. Could it be that a teacher who feels a particular need for success and fear of failure will tend to judge more favourably on all characteristics those children who do well and thus satisfy the teacher's need for success? The likelihood of this is certainly strong enough for teachers to be aware of its possible dangers.

One question arising from this discussion of person perception is whether there are certain types of people who are more susceptible to such influences and less aware of them than others. It seems that everyone is *likely* to be affected by mental set, first impressions, halo effect, but that some people are more ready to recognize further evidence than others and to alter their judgements accordingly. Adorno *et al.* (1950), in a large-scale study of personality along an authoritarian-democratic continuum, identified the authoritarian type as one who, among other characteristics, tends to hold stereotyped views of other people, failing to recognize individual characteristics, once he has labelled a person and slotted him into a preexisting category. If a teacher uses such categories as 'working-class children', 'the culturally deprived', 'West Indian immigrants' and attributes certain characteristics to all those he sees as belonging to any of these groups, his judgements are bound to be biased. Stereotypes are in fact wrong much of the time because they are over-inclusive. People holding them will not recognize contrary evidence. Frenkel-Brunswik (1948) describes such people as being 'intolerant of ambiguity', meaning that they are not ready to accept new evidence if it is inconsistent with ideas they already hold and are slow even to perceive change. A further unfortunate attribute of the authoritarian type is that he is not self-reflective. He tends to shy away from analysing his own feelings, motives, reasons for action and so is less likely to question the validity of the views he holds.

Implications of teachers' judgements for pupils' school careers

At the beginning of this chapter it was argued that some sort of categorization or typification was necessary and inevitable in any kind of social interaction. Several empirical studies were then examined to illustrate some of the bases on which teachers tend to typify children. However the consequences of such categorizations were found to be undesirable in that they had adverse repercussions for pupils' school careers.

Does this mean then that for some children typification is bound to have adverse effects which cannot be avoided? It would be useful to summarize the particular effects which typification by social class, stream, race and gender can have upon pupils in order to see how undesirable consequences might be avoided. One highly useful concept to draw upon is the notion of the ideal pupil. But by implication any pupils who do not conform to this ideal are automatically deviant in some way. They deviate from the ideal in terms of behaviour, being judged as unruly and disruptive in class. They are consequently not expected to behave as well as the ideal pupil and fulfil these expectations. Hargreaves' D stream boys are in fact unpopular with their peers if they conform to the teachers' standards of acceptable behaviour. Attitudes towards school of those pupils labelled as failures or belonging to an anti-school group tend to deteriorate so that they refuse to participate even in those activities which they enjoy and excel at. Because their status in school is low, they seek recognition elsewhere, often prematurely adopting adult roles, as did Lacey's pupils who drank and smoked on the school premises and refused to wear school uniform. With their rejection of school values and norms goes their rejection of anything the school might offer in terms of achievement and qualification. Teachers expect them to work slowly, to find difficulty in understanding material that is accepted by the ideal pupil, thus they are presented with less demanding tasks, their aspirations and motivation are reduced, and eventually their performance is lowered. The self-fulfilling prophecy has indeed taken effect. Pupils have conformed to the picture of themselves presented to them by their teachers. Naturally the same effect works positively. Children of whom high expectations are made live up to these and A stream children succeed. Does this mean that teachers were justified in placing them in an A group or that teachers' expectations raised their aspirations, resulting in superior performance? To talk of the effects of a self-fulfilling prophecy must involve some discussion of a pupil's self concept. If he sees himself as a failure, he becomes one. But what helps to create this self-concept?

If we accept Mead's notion of the self as a process rather than a structure, that is, something constantly changing and developing during the course of the individual's interaction with other people, particularly with those who are important to him, we can see that the way in which he learns to see himself is influenced partly by the way in which others see him and act towards him. When we use the term 'self-concept', we are usually referring to two elements: the self-image and self-evaluation (Burns, 1982). The self-image is descriptive and concerns what the individual sees when he looks at himself, while the self-evaluative element includes an affective component — how he feels about his self-image. Because this concept of the self is essentially an active process, the individual is seen as acting towards the world and others in it, interpreting what confronts him and organizing his action accordingly.

If we consider this notion of the self in relation to pupils' self-concepts in the classroom it follows that a child can only construct his self-concept by reference to the behaviour of other people towards him, both teachers and peers. Interactionist theory (the framework within which Mead writes) predicts that children perceived unfavourably by teachers and peers will develop unfavourable self-concepts, since through interaction they learn to see themselves as others see them — unfavourably.

Nash (1973), working within this framework, put this hypothesis to the test in his study of teacher expectations. On the basis of preliminary observations made in a small primary school over a period of a year, he set out to discover whether pupils' self-concepts, as illustrated by their behaviour in class, would vary according to the way in which they were judged by teachers. His hypothesis was that the behaviour of children in classes where they are perceived favourably by the teacher would be different from where they are perceived unfavourably. An investigation of how pupils behaved towards teachers they encountered in their first year of secondary schooling confirmed this hypothesis. Children who admitted to 'playing up' in class with those teachers they did not get on with and judged to be too soft or boring, behaved well and were said to behave well by teachers who judged them more favourably. Nash suggests that teachers' expectations will also affect pupils' academic behaviour in a similar way in so far as the teacher's interaction with any pupil will contribute towards his self-concept. A further empirical investigation supported this view. Children were asked to rate themselves and others according to their relative position in class. With very few exceptions their own estimate of their relative position in class corresponded to the teacher's view of them. It is interesting to note that when Nash examined friendship groupings, he found that cliques were made up predominantly of children either unfavourably or favourably perceived by their teacher. It seems then that teachers' views of children also affect their friends' views and expectations of them, so that an unfavourable self-image derived from teachers' views is even more reinforced by peers' views. Hargreaves too noted in his study of fourth-year boys that those perceived unfavourably by teachers tended to form friendships with one another and not with those judged favourably by teachers and vice versa. Very few friendship bonds were found between A and D stream boys.

Pidgeon (1970) has indicated two ways in which a teacher's attitudes and perceptions might influence pupils' behaviour. Firstly, if he regards certain parts of his curriculum content to be above a pupil, he simply will not attempt to teach it, but will select something less demanding (*cf.* Keddie, 1971). Secondly, if a pupil is led to believe that he is capable of little, he will have low expectations of himself, low motivation and consequently will achieve little. Nash's study lends support to these views. Through their interaction with teachers, pupils discover the teachers' views of them by the way in which teachers treat them.

Bearing this in mind, we might argue that it is simply not feasible to say that lower working-class children or West Indian immigrants perform poorly in school *because* they come from poor backgrounds unless we can confirm that they *still* perform poorly even when teachers behave towards them in exactly the same way as they behave towards children from higher social classes born of British parents. This clearly is an assumption that has never been tested, and in fact would be difficult to test, since subtle cues teachers might give to indicate a different judgement of their pupils are difficult to observe and record. But until such an investigation has been made it is dangerous to make such a judgement in good faith.

Whether individual pupils' self-images are affected by teachers' views depends to a certain extent upon whether they regard teachers as significant others. As we saw earlier, Fuller's study of black girls (1981) suggested that their very positive self-image was rooted in their own culture, so that they were able to discard the expressive culture of the school and to take what they wanted from it, that is, academic qualifications. They simply ignored their teachers' unfavourable attitudes and learnt how to play the system.

One very serious consequence of judging, labelling, and categorizing pupils lies in its implications for curriculum organization. When pupils are categorized and treated differently, even though often in the interest of apparent justice, it often follows that they are given access to different kinds of knowledge from a very early age. In other words, not only can a hierarchy of pupils be distinguished but a hierarchy of knowledge as well.

Young (1971) suggests that school knowledge can be seen as socially organized or constructed. At the risk of oversimplification, this implies that different kinds of knowledge acquire a different status. In our education system high-status knowledge has the following main characteristics: it is highly abstract, unrelated to everyday life, and ranks higher than practical activities. It is based on literary rather than on practical skills or oral communication; it emphasizes individual effort rather than group work or collaborative learning; it tends to be the kind of knowledge that lends itself readily to formal assessment. The assumption that some kinds of knowledge are more worthwhile than others has dominated the curriculum in schools in this country — certainly in secondary schools — until very recently. A stream pupils have been offered high-status knowledge characterized as above whereas lower stream pupils have tended to be denied access to this kind of knowledge and to be served a diet of practical skills and topic work to be carried out on a group basis.

Early Schools Council projects were fiercely criticized by some writers (for example, White, 1968) for offering low-status knowledge to pupils deemed less bright. However Bantock (1971) goes so far as to suggest that we should develop a cognitive-intellectual curriculum for able pupils and an affective-artistic one for the less able. He claims that an academic curriculum, based on literacy, is inappropriate for the large majority of working-class pupils who come from a background with a strong oral tradition. He accepts Jensen's (1969) distinction between two different levels of mental functioning — the conceptual level and the level of associative learning. Children who can cope only with the latter will be unlikely to manage the increasing level of abstraction characterizing curriculum content at secondary school, and therefore he suggests providing for them an alternative curriculum based on easily attainable aspects of everyday life — television, film, popular press, dance, and other practical skills. But how could teachers decide who, at a later stage, would be capable of these different levels of thought, even if a case can be made for them? Are the judgements made by teachers early in a pupil's school career going to commit pupils to or exclude them from kinds of knowledge which, it could be argued, are worthwhile for all?

Shipman (1971) argues vehemently against any kind of differentiated curriculum on the grounds that it produces inequality. He stringently criticizes a number of curriculum innovations involving topic-centred approaches, interdisciplinary enquiry, taking children outside the school, claiming that they can deteriorate into nothing more than a pot-pourri of trivia selected because they are believed to be of interest to pupils — but only to pupils categorized as less able. There is a real danger in separating the education of such pupils and denying them access to any contact with real academic discipline and moreover in bringing home to them the reality of their own lower status. Certainly credit is due to innovators for attempting to make the curriculum more relevant to everyday life and thus more interesting to pupils. But there is a twofold risk: firstly, sacrificing academic rigour of any kind, and secondly, maintaining the existing divisions between children of different abilities and different social classes.

Merson and Campbell (1974) also voice a particular concern about the effects of such differentiation, called for by some community education projects, in terms of the curriculum. They fear that the move towards a socially relevant curriculum which places little emphasis upon the universals of rationality or upon rigorous intellectual procedures and language style, far from preparing pupils for greater social and political autonomy, will serve rather to debar them from it. Community-educated pupils, they warn, are likely to be limited by their preoccupation with their own local needs, and will still need others who have had a more rational, universalistic education to be spokesmen for them in any public arena.

The introduction of the CSE in 1965 has again had a polarizing effect, in that brighter pupils are prepared for the GCE and are usually taught in separate groups from those preparing for the rather lower-status examination. It remains to be seen whether the new common examination at 16+, the GCSE, scheduled to begin in 1986, will in fact help to reduce the differences created by a dual system of examination.

Practical implications

We have argued so far about the effects of judgements made by teachers on their pupils during the normal course of a day's teaching. Although such impressions may have long-lasting effects, they are not usually formally recorded. They are undoubtedly open to various kinds of bias, but since they form part of an interaction process, they can constantly be modified according to the way in which pupils react, develop, and change.

On a rather different level are those judgements which are formally documented for specific purposes and are usually on permanent written record for others to consult and use. Once they are written down, they are not open to modification unless further material is added at a later stage. The process now ceases to be a two-way form of communication since what is committed to writing intervenes between the teacher making the judgement and the pupils being judged. The main types of formal judgement with which most teachers are concerned are record-keeping and report-writing, though secondary school heads and sometimes careers teachers will frequently be asked to provide employers with references or testimonials for school leavers.

The main purposes of record-keeping are to document children's interests, work and progress and to reveal any flaw which requires remedial attention. They also help teachers to develop and plan future work for their pupils. In addition they provide information about individuals for other teachers, the head, parents and possibly outside agencies. A more efficient and flexible system of record-keeping than the earlier oversimplified check-list approach is clearly going to be more demanding for teachers' time and attention and will necessarily involve qualitative judgements about children's emotional, social and moral development. This approach is obviously open to the biases already discussed, but in view of the importance of detailed record-keeping in a flexible teaching set-up, it is imperative that attention be given to the way in which information is collected and comments are formulated. Bierley (1983) offers an interesting account of how one infant teacher helped to develop a system which provided detailed day-to-day information on all the work undertaken by individual children. Teachers' comments are firmly based on specific achievements and activities so that general inferences and vague remarks like 'works well' are avoided. Bierley believes that, as children develop, they themselves should be able to take part in a record-keeping system and thus share in the assessment and evaluation of their own work.

To most secondary teachers annual or termly report-writing is an onerous, time-consuming and unpopular task. Most standard report forms even today still consist of a list of subjects with columns for examination results, sessional grades and perhaps position in class, and only enough room for each subject specialist to write a brief comment on a pupil's progress in a particular curriculum area. The language of school reports is telegraphic in nature, using clichés like 'works hard', 'could do better' or 'fair only'. Because these remarks are not specific, they convey little information to those reading the final document. Teachers' judgements and impressions of pupils which may already have been subject to distortion and bias are made even more stereotyped by the format in which they are normally required.

The aims of reporting are threefold (Jackson, 1971): to assess, diagnose and plan for the future. Most traditional reports stop at the assessment stage, but attempts to explore other methods of reporting include more than this. As early as 1965, Green suggested, as did Jackson (1971), adopting a two-way communication system between parents and teachers where parents are invited to make a written reply on their children's report form. They would thus have the opportunity of explaining a pupil's lack of progress and asking for further information. Some schools send such reports home well in advance of parents' evenings so that consultations can be based on issues which have already received thought and consideration by all those concerned. A further possibility, now practised by some schools, is to include a space for pupils' comments (Hargreaves, 1972), thus creating a three-way network of communication in which pupils, teachers and parents can participate. Yet another method adopted by some schools is to send a detailed personal letter to parents, commenting on their child's progress, with an invitation to reply (Roussel, 1973).

More recently there have been national moves to develop new kinds of assessment procedures to replace school reports and to provide some documentary evidence of achievement especially for those pupils who leave school without any formal qualifications. Such assessment should benefit pupils by helping them to make realistic choices and giving them an awareness of their strengths and weaknesses, parents by giving them a broader range of information and employers by showing them not only what has been attempted and achieved but also offering some comment on pupils' social skills (Evans, 1979). Such reports, known as pupil profiles, are designed to provide a documentary record of attainment, interests and aspirations and to include all pupils whether they are successful in public examinations or not. The Scottish Council for Research in Education (1977) already has a well-developed pupil profile system which includes comments on scholastic achievement and work-related social skills such as enterprise, perseverance, self-reliance and adaptability. The Record of Personal Achievement, developed by Stansbury, is well known and with many others is highlighted by Burgess and Adams (1980) who discuss the importance of a personal record for each pupil that bears witness to individual interests and achievements over the whole of his school career.

The value and effectiveness of these profiles depends largely on teachers' skills in forming and formulating judgements of their pupils. The more detailed and personal nature of such records involves an element of subjectivity that is avoided in the neutrality of public examination results. There is thus all the more need for care and understanding in compiling such profiles if bias and distortion are to be avoided. Teachers might indeed feel at risk because of anticipated parental pressure and the suspicion on the part of pupils that a biased subjective judgement might do them less than justice (Broadfoot, 1982). However, if, as Macintosh suggests (1984), profile compilation involves negotiation between pupils and teachers as well as an indication of the kind of evidence used to arrive at the comments recorded, elements of unfairness and bias should be minimized. It is important that teachers begin to acquire requisite skills during their initial training and that they continue to receive help on an inservice basis to develop and refine ways of judging, evaluating and assessing pupils' achievement.

Summary and conclusions

In this chapter we have first of all outlined briefly the nature of interpersonal judgements and have then shown with reference to empirical studies some of the ways in which pupils are categorized. The relationship between supposed educability and social class is explored, with some discussion of differentiation according to measured ability, race, and gender.

We have considered some of the factors that influence teachers' judgements of pupils, including their concept of the ideal pupil together with their educational aims and objectives and also their own personality make-up.

The implications of biases or distortions in judgement for pupils' school careers have been pointed out and finally some practical issues relating to report-writing and record-keeping have been examined.

CHAPTER 3

INTELLIGENCE, MOTIVATION AND LEARNING

We have considered in the first two chapters some of the effects of classroom interaction and teacher judgements upon children's attitudes to school and their school careers. We now need to look more closely at learning itself and to try to understand something about why children learn, about differences in ability, styles of learning and appropriate conditions for learning.

Most introductory textbooks written for students on courses of initial training approach learning from a purely monodisciplinary point of view, summarizing classic psychological theories of learning and attempting to apply empirical laboratory findings to classroom practice (for example, Stones, 1979; Child, 1981; Fontana, 1981). Such an approach, however, fails to offer a satisfactory analysis of what we mean by learning. Child explains that

> learning occurs whenever one adopts new, or modifies existing, behaviour patterns in a way which has some influence on future performance or attitudes (1981, p. 81)

But how does such a definition help us to understand ways in which children master concepts of time and space? How is the learning of aesthetic or moral values explained? Child points out later that

> No one learning theory provides us with all the answers (ibid., p. 93)

But answers to what? We need first of all to identify the kinds of question that are useful to ask and with which psychology, as an empirical study, cannot necessarily help us. In his studies of language acquisition in young children, Gordon Wells sees learning as first and foremost a process — a continuous making of meanings and an adding to and restructuring of the internal model of the world that each individual has already built up. The product in many cases is of less importance. (1982b)

When we talk about children's learning, we are thus primarily concerned with the capacity for development, not merely the ability to recall facts and information, with which most learning theorists occupy themselves. Learning includes not only the acquisition of basic and complex skills but also their application; it involves the understanding and critical evaluation of what has been learned; it implies the ability to profit from experience and to transfer what has been learned to new experiences as well as making choices and decisions involving values. Important too is the ability to evaluate one's own capacities. Learning is not a purely cognitive process but has also an affective element. We hope that children will come to care about what they learn and get some sort of emotional satisfaction from it as well as developing the capacity to express emotions appropriately.

Motivation and learning

In order to discover how it is that children want to learn and come to care about what they are learning, we need to ask what kinds of motivational question teachers are concerned with. These are mainly of two kinds: those referring to what has happened in the past and those concerning what might happen in the future. The first kind of question is asked when children behave unexpectedly or when they fail to meet teachers' expectations. We ask why a normally diligent pupil suddenly loses interest in his work or why an individual who is usually considerate towards others begins instead to disrupt the work of his fellow pupils. Questions of this kind seem to require a causal explanation as if there were some kind of unknown force making a child antipathetic to school. Such causal explanations of human behaviour give an impression of a passive, machine-like creature at the mercy of all sorts of influences which cannot be resisted. As such, these explanations are more appropriate to the realm of physical or natural sciences than to human behaviour, which is far more complex and less predictable. As humans, we usually have intentions and are usually more or less responsible for our own actions.

Extrinsic motivation

Behaviourist theories of motivation and personality explain human behaviour largely in terms of various forms of external stimulation leading to certain kinds of response. Learning is said to take place when such responses are repeated as a result of reinforcement or reward. Thus, according to supporters of stimulus-response techniques in learning (S–R), teachers need to offer appropriate incentives and rewards in order to motivate children to perform certain tasks and to behave in a socially acceptable manner. Prizes, good reports, examination success, housepoints and teacher approval are all examples of extrinsic motivation, offered in many classrooms to persuade children to learn. According to Skinner, the greatest advocate of S–R techniques in learning, the teacher's main task is 'to bring behaviour under many sorts of stimulus control'. He comments on the highly inefficient practices in schools that waste useful learning time owing to the clumsy nature of reinforcement procedures. He criticizes teachers not only for their inability to provide immediate reinforcement to each child for each correct response, but also for spending too much time attempting to redesign curricula instead of employing

> available engineering techniques which would efficiently build the interests and instil the knowledge which are the goals of education.
> (1968)

Skinner himself advocated the use of programmed learning in schools as a highly efficient way of ensuring that each correct response a child makes is reinforced, thus using time more economically than in the normal class-teaching context and providing motivation in the form of reward. A typical programme consists of factual content divided up into such small steps that in answering simple questions about pieces of information given, the learner seldom makes a mistake. Although Skinner considered it important not to make errors, it does deny children the opportunity to learn from their own mistakes and to come to understand flaws in their own thinking. Research has shown that programmed learning can be highly efficient in terms of retention, but how far could it encourage children to be active in their own learning, to pursue their own interests and frame their own questions? There is serious doubt too whether understanding is achieved with these methods of learning. The very essence of human learning is that it is not simply reproductive but is active, highly individual and unpredictable. Indeed part of the very value of learning lies in the unpredictable and unexpected.

Bloom (1971;1976;1978) adopts a similar view in discussing his concept of mastery learning. He describes this approach as a

> teaching-learning strategy that can succeed in bringing a large proportion of students to a high level of achievement and to high motivation for further learning. (Bloom, 1978)

It hinges on frequency of feedback, reward and evidence of success. Such techniques, Bloom admits, are more appropriate to those curriculum areas which are closed, sequential, convergent and where the content is largely predetermined.

The deliberate use of rewards for controlling children's behaviour has been fairly widespread with disturbed and delinquent pupils, especially in the USA. The use of such token economy methods — the systematic application of a reinforcement schedule — has spread in recent years. Earlier work on the scholastic performance of delinquent boys (Tyler and Brown, 1968) and more recently that of Hoghughi (1979) with severely disturbed adolescents in residential care are two notable examples of such procedures. Strivens (1981) outlines the use of token economies by teachers working with mentally handicapped children in special schools in this country. Individual programmes are devised for children who can earn tokens which they can then trade in for desired activities, such as playing with special apparatus, or for tangible goods, such as sweets or toys. For example, a highly disruptive child can earn tokens as a reward for periods of concentration on a task without disturbing others, while a withdrawn child is rewarded for making contact with his peers. Typical programmes emphasize the importance of success and teacher encouragement to accompany the tangible rewards. They are designed to be developmental, in that concrete rewards are gradually phased out as the child gains more control over his behaviour. Ideally all children should eventually become involved in the design of their own programmes. Although such schemes are clear examples of teachers controlling pupils' behaviour in a fairly mechanistic manner, Scrivens sees one important advantage in that they do provide experience of a consistent environment with predictable consequences which many children have lacked before they enter a special school. The desirability of the use of token economies, she argues, depends upon the extent to which teacher control is gradually reduced and emphasis is shifted from the control of behaviour to the acquisition of basic social and classroom skills.

Although many teachers, particularly those working with pupils who are emotionally disturbed or mentally handicapped, would agree with Child (1981) that 'extrinsic motivators in the form of incentives are a very necessary part of a teacher's life', there are those who are concerned about the passive kind of learning that goes on in classrooms where excess emphasis is put upon rewards for correct answers. Learning to give the right answer does not imply understanding of basic concepts and principles and indeed, as Barnes (1976) reminds us, frequently leads children to spend time trying to interpret cues as to the answer the teacher has in mind. Guessing strategies become highly sophisticated and time-consuming so that energy is spent in this way rather than on problem solving and reflective thinking. Stubbs (1976b) likewise criticizes the pseudo-dialogue he observed in many secondary classrooms where learning supposedly goes on when the teacher poses a question to which he already knows the answer. The ability to give right answers shows that information has been retained, but fragmentary pieces of information do not constitute knowledge nor is the repetition of them necessarily educative. Furthermore, undue emphasis upon rewards, be they in the form of tokens, good marks or teacher approval, is likely to devalue the nature of learning itself.

Intrinsic Motivation

Behaviour and learning activated by a stimulus or incentive and reinforced by a reward suggests that human activitites are capable of control by outside agencies. Within this framework learners are relatively passive and do little to initiate their own activities. However, many actions, particularly those of young children, are performed for their own sake: children actively explore their environment and display natural curiosity in all kinds of play and exploratory behaviour. They seem to be 'innately predisposed to make sense of their experience, pose problems for themselves and actively to search for and achieve solutions' (Wells, 1982b). Thus cognitive theorists such as Berlyne (1960), McV. Hunt (1960) and Bruner (1966) have for a long time drawn our attention to the importance of the intrinsic curiosity inherent in human beings. Berlyne (1961;1963) introduced the terms 'ludic curiosity' and 'epistemic curiosity' to refer to knowledge-seeking behaviour including questioning, observation and problem solving. Curiosity is initiated by perceptual or cognitive conflict where uncertainty is aroused by perplexity, doubt, ambiguity and cognitive incongruity. Conflict in this sense is occasioned by novel, surprising or puzzling situations. Epistemic or exploratory behaviour consists then in seeking information to reduce uncertainty and to make sense of a situation — thus the learner is motivated to discover something new for himself. Bruner (1966) views the satisfaction of curiosity as one important factor in cognitive growth and suggests that 'mismatch' between two experiences is one essential element for development. Piaget's theory of intellectual growth also depends on the notion of cognitive conflict, which prompts a child to question the illogicalities of his own thinking. Inhelder (1978), extending Piagetian ideas, shows that it is only when a child has a hypothesis that conflicting evidence prompts him to challenge this hypothesis and perhaps modify it. When young children, for instance, observe objects floating and sinking, they initially develop ideas about which objects are likely to float or sink — a hypothesis which might rest on whether the object is made of wood or metal or whether it is heavy or light. But having formulated this idea, subsequent experience and observation of floating objects produces conflicting evidence: for example, not all wooden objects float; not all heavy objects sink. This apparent contradiction or mismatch, according to cognitive theorists, acts as a motivating factor: the child's curiosity is aroused by the apparent discrepancy and he is impelled to pursue his enquiries further to resolve the conflict.

This is an interesting and plausible concept of motivation which sees the child as an active, exploring agent who purposefully seeks knowledge for its own sake. What he learns is not devalued by the extraneous reward offered on the S — R pattern. Moreover he is not learning responses to somebody else's (the teacher's) questions or problems, but is recognizing problems for himself and solving them for the satisfaction of getting to know more and making more sense out of his accumulated experiences.

Various sources of evidence suggest that this kind of intrinsic motivation is not only a plausible concept, but is also effective in school learning and can help children to understand and remember new material, and encourage them to search actively for new information, to attempt to solve problems for themselves as well as to recognize problems when they occur. But since children need constant help and guidance, teachers employ various devices to stimulate and maintain curiosity. The introduction of what is surprising or novel is, for example, frequently used in the teaching and learning of science. Thus children have to accommodate to and explain the surprising fact that although whales live and swim in water they are not fish but mammals. Before this is surprising to them however they have to have some familiarity with the biological concepts of fish and mammal, since at any stage of development knowledge of the familiar must precede recognition of the unfamiliar or novel. As Bruner reminds us, surprise favours the well-prepared mind (1961).

Once a child, even a very young one, begins to show an interest in the novel, he ventures into areas of greater complexity both in terms of perception and action. McV. Hunt (1971), in a discussion of intrinsic motivation in young children, attaches great importance to complexity in relation to children's interest and curiosity. In his view, a bored child is one for whom there is too little complexity in his environment. Just as a young baby will cease to pay attention to a very familiar pattern and become habituated to it, so an older child will cease to show interest in a skill he has learned unless it increases in complexity. Children will feel more challenged by greater complexity in dealing with number concepts than by being required to practise the same skills repeatedly in which they are already competent. In planning work for children it follows that what is surprising or complex for one child will not necessarily evoke the same response in another. If surprise is to work as a motivational device, each individual child's stage of conceptual development must be considered. The planning of work must be largely on an individual or small-group basis. It is interesting to note, as McV. Hunt suggests, that some children in the class may act as 'complexity models' for others.

The very concept of intrinsic motivation is indeed the basis upon which activity methods, discovery learning and enquiry techniques rest. All these approaches imply that the learner is not simply a passive recipient of what the teacher offers, but is himself involved in his own learning because he finds it intrinsically interesting and worthwhile. To say that children are actively engaged in their own learning or are discovering concepts and principles for themselves does not mean that they have to be moving about physically. Intellectual activity, reflection and problem solving are just as valid forms of activity. Learning by discovery, however, needs guidance from the teacher who can help pupils to recognize issues which they can pursue because there is some degree of uncertainty or ambiguity which intrigues them. The Schools Council Learning through Science Project (1978-1984) shows how children can learn science through observing, raising questions, enquiring and testing and tracing relationships in such a way that they become totally absorbed in what they are doing and need no extraneous rewards. Likewise MACOS, Bruner's social science programme for the 8 to 13 age range, is designed to stimulate children's thinking for themselves about what it means to be human. Curiosity is aroused by the course material which prompts learners to raise all kinds of questions about human behaviour and customs within a comparative framework. The satisfaction of curiosity acts as a reward, thus motivating the learner to go further. Competence, another aspect of Bruner's approach to motivation, implies the will to master a complex world; activities which lead to this mastery are also intrinsically satisfying (Bruner, 1966). Mastery and achievement are closely related and we need now to examine some of the work on achievement motivation.

Achievement motivation

As early as 1953, McClelland introduced the notion of achievement motivation in which ambition is the key concept. He suggested that all human beings have some sort of ambition or need for achievement which motivates them to aspire to standards of excellence and mastery, although some have a far greater need for achievement than others. Clearly the notion of achievement motivation is of interest to teachers and it has been suggested (McClelland, 1976) that, if the characteristics of high achievers can be identified, then teachers can attempt to develop these in pupils who are less achievement-oriented. A high need for achievement has been associated with early independence training (Winterbottom, 1958); children who have been encouraged to become independent of their parents in their very early years are likely to show a high need for achievement in school. And indeed McClelland (1972) developed training programmes to encourage achievement motivation in students of all ages. It is interesting to ask why pupils want to achieve: is the mastery of skills or areas of knowledge self-rewarding, thus acting as an intrinsic motivator, as Bruner suggests? Or do some children want to achieve in order to surpass others or to gain social approval? Ausubel (1969) recognizes three components in achievement motivation: cognitive drive which is task-oriented; self-enhancement which is ego-oriented; and affiliation, indicating dependence on others for approval. It would be impossible to determine which of these elements was most influential in any one individual. It must be acknowledged too that achievement motivation is not influenced only by parental expectations in the early years, but is to some extent determined by other social factors. It might be a mark of status within one's peer group not to do well in certain areas, as Hargreaves (1967) showed in his study of fourth-year secondary boys. D stream boys who attempted to work hard at school were unpopular with their fellow students. This may account too for gender differences in achievement: girls who regard maths and science as boys' subjects do not want to do well in these areas for fear of being thought unfeminine, while few boys aspire to do well in domestic subjects (Sarah, 1980).

But regardless of group pressures or norms, it is unlikely that an individual will want to achieve in every area. It is interesting to note that, according to

Weiner's notion of attribution (1977), pupils with a high need for achievement attribute their success or failure to their own effort and ability, while low need-achievers attribute failure to external causes such as bad luck or task difficulty. The latter do not generally persist in the face of failure while the former increase their efforts.

Social motivation

As we have already seen, motivation in the classroom is not only a matter of incentives, rewards or stimulating children's interests to encourage them to pursue tasks for their own sake. It concerns also the whole social context in which teachers and pupils are interacting. Of paramount importance is the establishment of a social atmosphere in which children will feel relaxed and will want to work and where they know that their efforts will be valued and judged fairly. Pollard (1985) points out that tasks should be socially as well as cognitively appropriate and this is particularly important in the multicultural classroom. In a discussion of social relationships he comments on the strategies adopted by teachers and pupils which lead to stable, routine practices and afford a framework within which pupils feel secure and where anxiety is kept to a minimum. One particularly important strategy is open negotiation where teachers and pupils recognize and respect each others' interests and concerns. The key features are good humour, friendliness, readiness to explain and reason, and flexibility so that spontaneous interests can be used as a basis for class activities. In this way, social distance is reduced and an appropriate climate established for children to want to learn.

Much has been written in recent years about the importance of the self-concept in education. Burns (1982) gives an extensive summary of self-concept studies and quotes evidence to suggest that a poor self-concept creates low self-esteem which is subsequently related to low motivation and under-achievement. Pupils with a poor self-concept generally exhibit behaviour of a fairly negative kind, characterized by frequent statements of self-criticism but also an unwillingness to accept blame for failure. They believe that others dislike them but find it difficult to accept praise if it is offered. As a result their motivation is depressed and they consider it not worth trying to achieve since failure is, in their eyes, fairly certain. By contrast, those with a positive self-concept are socially well adjusted: they are confident about their own competence, optimistic about their future and they set themselves realistic goals. They believe that they are well-liked by others and are able to accept both praise and criticism.

Kagan's early studies of the development of the self-concept in young children (1967) drew attention to the importance of developing a favourable self-concept. Children who have developed a negative self-concept before they even come to school show a high level of anxiety, have difficulty in making friends, adjust less easily to school, and are frequently hampered in general achievement. Teachers can reinforce the poor opinion a child has of himself, but fortunately they can also help to reverse this opinion and to create in the child a more positive view of himself and his capacities (Downey, 1977). Palfrey (1973) gives an interesting account of the way in which the expectations and judgements of head teachers can affect their pupils' self-concept, with a subsequent influence on their motivation and aspirations. Material for study was drawn from two small secondary schools in the same area. While the head of the boys' school considered his pupils unlikely to be favourably disposed towards school or to have any high scholastic or occupational aspirations, the head of the girls' school took a completely different view. Both head teachers made their expectations clear to their pupils, the headmaster implicitly, by offering little encouragement and showing little interest in his pupils, but the headmistress explicitly, by insisting on higher standards of behaviour and application to work and by taking a committed interest in the girls' progress and job choices. An investigation of the self-concepts of fourth-year pupils in both schools suggested that their heads' expectations had had an influence on their motivation in school and their aspirations for when they left.

Early studies of the performance of West Indian pupils had suggested that a poor self-concept was responsible for under-achievement (Coard, 1971; Milner, 1975). However, as we saw in Chapter 2, this assumption was challenged by the findings of Stone (1981) and Fuller (1981). Jeffcoate (1981) suggests that it is unhelpful to talk of any child having only a positive or a negative self-concept and that a more useful model would be to consider conflicting high and low self-concepts, especially in ethnic group children. Such a model, he proposes, can be a source of creative energy in enabling them to cope with their environment and the demands of the school.

A further social dimension of motivation stems from the way in which children are grouped in school. There is little doubt that the organization of the school can affect pupils' aspirations. Schools that are rigidly streamed create academic opportunities for the able children who can succeed in this area and thus follow a path through school that is officially encouraged. At the same time pupils in lower streams are automatically debarred from following an academic career. By being labelled 'nonacademic' or D streamers they have been designated as academic failures. It is not surprising then that many pupils in this situation create other kinds of school careers for themselves; they form anti-school or delinquescent subcultures, to use Hargreaves' term. Hargreaves' study (1967), as we saw earlier, examines the effect of streaming on fourth-year boys in a secondary modern school in which he worked both as teacher and researcher. He describes the constant hostility between the A stream boys who accept school values and the D stream pupils who reject all the school has to offer. Their growing dissatisfaction with school has led them to seek status and satisfaction elsewhere. Their rejection of the pupil role is manifested in the premature adult roles they adopt — flagrantly smoking and drinking on school premises for example. Similarly, as we discussed earlier, Lacey's study (1970) of a streamed grammar school shows how pupils become differentiated very early on, at the beginning of their second year, when they are streamed by ability. Early in their second year, the bottom stream pupils are considered difficult to teach and lacking interest in school learning and other school activities. These studies both suggest that pupils in low streams lack motivation, but we clearly need to ask how this lack of motivation originated. Lacey's findings give a clear indication that it can be created by the school. Thus motivation becomes an organizational matter rather than purely an individual one. Once pupils see themselves failing in what the school approves of they are apt to form anti-school groups and by a process of situational adjustment their attitudes become even more consistently hostile to school values.

Becker (1964) uses the notion of situational adjustment to explain how individuals easily turn themselves into the sort of person a given situation requires if they wish to become and remain part of it. Thus, for example, if an academically unsuccessful pupil finds satisfaction in being a member of an anti-school group, he adopts the habits and attitudes of members of that group so that he is accepted by them and is part of that situation, no longer an outsider. Similarly a pupil who wishes to be successful in school and to adopt its values adjusts to the situation by behaving well in class, doing his homework on time, wearing correct uniform, and participating in extra-curricular activities. But the school structure makes it very difficult for him to do this, if, in streaming its pupils, it places those who want to adopt school values in streams where the situation is hostile. Thus such pupils very often find themselves adjusting to a situation they originally found unsympathetic.

Once this process of adjustment (and therefore attitude change) has taken place, it can be difficult to escape because the individual finds himself committed by other social factors. Again we use Becker's concept of commitment to explain this. He considers that a person is committed when we observe him pursuing a consistent line of activity in varied situations, for example, consistently rejecting school values. Commitment is maintained by fruitful rewards acquired in the situation, by relationships formed with others, by high status within the group and so on, all of which Becker refers to as side-bets. Although, however, as we have seen, the structure of the school can lead to little but failure for those pupils who are placed in low streams, we cannot feel assured that in an unstreamed situation these pupils would be any more committed to school. Adolescents' commitments outside it are likely to be strong in any case. The attractions offered by pop-cultures, presented to them most successfully via the mass media, require them to make less effort than the intellectual challenges provided by the school. Fletcher (1984), commenting on the nature of peer groups where children share the same influences and have the same cumulative experience of pop music, youth idols, fashions, gang membership, claims that this kind of informal organization can be the source of disaffection with school. The peer group, even though its roots are in social influences beyond the school, can then act as a kind of negative motivating factor.

The ways in which children are grouped within the school and within the classroom itself can affect their attitudes towards learning. The traditional model of class teaching with all children sitting in rows facing the teacher gives rise to the expectation that children work alone and not with their neighbour. In those schools where position in class is still recognized as important, the atmosphere can be highly competitive. Ausubel (1968) describes competition as 'a form of ego enhancement motivation involving self aggrandising activity in which the individual vies with others for hierarchical pre-eminence', whereas cooperation with others is group-oriented and individuals work towards a common goal. Research into the relative merits of competition and cooperation was conducted by those interested in group dynamics as long ago as the 1940s and 1950s, but, as far as classroom practice is concerned, has proved not particularly illuminating. Early laboratory studies (Deutsch, 1949; Stendler et al., 1951) suggested that motivation was higher and attitudes towards work more favourable when students worked cooperatively. There is, however, no convincing evidence to show that either cooperation or competition leads to more effective learning. Although Ausubel (1968) claims that both devices are active motivators, there are certain reservations. The very nature of competition ensures the success of some and the failure of others. Not all children in a class can come top and very often the same ones will fail all the time. Since continued failure leads to low self-esteem and depressed motivation, they will soon become frustrated and are likely to give up. Even children who are manifestly successful are likely to suffer ill effects and either resort to cheating in order to maintain their position or become so obsessed with self-aggrandizement that they lose sight not only of the intrinsic worth of what is being learnt but also of human values. High achievement and the prestige that accompanies it become the main criteria of human worth.

Cooperative or collaborative learning, one of the key features of British primary education, was strongly advocated by the Plowden Report (1967) in its recommendation that group work should occupy an important place in the educational experience of young children. Some advantages acclaimed for working in small groups are that children will help one another realize their own strengths and weaknesses as well as those of others. They will gain from opportunities to explain to others in the group and afford support to those who are nervous or insecure. Apathetic children might be stimulated by other members of the group and opportunities for talk and discussion are rich. Group work is appropriate for enquiry-based learning where children feel less inhibited in putting forward ideas than they would in front of a whole class. Group work then seems the ideal organization for collaborative learning, where each child learns to help others rather than vie with them. Recent studies however (DES, 1978; Galton *et al.*, 1980) have shown that grouping is less widely practised than protagonists of the progressive movement would like or that its critics claim is happening. The ORACLE studies revealed that grouping in the sample of primary schools studied was used largely as a managerial device rather than as a means of genuinely collaborative learning.

Barnes (1976; 1977) is a strong advocate of small-group work in secondary schools, claiming its advantages for exploratory talk and thinking. His own research suggests that the group is a valuable unit for learning, yet again there is little evidence of its use in practice (DES 1979).

To conclude this section on motivation we need to remind ourselves of two important issues. Firstly, if one of the reasons for learning and indeed for education itself is to achieve some kind of excellence, then all children, but especially those approaching the end of their school career, need to be assured that society itself values excellence and high standards of integrity and morality. If all they see is fierce competition for material rewards, they are likely to attach importance to these rather than to pursuing activities for their intrinsic interest and worth. Secondly, they must be able to see some place in the structure of society for their own efforts. There may be little point in encouraging children in school to develop a high need for achievement if there is no place for what they have achieved in the world outside school.

Intelligence and learning

One of the main aims of education, though not the only one, is to promote children's intellectual abilities and provide opportunities for their cognitive development. As teachers, we talk about intelligence and abilities and recognize that not all children are similarly endowed and that they do not all learn or develop at the same rate. Before we look at approaches to the study of intelligence it will be helpful to look at the general concept, which is both evaluative and descriptive.

It is used evaluatively in that it is considered a prized ability. It is generally thought better and more valuable to be intelligent than unintelligent for obvious reasons. It must be stressed however that the term 'intelligence' is a *morally* neutral one. There is nothing inherently moral in being highly intelligent. Such misuse or misunderstanding of the term can have unfortunate repercussions for those about whom judgements are being made. In a school system that values intelligence and achievement above all else, teachers might easily be misled into judging an intelligent pupil as a better person all round.

If, on the other hand, we use the term 'intelligence' purely descriptively, we need to know what characteristics are being picked out, and how to recognize intelligent behaviour.

Ryle (1960) suggests that to act intelligently is to think about what one is doing. Thus it would not be possible to act intelligently by accident or by chance. A young child for example might accidentally do something that for his age would appear exceptionally intelligent, but if it were not incorporated into his learning patterns and were not repeatable, in other words, if he could not yet learn from his own experience, this would not count as intelligent behaviour, but only a chance happening. Thinking about what one is doing is clearly seen in the performance of motor skills which very often give the appearance of being performed automatically, as if by habit. Yet it is only because the performer has thought about what he was doing in learning the skill that he can cope with disruptions, even serious ones, without a subsequent breakdown in performance. A skilled driver is usually able to cope with an unexpected hazard on the road because he is thinking about his actions, even though performance under normal conditions appears so smooth as to be deceptive.

It is important not to confuse the ability to carry out a complex skill which has been learned with *any* kind of complex routine. MacIntyre and Nowell-Smith (1970) suggest that this would be a mark of intelligent behaviour. But if it is, then the statement must certainly be qualified. Sticklebacks carry out highly complex routines as in courting and mating behaviour, yet this is instinctive and unadaptable rather than intelligent. Similarly, obsessives perform such complex routines that one minor false step causes them to go back to the beginning of the whole ritual again — hardly intelligent behaviour since it is both maladaptive and unadaptable. This kind of complex routine fails to be intelligent because it betrays no intentionality or purpose. It is merely fixed and rigid and could not be adapted to suit any particular purpose.

It seems then that intelligent behaviour must be intentional and that it must be adaptable to a specific purpose in the mind of the person himself. A machine could be programmed to carry out apparently purposeful activities but could not be called intelligent on these grounds. Behaviour judged as intelligent must of course be related to the age of the person concerned or to any special problems that he has. Thus it would not be particularly intelligent of a normal adult to climb on to a stool to get an object out of reach, but it would be considered intelligent for a two-year-old to do so.

Two theoretical perspectives

Approaches to the study of mental growth or intelligence have been of two kinds: the psychometric view concerned with the measurement of abilities and the developmental view, concerned with the structure and growth of cognitive abilities. These approaches are in practice complementary rather than contradictory and can both help to guide teachers in their assessment of children's abilities and progress as well as in the planning of their work.

Psychometry is concerned with mental measurement. The main interests of psychologists such as Galton, Spearman, and Burt lay in examining individual differences in measured intelligence and in attempting to discover what kinds of abilities go to make up what we call intelligence. Around the turn of the century there arose a pressing educational need to detect those children who, because of apparent dullness, were not able to profit from normal schooling. When Binet was asked in 1904 by the Paris Education Authorities to assist in discovering such children, he began to develop individual tests of ability, designed specifically to rank children of the same age according to their relative brightness. Without going into detail on the history of mental testing, suffice it to note that many more individual and, later, group tests were developed for similar purposes. The Army 'Alpha and Beta' tests in 1916 were constructed to test and place recruits to the US Army. After the war and in the 1920s such tests were used to help to select bright children for secondary schools and able adults for civil service positions and for similar selective entrance purposes. They were designed then to measure certain cognitive abilities which were thought to be largely independent of direct teaching, and although it was never claimed that purely innate capacity could be measured, the tests were assumed to give some indication of a child's innate ability to reason.

Some definitions of intelligence reveal the kinds of ability intended to be tapped by such tests. Burt's definition of intelligence (1955) as an 'innate, all-round cognitive ability' suggests firstly an emphasis on abilities a child is born with, although in a later article (1966) Burt reminds his critics that he never denied the importance of environment. Secondly, it implies that these abilities are of a general, nonspecific nature (*cf.* Spearman's 'g' factor) and thirdly that they are cognitive only, excluding by definition motivational elements.

Vernon (1969) sees intelligence as referring mainly to the ability to grasp relationships and to think symbolically, again with an emphasis on the cognitive side. But we must remember that a person's inclinations and motivation are probably just as important in determining his achievements, including achievement on an intelligence test, as his abilities. Stott (1966), for example, suggests that a child's ability to solve any problems, including those in an intelligence test, depends partly on the 'effectiveness motivation' he has developed in the past. Stott and Albin (1975) compiled an 'effectiveness motivation scale' designed to tap manifestations of effectiveness in preschool children over a wide range of activities. Since however it is far easier to observe and measure what a person can do than to assess his willingness to do it, the effort he puts into it or his reasons for doing it, psychologists have tended to concentrate on the cognitive aspects and to neglect the motivational components of intelligence. It is therefore interesting to come across an early definition of intelligence by Wechsler (1944) who includes 'acting purposefully' in his definition. Indeed, differences in motivation may account for some discrepancies in measured intelligence, such as those noted by Watson (1970) in his studies of West Indian children in East London. These children's scores were higher when tests were administered by a member of their own race than by a white tester. This kind of situation serves to remind us how difficult it is to separate ability from motivation.

The nature-nurture debate over the origins of intelligence is largely of historic interest to us today in relation to educational practice. But despite the fact that the argument is unresolved, it is important to realize what a powerful influence was exerted on practice and policy by the weight of evidence produced in support of innate determinants. Evidence that a certain proportion of measured intelligence is attributable to either innate or environmental factors can only be indirect, and is obtained mainly through twin studies. A wide-scale survey of such studies by Erlenmeyer-Kimling and Jarvik (1963) showed a higher correlation of scores between identical twins (with the same genetic constitution) than other siblings, although most studies suggested some influence of environmental factors. Burt's work (1966), now largely discredited because of the dubious nature of his findings, some of which appear to have been fabricated (Hearnshaw, 1980), purported to show that despite marked differences in their environmental conditions the scores of monozygotic twins showed a very high correlation. More recently the nature-nurture debate has been reopened in a different context, that of racial differences. Jensen's outspoken article (1969) on racial differences in measured intelligence, with its implications of Negro inferiority, was followed by a series of attacks on his assumptions, methodology and conclusions. What originated in the 1930s as a theoretical discussion on the relative importance of genetic and environmental determinants of intelligence seems to have been revived as an ideological and even political debate over the supposed intellectual inferiority of some races. The debate still continues today, although participants now agree that there can be no clear verdict in either direction and that it is impossible to state with any reliability what exact contribution genetic and environmental factors make to intelligence (Vernon, 1979; Vetta, 1980).

Of interest in this context is Hebb's view of intelligence (1949) which points to the importance of early stimulation for further growth. He conceives of intelligence A as the innate potential for development. This is a genetic component and, since it can never be observed or measured, is purely a hypothetical construct. Intelligence B is seen as 'the functioning of a brain where development has gone on'. Intelligence A then gives the potential for growth, but is manifested only if and when growth takes place. Since growth is not the same as maturation, it depends on some sort of nurture in the form of environmental stimulation. Hebb's own work on brain-damaged patients suggested that early stimulation was most important. Those suffering from later brain damage were far less impaired in terms of thought processes and problem solving than those who suffered similar damage early in life.

This hypothesis received confirmation from two further sources, again by work stemming from Hebb's laboratory. Experimental groups of rats were reared in a 'stimulating' environment, that is, one where the animals had freedom to roam and explore, where plenty of interesting objects were provided to arouse curiosity. Control groups were reared in a restricted environment, that is, in cages where they had little freedom and no new objects to explore. On subsequent tests, the experimental groups were found to be superior in maze learning (a kind of rodent intelligence test). The wide variety of stimulus variation experienced by the experimental animals early in life had given them a head start over the impoverished controls.

The second source of positive evidence supporting the early stimulation hypothesis was the vast amount of work on sensory deprivation, or reduced sensory input, to use the later and more accurate term. Subjects, both human and animal, deprived of sensory stimulation (visual, auditory, or tactile) in early life were found to remain permanently retarded while even adult subjects (as in the well-known coffin experiments) showed impaired vision, with impaired problem-solving ability, for some time after they emerged from the restricted and monotonous environment to which they had agreed to be subjected.

It may not be very helpful to extrapolate from animal or laboratory studies in an attempt to find evidence to support a hypothesis about human growth in natural conditions. Nevertheless such evidence does suggest the overriding importance of early experience for development.

If then, early stimulation is required for the functioning brain to grow, as it seems certainly is the case, this suggests that however small the effect of the environment might be on the development of innate potential as compared with an inborn component, it is the quality and nature of the environmental influences that are important. And for teachers concerned with practice, no less than psychologists concerned with providing a theoretical explanation, the important question is: what exactly is it that makes an environment stimulating for a particular child at a particular stage of development?

Although research evidence seldom forms the basis of policy making it is interesting to note that in this country tripartism was supported by the kind of evidence and view of intelligence that we have been discussing. The belief that intelligence is largely innately determined and can be reliably measured was at the basis of the recommendations of the Norwood Committee (1943). After the reorganization of secondary education in 1944, when most LEAs chose to adopt the tripartite system, not only were children selected for different kinds of secondary education but were again grouped by ability within the school.

During the 1950s attention turned to the importance of environmental factors in intellectual development and one of the consequences of this was to attribute the failure of working-class children to lack of stimulation in the home. Such children were labelled 'culturally deprived' (Riessman, 1962).

Thus programmes of compensatory education were developed in this country in the form of special provision for schools in Educational Priority Areas (Plowden Report, 1967), and such programmes as Headstart (Bereiter and Engelmann, 1966) were developed in the USA.

This sort of question which arises from Hebb's work seems to provide a useful link with our other broad perspective on intelligence — the developmental approach of Piaget. It is partly because of the influence of Piaget's work that educators have begun to think of intelligence as more than a mental faculty which simply matures as children grow up. Piaget (1950; 1952) has conceived intelligence in terms of a cumulative building up of complex schemata through the impact of the growing organism and the environment on one another. It is important to consider the origins of the Piagetian approach to intelligence and to remember that whereas intelligence tests were practical tools used to obtain data for educational purposes, Piaget's tasks were designed to test his hypothesis about the child's thinking and concept development. They were intended to explore and reveal differences which became apparent at various stages in any one child's development and were concerned therefore with intra-individual rather than inter-individual differences.

The Piagetian conception of intelligence is then essentially developmental and structural in nature. In his system, intelligence is broadly conceived as an adaptation to the physical and social environment. Since it is developmental, it shows the acquisition of knowledge in terms of adaptation to the environment along certain stage sequences. As children develop and interact with their environment, the structures built at an earlier stage evolve gradually into an integral part of the structure of a later stage. An infant first learns very slowly about the permanence of objects, for example, that a ball he has been playing with does not cease to exist when he cannot see it. This notion of permanence, his first step towards invariance of objects, is necessary to the notion of conservation of quantity which is learned during the stage of concrete operations. If the learning of one concept (in our example, permanence) is essential to the understanding of more complex concepts at a later stage of development, then it follows that the sequence of development must remain constant. The permanence of objects could not be learned *after* conservation of quantity since the understanding of permanence is a necessary condition of conservation. Similarly concrete operations form a basis upon which formal operations can later be learnt. To understand the notion of ratio, for instance, the child has to be able to compare different quantities and consider them in relation to one another rather than an absolute.

In Piaget's detailed description of the stages through which children pass from birth onwards, it emerges that what is of particular interest to him is not so much the products of thought, such as the answer a child gives to a conservation problem, but the processes of thought, namely the methods children use to respond to their environment or the kinds of attempts they make to solve problems set them. This suggests a qualitative approach to the development of intelligence, characteristic of the interest in developmental sequences within any one child, rather than a quantitative approach concerned with comparing measured differences between children.

The period of sensory motor or practical intelligence is characterized by a gradual moving away from a world in which the self is undifferentiated from the environment, to one which the child can experience and begin to understand through his actions. He comes to this understanding by first of all making purely perceptual and motor adjustments to objects about him. During this period (lasting for roughly the first two years of the child's life) he is seen to develop from an organism governed purely by his reflexes to a human being whose behaviour is beginning to show intentionality. A young infant will, for example, first look at his own hands when he drops an object he is playing with, and only gradually after much experience in handling objects will he begin to search for it when it is no longer in sight. But he is so far able only to perform actions, not represent them. His understanding of the world is limited to his own physical interaction with it. When he begins to go beyond the purely motor stage, the beginnings of some symbolic representation are apparent.

The child now enters the stage of preoperational thought in which he no longer has to rely on action alone, but can cope with representation. One example of representation is pretending. A child who pretends that a newspaper is a pillow will lie down with his head on it and 'go to sleep'. According to Piaget, the preoperational period is characterized still by egocentrism. A child cannot imagine what an object would look like from a different angle; he would draw it as it looks to him if asked to imagine himself in another position. He still tends to centre on only one aspect of a situation, such as the height of a column of water, disregarding its breadth. Thought at this stage tends to be static, because the child cannot understand the link between successive conditions and see them as a coherent whole. It is not unnaturally very similar to sensory motor intelligence upon which it is based.

During this period he shows the first signs of being able to deal with the potential as well as the actual, that is, to develop operational intelligence, in that he can predict what *will* be the case even if he has not yet experienced it.

If confronted with, say, a series of straws of different lengths placed in order from short to long, he will be able to predict accurately that to continue the series he will need a longer one. But he still cannot say what *might* be the case; he cannot yet deal with the hypothetical which probably belongs to the stage of formal operations. Indeed this is probably the most important general characteristic of formal operational thought. Only as a result of being able to deal logically with reality, the concrete, the here and now, can the adolescent, as he now is, conceive of reality as a part of what might be.

He is now able to deal not only with what is, with the here and now, but also to imagine what might have happened in the past or to conjecture about what could occur in the future. This implies that he must set up a series of hypotheses which in turn he confirms or rejects. This process clearly rests on the notion of invariance which he has already learned and on the ability to perform combinatorial operations. Similarly classification, seriation and correspondence which he learned at the concrete stage now enable him to develop propositional thinking. He is able to spot the logical flaw in the following, by being able to form sets and subsets, that is, to classify.

All X's are Y's
Here is a Y
Therefore it is an X

According to Piaget's scheme, then, a child is seen as developing through several stages of thinking, each more complex than the last and each one built upon and incorporating the previous one. Piaget postulates no fixed age limits for this development, but maintains that the sequence is constant. The ages he suggests give only very rough guidance. Nor does he imply that everyone goes through all the stages and finally achieves formal operations.

The main characteristics of Piagetian theory are firstly that cognitive development can be traced through a recognizable sequence of stages that is invariant. Although rates of development differ and not every individual attains the final stage, the sequence appears to be universal, as cross-cultural evidence has shown (Bruner, 1966). Further, there are no discrete cut-off points between the stages but a certain degree of overlap.

However amongst the plethora of Piagetian studies carried out during the past decade or so (for example, Modgil and Modgil, 1981) criticisms have begun to be levelled at the stage-theory concept itself. Brown and Desforges (1977) point out that if a stage concept is to have validity, there must be a substantial degree of homogeneity within the behaviour of most children for the greater part of each stage. They cite fairly early studies which were able to demonstrate considerable heterogeneity with individuals of all ages (Hamel, 1974; Schwebel, 1975). The universality of the stage theory has also been questioned by some cross-cultural studies which showed variation according to the nature and priorities of any particular community (Price Williams *et al.*, 1969; Ashton, 1975). But to question the stage theory is not to deny some sort of coherence in cognitive growth. Intellectual growth can still be systematic even though the original stage description might be inadequate.

Further criticisms have been made of Piaget's research procedures, especially in relation to the role of language. Donaldson (1978) points out that in Piaget's own work and in replication studies children were required to work in accordance with the researchers' language rather than with their own. She draws attention to the way in which questions were framed and suggests that the very wording of the question led children to believe that a particular kind of answer was expected of them. Especially unclear is children's understanding of comparative terms such as 'more', 'less', 'taller'. She further criticizes the neglect of social context in Piaget's experiments. Where a child and adult are in dialogue, she claims, the child feels under pressure to opt for one of a limited number of solutions to the questions he is asked. For example, in asking whether the length of two parallel rods has changed when one is moved, the adult is drawing attention to specific cues, suggesting that there is in fact something different he or she has to look for. Thus, in responding, the child takes into account the whole context in an attempt to interpret what the adult means. In her own work with children Donaldson showed that, by altering the experimental procedures, very different results were obtained. Young children, for instance, do show some evidence of deductive reasoning long before they have developed the general ability to think logically.

While it is important to remember that his interest lay in genetic epistemology, and that Piaget did not set out to provide teachers or educators with a theory of instruction or indeed any pedagogical guidelines, there is no doubt that his work has had an enormous impact on teachers' professional thinking, especially those concerned with primary education. Indeed the Plowden Report (1967) acknowledged its debt to Piagetian thought and many of its recommendations for practice were supported by reference to Piaget's work. Practices generally regarded as progressive either stem from Piaget's ideas about cognitive development or are justified by reference to them. Some examples are: treating individuals as active participants in their own learning; providing active experiences in the classroom for children at the stage of concrete operations; attempting to match curricular provision to the individual's state of development and being concerned with children's capacity to think rather than with an end-product. Teachers who adopt this view of the development of intelligence or cognitive growth favour individualized learning, discovery and enquiry techniques. Several curriculum projects developed during the past decade have acknowledged their debt to Piaget. For instance, the Teachers' Handbook for the Nuffield Mathematics Project (1975) is dedicated to Jean Piaget; in The Schools Council Science 5—13 (1975), work for children is sequenced according to Piagetian stages. And although Piaget's ideas have had a particular influence upon mathematical and scientific areas of the curriculum, attempts have also been made to apply the stage theory to religious education (Goldman, 1964); history and geography (Peel, 1972).

But despite the influence of Piaget's work, its relevance for educational practice has always had its critics and recently has been even more contested. Brown and Desforges (1979) point out how professional discourse has been unduly influenced by assertions about stages and readiness, with the result that teachers have tended to underrate children's capacities for reasoning and abstract thought. Some critics claim that Piaget's work is more useful in telling us what children cannot do than in suggesting ways of developing what they can do. Duckworth (1979) highlights the dilemma that educators face in attempting to apply Piagetian thinking to practice. She points out the impossibility of diagnosing each child's intellectual development and constructing individual programmes of work to match — hardly practical when one teacher is responsible for thirty or more children. A solution is to offer learning contexts in which children can experience their world in different ways, whatever their intellectual structure. If teachers can create such opportunities where children have the freedom to use their own methods of attaining an ultimate goal, then this will account for personal differences. Emphasis is again on the individual's processes of thinking and learning rather than on the outcome.

Many educators who have attempted to base their work on Piaget's research not only have encountered the difficulties discussed above but also have realized that there are other limitations. Piaget pays no attention, for example, to emotional blocks that may prevent a child from learning. Egan (1983) considers the theory limited because it fails to take into account the importance of fantasy in children's cognitive growth. Nevertheless, despite the growing body of criticism, it must be acknowledged that Piaget's influence on education, particularly on the ideology of primary education, has transformed the way in which we view children's thinking and learning. Our debt to him is one which cannot be ignored.

The work of Jerome Bruner

Turning now to the work of Bruner, we find that he deliberately set out to link his theory of cognitive growth to an understanding of both knowledge and instruction. Bruner argues that intellectual development is a means of mastering the environment by reducing and ordering its complexity. We do this by developing strategies in order to categorize objects, events and ideas. Children learn to master their world firstly through the senses and direct action; secondly, through images and visual representation and finally by symbolic means, namely language. These he refers to as enactive, iconic and symbolic modes. Although these three modes emerge sequentially, he is not proposing a stage theory of development in the Piagetian sense: all three have evolved by the time a child comes to school and each one continues to function and interact with the others. In infancy and early childhood the individual learns to master his or her world by touching, feeling and manipulating objects; he or she acquires the simple skills of walking, climbing and running. Bruner (1973) talks of play practice through which a child consolidates these simple skills, often being helped by the presence of a 'complexity' or 'competence' model in the shape of a peer or adult. Then gradually he or she learns to free himself or herself from the concrete world of the here and now and to use less direct means of coping with his or her environment: with the help of pictures, images and representative objects he or she can enter the realms of pretence and fantasy. Bruner admits that we understand little of the development of imagery and iconic representation but that it seems to grow out of practice in the enactive mode. Subsequently it is with the help of language that he or she is released totally from the concrete world. He or she is now able to reflect on the future and the past and also to think hypothetically about what might be in addition to what is. Children best attain this stage, Bruner claims, when their iconic thinking (intuition and guesswork) is not inhibited by a rigid framework of objectives and questions demanding precise answers. Once all three modes are acquired, they can all be used, sometimes simultaneously but sometimes separately, according to the nature of the situation or task in hand. Bruner takes an interactionist stance in that he regards the role of culture as an important factor in cognitive growth. This is not a purely individual matter of maturation, depending on the individual's genetic make-up, but rather it depends upon how a culture assists him to develop his potential. Every culture helps to promote cognitive growth by providing what Bruner calls 'amplifiers' appropriate to each of the three modes. Amplifiers of action are tools, equipment and utensils; those of the senses are signals, diagrams and pictures; while those of thought processes are language and number. Since different cultures have different priorities, he points out, there is no reason to suppose that intellectual development is universal in its rate or nature. Nontechnological societies, in contrast to our own, attach greater priority to direct action than to telling or instructing out of context. Skills that a young child learns, for example, fishing, sowing, reaping, are acquired directly by watching adults and working alongside them. There is thus little need for the symbolic mode where children are taught by being told out of context.

It is because of his claim that cognitive growth needs the assistance of culture, that Bruner sees the task of the school (an instrument of culture) as providing this support in the form of appropriate amplifiers. He therefore links his theory of cognitive growth which is purely descriptive to a theory of instruction which is prescriptive and normative. This theory is thus designed to improve and develop children's thought processes rather than merely to describe them. The task of the school is then to structure knowledge in forms that children can master at any given level of development — hence his notion of a spiral curriculum based on concepts to which the learner returns again and again at ever greater levels of complexity. 'In time, one visits and revisits the same general principles, rendering them increasingly more abstract and formal, more precise, more powerful, more generative' (1971, p. 38).

Bruner attaches great importance to processes of learning and claims that the best way to learn a subject is by doing it rather than being told about it. Thus learning by doing, discovering and enquiring is inextricably linked with his understanding of instrinsic motivation. One way in which teachers can stimulate thought and encourage pupils to explore further, is to work with conjectures and hypotheses, prompting pupils to suggest what might occur under certain circumstances or what might have happened, given different conditions. Man: a Course of Study affords children the opportunity to speculate and to go beyond the information given in order to generate modes of thought, understanding and opinions of their own. As we saw earlier, the aim of this course is to provide a context in which children can question, analyse and discuss important issues about the nature of man, rather than assimilate passively a collection of predigested facts. Edwards (1983) gives an interesting outline of how this project is used within a Humanities programme in a secondary school.

Other recent thinkers

It would be wrong to conclude this discussion without reference to the work of Eisner, who proposes a theory of cognition that is rather broader than that of Piaget or Bruner. Like Bruner, he is concerned with relating his theory of cognition to teaching and curriculum planning (1982). His thesis is that any theory of cognitive growth must include an affective component. He therefore pleads for a reconsideration of the part played by the senses and feelings in cognition itself, claiming that concept formation depends upon more than purely intellectual processes. The mistaken view that the cognitive is separable from other types of mental functioning has, in his opinion, done a disservice to education and the developing child.

Eisner's theory of cognition is based upon three broad concepts: forms of representation; modes of treatment of these forms, and syntaxes or arrangements of them. He introduces the notion 'forms of representation' to denote the ways in which we make public our private concepts so that they can be shared by others. Such forms of representation may be visual, auditory, kinaesthetic and so on and are expressed in terms of pictures, music, dance, drama. The choice of form an individual makes is determined by his skills and experience in that area and the appropriateness of the form to what he wishes to express. Thus one person may be able to express himself more clearly in pictures, another in music, another in words, while at times a combination of forms may be called for. The implications for the curriculum are twofold: firstly, if it is heavily biased towards the spoken and written word, then those pupils who would naturally use an alternative form are at a disadvantage in school; and secondly, since early experience has been shown to be crucial in perceptual development, the earlier we begin to help children develop a range of modes in which to express themselves, the better it will be for their cognitive development. To help all children develop a wide range of forms of representation is to equip them with intellectual capacities and resources that will liberate them as human beings rather than constricting their growth, as often happens in our present education system.

Eisner develops his theory of cognition by outlining three ways or modes in which forms of representation may be treated: the *mimetic* initiative which conveys what has been experienced in any particular sense in reality; the *expressive* which conveys feelings about what has been experienced; and thirdly the *conventional* mode which expresses what has been agreed upon within a culture. For example, as Eisner illustrates, an auditory experience can be treated mimetically in a piece of music suggesting a rider on horseback or expressively in music conveying feeling and atmosphere rather than a specific programme. To some music, on the other hand, a conventional meaning has been attributed, such as a national anthem or hymn.

To demonstrate the ways in which forms of representation are arranged (syntaxes) Eisner suggests a continuum, one end of which is arranged according to an agreed code or set of rules which must be adhered to in the interests of common understanding — for example, in arithmetic, spelling or punctuation. At the other end are those forms where the syntax is figurative rather than rule-bound, for example in the fine arts, dance, poetry, all of which are open to individual variation and original expression. It is here that idiosyncratic styles, personal deliberation and judgement come into play.

The kind of curriculum reform that Eisner would like to see is based upon his theory of cognition, and demands firstly a modification in the scope of content and secondly a change in the manner in which that content is taught. He suggests that more attention be given to subject areas such as the fine arts that help to cultivate and refine the sensibilities; pupils should be encouraged to develop poetic, literary and metaphorical ways of communication which permit personal judgement and awareness and therefore invite the learner to think imaginatively rather than learn to expect clear-cut solutions to problems. Pupils should be challenged to convey their understanding in diverse ways — through film, drama, dance, music, as well as through language. Only in this way can real meaning be given to the notion of developing each individual's potential in the interests of equity and parity in education. In addition, new forms of evaluation must be evolved which are compatible with this kind of curricular diversification. A shift away from quantitative to more qualitative styles of evaluation is needed and a willingness on the part of teachers and educators to recognize that any one style is on its own necessarily incomplete.

In an earlier article (1979) he had pointed out the value of participation in artistic activities, with painting as his special example, for a wide range of learning processes. He argues that such activities help to clarify thought for the individual, enabling him to develop competence and standards of judgement, to communicate to others ideas that can perhaps only be expressed through visual form, and to express feelings by the use of visual images.

As Eisner reminds us, the world of images, senses and feelings is one that by and large has been neglected by most theorists concerned with cognitive development. Egan (1983), wishing to restore balance, argues that fantasy is the most energetic aspect of young children's thinking and as such should be included in any theory of cognitive development. He claims that some of the most profound and fundamental concepts, such as love and hate, fear and security, good and bad, are experienced by children in their fantasy play and are embedded in the stories they read. Children's fantasy, he argues, is typified by settings and characters which appear to be totally removed from their everyday experience, for example witches or goblins, but who embody these universal human concepts. Thus while children seem to be more absorbed by the content of a fantasy world than by the real world, the basic human issues are very real indeed. Experience through fantasy is real to them not because of the content but because of these underlying abstract notions. Children who have not yet developed conservation and might therefore be seen to be at an immature stage of cognitive development within a Piagetian framework, might be experiencing a very vital intellectual life, trying to make sense of the important issues they encounter in the world of dragons and witches. To take children from the known to the unknown would mean, within Egan's frame of reference, to take them from what is familiar to them in the world of fantasy to the real world. This would be to extend their understanding of the basic conflict between good and bad, right and wrong, to manifestations of these in real life. This can best be achieved in an atmosphere where children feel free and uninhibited and not constrained by the rigidity of a preplanned programme in school.

Cognitive styles

We have so far in this chapter looked at theories of cognitive development and considered some of their implications for educational practice, while in a previous chapter we examined differences in teaching style. But what about differences in learning or cognitive style? Although intellectual development may progress in roughly the same way in all normal children, research has shown that approaches to problem solving are likely to differ. In laboratory-based experiments on problem solving, researchers have been able to identify different cognitive strategies or styles. Pask and Scott (1971) distinguished between a serialist and a holist approach to learning: serialists characteristically learn in a step-by-step manner disregarding digressions and what they consider irrelevant information. When asked to explain what has been learned, they tend to frame their argument in the same way as it was presented to them. Holists, in contrast, prefer a variety of approaches to a problem. They allow themselves to be diverted by interesting but apparently irrelevant information and like associating ideas in novel ways; they can accept that a problem may be solved in several ways and do not strive for clear-cut solutions.

Witkin (1977) used the terms 'global' and 'articulated' to refer to differences in perception and thinking that emerged from his battery of experiments with adults and children. Those with a global style find difficulty in separating relevant from irrelevant information in a problem and are more likely to be influenced by context or surrounding. Those with an articulated style are better able to focus on relevant details and adopt an analytical approach to learning and problem solving.

Of particular interest to teachers is the work of Kagan (1966), who proposed a 'reflectivity-impulsivity' dimension. The reflective child spends time working out the right answer before committing himself or herself in front of others; he or she likes to be right first time, so is cautious of making a response if he or she feels uncertain. The impulsive thinker is less cautious and likes to respond immediately, as if depending upon others — teachers or peers — to evaluate his answer.

Guilford (1968) distinguished convergent from divergent thinking: the convergent thinker is one who seeks a single solution to a problem, who likes the security of what is known and usual and tends to shy away from the risk and uncertainty of the unknown. Divergers seem to enjoy the ambiguity of unfamiliar situations and problems: they seek a variety of possible solutions and prefer unconventional responses which may seem bizarre. In his early work (1950) Guilford compared divergence with creative thinking and it was this interest that gave rise to the plethora of studies carried out in the 1960s. Most researchers (Guilford, 1950, 1959; Getzels and Jackson, 1962; Torrance, 1964) were working within a psychometric framework and thus concentrated on attempting to compile objective tests to distinguish between creative or divergent thinking on the one hand and convergent thinking on the other. These took the form of open-ended tests, including problems of word association, unusual uses of objects, hidden shapes and so on, designed to reveal fluency, flexibility and originality in thinking. Researchers talked about creative performance on tests but although clear differences in cognitive style were apparent in individuals' responses, it is doubtful whether the ability to attain high scores on open-ended tests bears any relationship to creative performance. Children who think divergently are not necessarily better able than convergers to write a poem, paint a picture, build a model or indeed to perform any of those activities which a layman might call creative. Nor can the tests predict creative performance later in life. The ability to give an unusual answer to a test question may reveal a difference in willingness to take risks or even a desire to appear bizarre. The fact that convergent thinkers do not give unusual answers does not mean that they have no creative ability.

After all, to some highly intelligent children the test may appear trivial and not worth bothering with.

Before we conclude this chapter with some discussion of the concept of creativity in education we must ask about the relevance of cognitive styles to classroom practice. It must be acknowledged first of all that differences do not imply that one style is superior to another, and that different styles may be appropriate to different kinds of learning. While it is not feasible to match teaching style with cognitive style, even though some writers have suggested this (Witkin, 1969), it is useful for teachers to be able to recognize and understand that not all children think or approach their work in the same way.

To raise questions about creativity in education or even different modes of thinking requires further analysis of the concept of creativity. As we have seen, intelligence is far more than performance on a test; similarly creativity must be more than test performance. What is needed then for the understanding of the relationship between creativity and intelligence is some kind of conceptual reorientation.

Jackson and Messick (1965) attempt to construct a hierarchical model of creative responses which seems to go further than previous attempts in picking out what might be called a creative performance. Intelligent responses, they suggest, are characterized as being correct in that they satisfy objective criteria and operate within the constraints of logic and reality. Creative performances by comparison are more difficult to recognize because they have to satisfy subjective criteria and are thus open to a wide variety of judgemental standards. Jackson and Messick use the term 'good' to characterize such creative responses and attempt to analyse what constitutes the good in this sense. Their first prerequisite for a creative response or performance, whether it relates to an artistic or scientific product, is the novel, the unusual in the sense of being strikingly different from other products of the same category. A young child's painting, for example, might show features that are unusual for children of his age but would not surprise us in an adult's work. For a creative response to be merely unusual though is not enough. It might be nothing more than odd or bizarre or even totally inappropriate. Appropriateness then is a second or higher-order criterion. Thus to be creative a product must be both unusual and yet appropriate to the context. But at this stage the level of creative excellence must be examined. To distinguish levels of creative excellence requires two further criteria: that of transformation of ideas or materials to overcome conventional restraints and condensation of meaning and association. These criteria are both difficult to define and to recognize. Transformation involves not just a restructuring of old ideas but a creation of new forms that generate reflection and wonder in the observer and stimulate him to further thought. Condensation is characteristic of the very highest levels of creative performance. It implies an intensity and concentration of meaning, intellectual or emotional, that can evoke constant contemplation — such as Tolstoy's *War and Peace* or a mature Haydn symphony.

We are not impressed or even awed only at the moment of contemplating a great work of art or a body of scientific theory, but we return to it again and again to discover new features, values, and relationships. For this reason it seems important to offer children aesthetic experiences. If they have the chance to listen to music or to look at paintings and buildings, and at the same time to learn something about the traditions behind them, they will learn to appreciate the values inherent in them.

Degenhardt's three main criteria (1976) for recognizing a creative product are interesting and useful as a complement to those set up by Jackson and Messick. He suggests, as they do, that what is created must be novel, at any rate to the creator. Secondly, that what is created must be of some value and, thirdly, that it must be intentionally created. In other words, the creator must have some idea of what counts as valuable in the field in which he is working and must also to some extent have mastered the appropriate skills and techniques so that he has a good idea of what he is after.

Creativity has traditionally been associated with the notion of creating something quite new, as if out of nothing. Such a concept of creativity, Elliott (1971) suggests, stems from the divine myth of creation, but a newer concept of creativeness allows far more flexibility in what can be included as creative acts, products, or thinking. This newer concept sees creativeness as developing novel ideas and either using them to solve problems for which there is no adequate response in terms of existing knowledge, methods, or techniques, or simply making them available to others. This notion of creativity can be thought of as part of what we understand by imagination.

It seems from this kind of analysis then that all teachers should discover what creativity means to them and what could count as a creative response in any particular sphere of children's activity and learning. This kind of approach is surely far more profitable than attempting to measure certain test responses, where one's thinking can so easily become enmeshed in the intricacies of scoring and standardizing. As soon as a testing approach is adopted, the notion of comparability in creativity arises. This of all areas in education is surely not one where an element of competitiveness is at all appropriate. It is interesting to remember, as with intelligence, that the term creativity can be used descriptively as well as evaluatively. If we are merely describing a child's thinking as being creative, we wish to point out certain characteristics of that style of thinking without implying that it is better than any other style. In using the term evaluatively, it implies that creative thinking is something worthwhile and something that we want to promote in children. Whereas teachers would clearly not want to promote or develop any kind of learning or skill that they did not consider worthwhile, it would be a mistake to undervalue those achievements which were not considered creative in favour of those that were. After all, in order to be creative at a high level of excellence, a person must have mastered certain basic skills and have acquired a certain verifiable body of knowledge. A boy cannot be creative in the design workshop, for example, unless he knows something of the properties of the materials he is using and recognizes the constraints they impose upon his freedom to create. Similarly he cannot work upon his materials until he has mastered certain skills and techniques of handling the appropriate tools. Just as there has been a danger of associating moral values with intelligence, a morally neutral term, a similar risk can arise with creativity. Not all children are as creative as others, just as not all are equally intelligent. But those who are less creative (or less intelligent) are not worse people for that.

In recent years in nearly all statements made by teachers, psychologists, educationists about the need for flexibility in education there has been some criticism — at times very heated and at times justifiable — about the iniquities of an education system, both in this country and in the USA, which requires conformity, conventionality, and regurgitation. It must be remembered, in making a distinction between the two groups, that there is no clear cut-off point. Convergers are those who show a *bias* in this direction. In Hudson's study there were those who gained a higher score on an intelligence test than on open-ended tests regardless of how high each score was.

However, if some pupils do show a bias towards convergence and others a bias towards divergence, it is interesting to discover whether schools can and do cater for both. A school system which is geared towards the passing of examinations and the attainment of qualifications, especially at secondary level, would seem to emphasize the ability to produce right answers or perhaps what the examiner wants. Thus convergent thinking would tend to be at a premium. Anxiety on this count, stimulated by such as Guilford and Torrance in the USA and by Hudson, Haddon, and Lytton in this country, has served to alert teachers to the dangers of undervaluing one type of thinking. If teachers are less favourably disposed towards divergent children, these children may soon learn to conceal such originality as they have by withdrawing into themselves. Thus potential creativity is stunted early in their school careers.

Schools, however, are not all the same in their social climate or aspirations. Haddon and Lytton (1968) compared two types of primary school, one using more conventional formal methods with an emphasis on achievement, rigid timetabling, and instruction, and the other a more progressive type of school, placing great emphasis upon self-initiated and creative learning. The schools were matched for socio-economic status and the children matched on verbal reasoning scores. Children in the informal schools showed higher scores on open-ended tests than those in the formal schools. Whether these are tests of true creative thinking is in doubt, but the indication that some children were more willing to venture unusual answers does perhaps reflect the freedom to learn that they had experienced in their schools where they moved freely about the classroom, had free access to the school library, and worked much of the time without supervision.

Critics of the traditional authoritarian type of education who have been writing recently within a sociological framework have contrasted two opposing paradigms in the social sciences which have formed a pattern for education (Esland, 1971). One is the psychometric paradigm which as we have seen in our discussion of different concepts of intelligence has been concerned with intelligence testing and a consequent imputation to children of specified levels of academic potential and achievement. This view diverts attention from children's thought processes and individual differences in modes of thinking and has led to a passive view of learning in which the individuality of the pupils, their interpretation of their world, and the meanings they attach to their learning experiences have been neglected to some extent. The phenomenological paradigm which Esland and others would like in its place is one which is concerned with individual ways of knowing, where an active rather than a static notion of the mind is emphasized. Processes of thought are 'seen to be part of a highly complex personal system of interpretations, intentions and recollections' (Esland, 1971). This view of development suggests that learning is a growth process, subject to an individual and personal interpretation, and that the mind is capable of unlimited development in many directions.

This view of education with its interest in classroom interaction without rigid teacher control would seem to provide an important conceptual and practical framework, not only for cognitive development along Piagetian lines, but also for the growth of creative thinking. After all, one of the most unfettered and therefore least threatening occasions when creativity can begin to develop in young children is when they are at play.

Although we cannot teach children to be creative, we can provide conditions in which creative abilities can develop, by ensuring that teaching, like play, does not stifle children's imagination by its rigidity and inflexibility. In suggesting what practical action teachers might take if they wish to create a school climate favourable to the development of creative thinking and abilities, Torrance (1967) makes proposals that anticipate just those attitudes being advocated by Esland and others within a phenomenological framework in the sociology of education. Torrance's suggestions are that teachers should be respectful of children's unusual questions and ideas, showing them that these ideas have value. They should provide opportunities for self-initiated learning and for periods of nonevaluated practice, indicating that whatever children do may be of some value and is not constantly going to be assessed by some absolute criterion of correctness set up by teachers. This emphasizes not only the need to value children in their own terms, by acknowledging the worth of common sense knowledge they bring with them into the classroom, but also acknowledges the importance of freedom and flexibility to develop and grow. These seem to be not only the cornerstones of both cognitive and creative development but also part of what is meant by education.

Summary and conclusions

In this chapter we have first of all examined the concept of learning and then explored some of the important determinants of learning — motivation, ability and intellectual potential.

We have discussed questions of rewards and incentives, referring to theories of extrinsic motivation and showing how these have been applied to human learning by illustrating from classroom practice. Intrinsic motivation was then compared and contrasted with a system of reinforcement and reward. Motivation, not only an individual matter, is shown to be influenced by social and organizational factors within the school. We have then tried to show the interrelationship between motivation and ability and have examined two broadly contrasting views of intelligence and intellectual development. We have not only discussed the well-established work of Piaget and Bruner but have also referred to some of the more recent approaches to cognitive growth and cognitive style. Finally we have examined the relationship between creativity and intelligence and have pointed to some of the problems encountered in trying to analyse the notion of creativity.

CHAPTER 4

LANGUAGE AND LEARNING

Language is at the very core of human experience; it is a public system of agreed signs and symbols which humans have created in order to communicate with one another and to make sense of their worlds. Since most of the learning that goes on in schools is mediated through language it is essential that all teachers develop a thorough understanding of the processes of language and the ways in which children learn and use it.

Studies of language have proliferated over the past two decades or so, but particularly since the publication of the Bullock Report in 1975 which outlined the central role of language in learning. More than ever before, teachers have come to accept that they are all responsible to some degree for the development of language in their pupils, regardless of the age range they are concerned with or their subject specialization. We shall attempt in this chapter to guide readers through the vast amount of literature reporting research findings and making recommendations for educational practice, by examining some basic issues in the language field.

Functions of language

It is useful from a practical point of view to bear in mind the distinction between *language* as a public system of symbols, agreed upon by common usage, and *speech* which refers to an individual's use of language. In this chapter we shall be concerned with the ways in which children acquire and use their language and in discussing classroom practice shall concentrate on spoken language rather than reading or writing. The language a person uses has many functions and indeed even one utterance may have more than one. For example, a child may be seeking to establish a relationship with his or her teacher or peers, while at the same time conveying information. Recent research has shown a move away from the study of the formal properties and structure of language to its uses and functions. Studies have centred thus on dynamic aspects of language, acknowledging that there is more to it than the rather more static features of code and syntax. Long before they come to school, children are beginning to use language to bring about changes in their environment, to interpret their world, to communicate with others and so on. Teachers have relied traditionally on the communicative functions, especially if their teaching is based on a didactic transmission model. Halliday (1973) suggests, however, that this function is late to develop and is never dominant in the language of young children. In his view children know what language is because they know what it does; they know how language is instrumental in helping them realize their intentions. He outlines seven main functions of language: the instrumental, the regulatory, the interactional, the personal, the heuristic, the imaginative and the informative. The instrumental is the first to emerge in the young infant, who can get things done for himself or herself by utterances that are not yet recognizable as words. He or she later learns to use language to regulate or control the behaviour of others. Interactional language is used to signify relationships with others and indicates degrees of familiarity, group allegiance or social distance. We use language in a personal way to express our own individuality, our feelings and emotions. Any attempt then to impose a uniform standard of dialect or pronunciation upon children at the expense of their personal expressive style runs the risk of undermining self-esteem and self-worth. To seek facts and information in order to find out about the real world is to use language heuristically, while an exploration of the world of fantasy requires the imaginative use of language; this also expresses pleasure in the words themselves and can be seen in children's delight in riddles, puns and chants as well as in their games, stories and pretence play. Finally language functions informatively to give information and express propositions. While it would be impractical for teachers to try to chart these functions for each child, as if categorizing each utterance on a checklist, Halliday suggests that we do need to recognize a whole range of uses and give children opportunities to develop language in all areas. Children who are linguistically restricted are likely to be those whose personal and heuristic functions in particular are deficient and, while this may be explained in terms of early social experience, the teacher's task is still primarily a linguistic one. Thus, in planning a language programme, teachers need to take into account not only children's own linguistic background but also the linguistic demands that will be made upon them by the school and eventually by society. Frank Smith (1982) reminds us that language is always accompanied by a metalinguistic or nonverbal mode which frequently reinforces the words themselves and indeed can sometimes replace them. Thus facial expressions, posture, beckoning, waving or smiling can indicate the speaker's intentions. Again it is important to recognize the significance of nonverbal means of communication which can have subtle nuances and cultural variations.

Joan Tough (1977a) likewise constructs a model of language functions based upon her investigations of the language used by groups of children of three, five and a half, and seven and a half at home and in school. She sees four main functions: the directive, the interpretative, the projective and the relational. In a comparative study of children from advantaged and disadvantaged homes (distinguished by parents' occupational and educational background), she found that children from both kinds of background used language to a similar degree, but that disadvantaged children were far less likely to use it for analysing and reflecting on past and present experiences or for projecting beyond the present to the future or to the possible or hypothetical. The main purpose of the Schools Council programme directed by Tough (1976; 1977b) was to help teachers identify the linguistic needs of young children and to develop skills involved in fostering their language development. Teachers were encouraged to engage children in pupil-teacher dialogue which would extend, probe and give focus to their experience and imagination. One important aim was to create experiences that challenge children to use language for imaginative play and for reflecting upon events and behaviour.

Although Tough's work has been criticized by later writers (Wells, 1982b; Tizard and Hughes, 1984), as we shall see later, her approach on a practical level as well as that of Halliday on a theoretical level with an emphasis on uses and functions of language has exposed the inadequacy of earlier investigations which were based largely on vocabulary and syntax.

Early language acquisition

Before we go on to discuss ways in which the various functions of language can be developed in school, it is important to have some understanding of how young children learn language and to see how practice can be affected by different theoretical approaches to language acquisition.

One theoretical explanation which is readily adopted by the layman because it appears to be common sense is in terms of imitation and reinforcement. Within this behaviourist framework, learning is explained in terms of rewarding the child when he makes a correct utterance and either ignoring him when he is wrong or correcting him in the hope that he will be able to imitate what the adult holds to be correct. Praise (reinforcement) follows when the child gets it right. However, this kind of explanation, put forward by Skinner and Mowrer, which sees the major part of any learning process in terms of rewarding correct responses, as we saw in the previous chapter, fails to explain the active nature of language learning. Imitation and reward could satisfactorily explain the learning of vocabulary and the naming of objects, but if these were the sole mechanisms at work, how would they explain how children come to utter sentences they have never heard before? Certainly this sort of model seems to underlie the practice of didactic teaching, rote learning and what Holt (1964) disparagingly called 'right answerism'.

But the very fact that all children have acquired the basic rules of grammar of their native language and have mastered its syntactic complexity before they come to school suggests that such rapid learning is partly supported by some innate mechanism which is exclusively a human characteristic. Thus McNeill (1966) postulated a 'language acquisition device' (LAD) which not only enables us to learn the syntax of our own language rapidly, but also helps us to recognize pseudo-sentences as grammatically correct, independently of their meaning. Chomsky's much quoted nonsense sentence — 'Colourless green ideas sleep furiously'. — is nevertheless recognizable and illustrates this point. Chomsky's (1959) recognition of the fact that by the age of four most children have acquired the basic rules of morphology, such as the formation of plurals and past tenses, gave rise to a whole series of studies focusing on grammar and syntax in the speech of young children. Fraser, Bellugi and Brown (1963), Cazden (1968) and others designed experiments to demonstrate that, even when presented with nonsense words that they could never have heard before, young children would apply rules that they had apparently worked out for themselves: for example, one wug; two wugs. McNeill's study of language learning in a two-year-old shows the creative and innovative nature of the process. The child builds up a limited store of words which he then uses in various combinations to create novel utterances within his own simple but already structured linguistic system. From original phrases learned from adults, like 'the chocolate's all gone' or 'more milk', a child creates his own simple meaningful units by using the same pivot words in a different context. 'All gone outside' thus indicates that the door is closed, while 'more page' means that he wants his mother to continue reading to him.

Brown and Bellugi (1964) suggested that there is a strong developmental factor at work, reminiscent of some kind of readiness device, since three-year-olds in their study, when asked to imitate a sentence spoken by an adult, contracted it to their own type of syntactic pattern, while retaining the meaning. Thus 'the cat wants to go out' is reduced to the telegraphic form 'cat out'.

Studies of this nature certainly pointed forward to a deeper understanding of young children's language, indicating as they do the dynamic nature of language learning, regardless of the complexity of the particular native language (Slobin, 1973). One important aspect was however still overlooked, namely the social context of language learning. Hymes (1970) points out the importance of communicative competence, that is, the ability to use and understand speech within a particular context. Such competence is nurtured by the social experience, needs and motives of the speaker. There are rules of use, he suggests, without which rules of grammar would be pointless, since what is grammatically the same sentence may be a statement, command or request, depending on the social context in which it is used. Children begin to follow these rules very early on and thus acquire not only a knowledge of sentences as grammatically correct but also as socially appropriate. They learn when to speak, how and to whom to speak. The notion of communicative competence gave rise to a whole series of important language interaction studies especially with very young infants. Such mother-baby studies showed quite clearly that infants begin to develop and use communication skills long before they can verbalize. Investigators such as Bruner, Trevarthen and Snow have suggested that prespeech communication plays an important role in the eventual interactive competence of young children. In her observations of very young babies, Snow (1977) found evidence of communicative moves as early as three months when baby and mother participate in pseudo-dialogue. The mother (or caregiver) reacts to the baby as if he is responding to her questions and statements. In aiming to get the child to take a turn in the 'conversation', the mother frequently uses questions, tag questions and greetings and if the baby fails to respond, she does it for him. He is thus taught to respond and take part in reciprocal communication. Trevarthen (1977) likewise found that two-month-old babies are capable of initiating conversational exchanges and suggests that the first six months of life are devoted to this kind of 'inter-subjectivity' where both partners are concerned only with each other. The child then is already becoming a social being at this very early stage and is learning the conventions that underlie the use of language long before he can use words. Bruner (1974) comments that a mother's interpretation of her child's communicative intent keeps the verbal interaction going. Language acquisition, he claims, 'occurs in the context of an action dialogue in which joint action is being undertaken by infant and adult'.

The significance of these studies for later development is interesting. Not only do the results suggest that the quality of this early interchange is likely to affect a child's ability or readiness to use language later on but they also raise questions about Piaget's notion of egocentricity. Observations make quite clear that infants are interested in others and do engage in reciprocal action with their caregivers by eye-contact, gestures, turn-taking.

Gordon Wells (1971-1984) has explored conversations between mother and child in the preschool years. The Bristol Language Development Study, of which he is director, was set up to observe and record the conversation of young children with their mothers in the home. Children aged fifteen and thirty-nine months were studied (128 children in all) and observations made at three-monthly intervals over a period of two and a quarter years. He found that all children tested (with the exception of two) engaged in conversation with the caring adult and had mastered meanings and the syntactic structure of sentences by the time they went to school. Observation showed that children frequently initiate conversations, many of which arise from the interest of the moment and within the context of normal household routines. For most of the time parents treat children as equal partners in conversation, encouraging them to take the initiative and helping them to extend the topics they embark upon. Conversation is regarded as a joint activity and although the mother frequently adjusts her speech to the child's level of development (the use of 'motherese'), she continues to provide a 'scaffolding' within which the child constructs his own understanding of meanings and his own model of the world that is expressed through language. Wells (1982a) calls this an apprenticeship in meaning and comments that 'the most effective talking and learning will take place when adult and child engage together in an apprenticeship in meaning', which rests on a reciprocal, negotiating style of interaction. A situation which affords ideal conversational experience for young children is one where the adult expresses an attitude of reciprocity and treats the child as someone who has something important to say, supporting his attempts to communicate and extending his contribution. A style that is dominating does not allow the child to take his share and is therefore not very helpful. These studies show a substantial similarity in the early conversational experience of children across all social classes, but as in the mother-baby interaction studies, it may be assumed that differences in the ability to use language are attributable to differences in quality of such experience.

Support for the validity of these findings is provided by the work of Tizard and Hughes (1984) who examined the conversation of thirty children from working-class and middle-class backgrounds in their homes and nursery schools. Again, all homes provided a rich linguistic environment, with working-class conversations proving to be as prolific as those in middle-class homes. All children asked vast numbers of questions and frequently took the initiative in dialogue; all mothers talked with their children during the normal course of household activities and most of them spent time telling stories.

In view of this, it is all the more surprising that when the same children entered school, some of them, particularly those from working-class homes, appeared to be linguistically disadvantaged. Tizard and Hughes found that all children became more subdued when they began nursery school, but that this passivity was more marked in their working-class sample. They suggest that the intellectual challenge provided by the home was lacking in school because of the teachers' style, which even with young children tended to be didactic and did not allow children the opportunity to take the initiative. Even storytime became more like a lesson with the teacher asking questions to test children, rather than challenging them to extend their own use of language and powers of thought. Wells (1982a) likewise attributes the apparent linguistic disadvantage of some children to the inappropriate kind of interaction they experience in school. Teacher-dominated conversation, with extensive use of closed questions, tends to lead to loss of confidence and feelings of inadequacy. Teachers' low expectations of children who are reticent because they have not yet learnt the rules of the game of school talk are likely to lead to a self-fulfilling prophecy. Both Tizard and Hughes, and Wells advocate more leisurely conversations in school which are open to a greater degree of spontaneous pupil participation. The classroom context should help children to go beyond the here and now and to reflect upon events, thoughts and feelings, so that language is used to explore imaginative and hypothetical worlds and to engage in what Wells calls 'disembedded' thinking. Teachers, he advocates, should be able to listen attentively to what children have to say and to discover what it is about their experience which makes them want to share it with an adult. They should learn how best to question children in order to extend their thinking and to foster reflectiveness rather than using display and probing questions. Many teachers, even of very young children, he observes, are too concerned with transmitting information, so that as a result, children come to think that real learning involves only tasks that the teacher has prescribed. Their own experience is likely to be undervalued by the teacher, so that it is better to play safe and do what the teacher wants rather than engage in spontaneous conversation or self-initiated enquiry.

The earlier Schools Council curriculum project directed by Joan Tough, has already been cited as an example of one attempt to help teachers to recognize young children's linguistic needs and to help them to acquire skills to promote language development in the nursery classroom. Tough's longitudinal study of young children's language had shown that groups of children drawn from two different social backgrounds were already using language in different ways by the age of three. Although there was little difference in the quantity of talk recorded or in the fluency of the children, those from advantaged homes were able to use language to express a much wider range of meanings. They were able to reflect on their present and past experiences, to consider possible alternatives, to plan and predict, and to attempt to explain why things happen, unlike those from disadvantaged homes. These differences are thought to be indicative of differences in thinking and understanding that would affect their progress in school. Thus a three-year project was set up in 1973 with members of the project team drawn from nursery and infant teachers. Two publications resulted from their work: the first (Tough, 1976) outlined a classification of language use (discussed briefly earlier), designed to help teachers to identify children's language functions. The second (Tough, 1977b) explores ways in which teachers can extend children's thinking and language skills and contains many examples of teachers talking with children during various classroom activities.

Wells (1977) however is highly critical of the work of Joan Tough, partly on account of her methodology and partly because of the kind of recommendations she makes to parents and teachers. Although the selection of children from widely different social backgrounds reveals broad social class differences, Wells' own findings show much smaller differences when the full range of background is examined. He doubts the validity of making generalizations about children's habitual use of language from one limited sample and maintains that it is not reasonable to infer that because a child does not choose to use language for a particular function within an interview, he or she cannot and does not in other situations. He also comments on Tough's method of categorization, and her neglect of the affective and social aspects of experience. His most serious doubts however concern meaning-making and communication: these, he says, seem to be based on what count as satisfactory answers to teachers' questions, indicating an outdated didactic setting of the primary classroom. In his view Tough's work is open to debate because, at a time when researchers are increasingly concerned with the business of communication, she gives insufficient attention to the interactional nature of this communication. Although she stresses the importance of dialogue as a means of extending children's language and thinking in school, her notion of dialogue is modelled on a question-and-answer technique, much criticized by Barnes and others in their observations of secondary classrooms. In such a setting the child tries to produce the answer he or she thinks the teacher wants and is thus denied the opportunity for spontaneous conversation with genuine collaboration, reciprocity and sharing of meanings. Wells' own studies show too many exceptions for him to be able to trace a simple relationship between social class, linguistic skills and educational success. His own recommendations for classroom practice, as we have seen, emphasize very strongly the need for the development of communicative competence.

The tendency for the question-and-answer mode of teaching to persist in many nursery and infant classrooms is attributed also by Tizard and Hughes (1984) to the impact of Tough's work on the practice of so many teachers. Indeed, her work was highly successful in disseminating information about the project since it used a proliferation of centres model and involved teachers from all over the country in its workshop sessions. Tizard and Hughes are particularly critical of moves to persuade parents to act like teachers. They also advocate more participation by parents in the education of their preschool children and a greater degree of parent-teacher collaboration, provided that the overall aim is to promote leisurely conversations where children are active participants.

There have indeed been many local moves to persuade parents to become more involved in their children's language development before they enter school. Raven (1982) describes an Educational Home Visitors scheme carried out in the Lothian region, the aim of which was to encourage mothers to play a more active role in promoting the educational development of their children. He comments that in any kind of intervention programme the important issue is what kind of talk mothers engage in with their children. In the conversation of parents of low social status he notes the frequency of questioning in order to test children — not an ideal means of extending their language. Chazan (1982) looked at home-visiting programmes as part of the West Riding EPA project and suggested that the language of some children (18-24 months) was restricted because mothers all too often anticipated their children's needs, so that they were not obliged to use language to get things done for themselves. One of the outcomes of this home-visiting scheme was that mothers began to realize that they could play an active part in developing their children's linguistic skills by joining in their activities. Yet another study (Donachy, 1976) describes a four-month programme, designed to help mothers participate in their children's learning, with the desired result that they became more aware of the natural teaching opportunities that arose during the course of ordinary household routine.

Young children themselves seem to show a fascination for language at a very early age; studies of language awareness suggest that long before children go to school they begin to take an interest in and reflect upon their own utterances. Evidence that very young children play with spoken language and practise new words and phrases is documented in Weir's study of her own child (1962), heard practising words in her cot at night. Slobin (1978) provides us with a case study of the early language awareness in his own daughter. Between the ages of two and six, children are observed to comment on the speech of themselves and of others, to ask explicit questions about speech and language, to correct themselves and to rephrase their own utterances. Clark (1978) claims that children begin to make judgements about language and are sensitive to the appropriateness of certain ways of speaking according to the social context in which they find themselves. They also practise and play with language, taking pleasure in puns, riddles and play on meanings. Indeed the now classic study of children's rhymes, chants and games by the Opies (1959) shows the aesthetic delight children take in varying and modifying rhymes. Bruner's research with preschool children (1975) explores the games and rituals shared by mothers with their babies and sees in these interactive games the seeds of meaning and aesthetic pleasure. Later linguistic disadvantage might in fact be due partly to lack of opportunity for such play in the early years.

Language variation

Social class and the notion of linguistic deprivation

We have already noted that some social class differences are apparent in the ways in which young children use language, but the differences are not nearly as marked as had been suggested by earlier work, notably that of Basil Bernstein (1973), whose explanation of working-class under-achievement was couched in terms of linguistic codes.

Social class, always a problematic term, was seen for his purposes as consisting of two broad subgroups; the working class: where neither parent has had a selective secondary education or any skilled training, and the middle class where both parents have had a selective secondary education and hold nonmanual jobs. There is too a transitional or upwardly mobile working-class group, some of whom have had some experience of selective secondary education or have been trained in a specific skill. The marked differences in language, social relationships and control that Bernstein discussed refer mainly to the two extremes of these subgroups — *lower* working class and middle class. Scant justice can be done here to the evolution of Bernstein's theory. It is essential that those concerned with such linguistic differences should certainly pursue some of the summaries of his theory to help them to tackle his original papers, if his ideas are not to be misinterpreted, as, sadly, they have been by those who are only superficially familiar with them. Working on the hypothesis that lower working-class children would be less linguistically competent than their middle-class peers because of the greater stress laid by the middle-class parents on language, he established that, on a verbal test of intelligence (Mill Hill Vocabulary Test), working-class adolescent boys scored significantly lower than a comparable middle-class sample. On a nonverbal test (Raven's Progressive Matrices) the discrepancy in performance was not significant. He went on to argue from these findings, albeit from a very small sample of subjects, that a great deal of potential ability is being lost in that working-class pupils may have failed to reach grammar school because of their poor performance on the selection tests which are mainly verbal.

Differences in the kind of speech system or language code that children develop are part of the process of socialization. According to Bernstein, families from different social backgrounds have different attitudes towards child rearing and thus different kinds of relationship are formed between parents and children: these relationships in turn affect the use of language. Several general conclusions emerge from empirical studies carried out by Bernstein and his co-workers, indicating where these early differences originate. From an analysis of replies given by fifty working-class and fifty middle-class mothers, all randomly selected, Bernstein and Henderson (1969) drew conclusions about the ways in which the different types of social interaction that develop duly affect the child's dependence on and use of language to express his needs. Clearly there will be exceptions. Not all apparently working-class or middle-class mothers will conform to a general sterotype, so it is important to remember that what follows indicates only a general tendency. Middle-class mothers are less likely to use coercive means of controlling their children (including smacking or unelaborated commands) but will tend to explain to their children why they regard their behaviour as undesirable. They are more likely to enter into and encourage conversation with their children and will attempt to answer difficult questions rather than evade them as many working-class mothers do.

Jean Jones (1966), again using a questionnaire technique and drawing from a sample of 360 mothers, found that middle-class mothers tended to prepare their five-year-olds for a more active role in school than working-class mothers. They read to them, encouraging them to join a library, talked to them about school and showed their children similarities between home and school, recognizing the educational significance of toys and play. In terms of language development, this active role adopted early by middle-class infants would make them more ready to talk to their teacher. Robinson and Rackstraw (1967), dealing with the way mothers coped with children's questions, found that working-class mothers were less likely to reply accurately to children's questions or even to answer them at all. They were less likely to explain or give elaborate answers and more likely to appeal to tradition in getting children to conform or obey. What emerged then from these various studies was that children were socialized differently according to the family subculture and that the emphasis put upon speech and language during the socialization process differed according to social class.

What then were the educational implications of such differences in early socialization and its effect on the use of language? Bernstein suggested the possibility of two different language codes. The restricted code is characterized by short sentences, frequently unfinished and with poor syntactical structure; by frequent use of short commands and questions; by limited use of adjectives and adverbs; by avoidance of impersonal and passive forms; and by use of clichés and idiomatic phrases without variation according to context. The restricted code speaker does not make himself explicit through language but relies heavily on gesture and intonation, and appeals to the listener in terms of 'You know what I mean?', 'See?' and so on. The elaborated code, because of its greater structural complexity, is one in which the speaker does make himself explicit, without having to rely on nonverbal cues or the shared sympathy of the listener. Because of fewer clichés and well-worn phrases, the speech used by elaborated-code speakers is at once more personal and less predictable. From this brief description of the codes it can be seen that a restricted code is more likely to be used when people share common experiences and are well enough acquainted with one another for meanings and intentions not to have to be made explicit. It would normally be used by any speaker within his own family or with close friends for example.

Bernstein suggested in his early work that most working-class speakers, as a result of the way in which they have experienced socialization in the early years were confined to a restricted code, while middle-class speakers have access to both. Since formal school learning requires children to make themselves explicit through language, those who can do so were supposed to be at an educational advantage. One way in which working-class children fail to make themselves explicit in words is that meaning for them was thought to be implicit, context bound, or particularistic, whereas the middle-class child can operate in a context-independent situation.

Bernstein's work has been stringently criticized on methodological grounds (see especially Coulthard, 1969). No doubt much of this criticism is justified, but anybody who pursues the *development* of such a theory as Bernstein's (amply documented over the past two decades) must acknowledge that the investigator is bound to stumble and make modifications in groping his way towards further understanding. Research methods indeed would not develop at all if errors did not give rise to modification and eventually to improvement. But of greater concern here in the context of language in education are the implications Bernstein's work has had for educational practice, many of them unfortunately based on a misunderstanding of his basic tenets. His early papers, published towards the end of the 1950s, came at a time when teachers had been made aware of gross inequalities in educational opportunity in this country. The idea that working-class children were failing because of their linguistic disadvantage was seized upon eagerly by teachers, to explain why such children, in spite of the teachers' efforts, were not succeeding in school.

Linguistic deprivation

However, it was unfortunate that Bernstein's notion of a restricted code gradually came to be regarded as an inferior kind of speech, as some sort of nonstandard, second-rate language which made school learning difficult and impeded logical thinking. In spite of Bernstein's comments (though perhaps not pointed or forceful enough in the early papers) that a restricted code was not to be regarded as second-rate, and that one code is not *better* than another, since 'each possesses its own aesthetic, its own possibilities' (Bernstein, 1971), the implication seen by his critics, and by teachers, many of whom became half-familiar with his theories, was one of linguistic disadvantage or even deprivation. And the idea of linguistic deprivation as one aspect of cultural deprivation was not without support in educational circles, particularly in the USA where compensatory educational programmes had been in operation from 1960 onwards. One of the assumptions upon which compensatory programmes were based was that certain disadvantaged children have difficulty in school because of poor language development and that remedial methods can help overcome these difficulties. The hampering effects of children's early impoverished home environment were thought to be reversible by the use of certain training or enrichment techniques.

The emphasis placed on language in American compensatory programmes must be attributed partly to the assumed interdependence between thought and language though, as we saw earlier, the nature of this relationship is by no means clear. Nevertheless, great emphasis was placed upon language in the American preschool intervention programmes, such as the Bereiter and Engelmann language development programme. The basic aims of this programme were to develop in preschool children sufficient understanding of language for them to grasp 'identity statements' and their negative counterparts ('this is a cat'; 'this is not a dog'), to accelerate their concept learning and to enable them to understand from their teacher when they are right or wrong. Four-year-old children worked with one teacher in groups of five for twenty-minute periods a day. Effort was concentrated on helping them to classify objects by showing them pictures and bombarding them with questions, to which they were taught to respond in chorus. It is thus a programme based on drill in sentence structure and use of words and as such has been used to teach standard English to Negro children and other nonstandard English speakers. Other programmes, such as that of Blank and Solomon (1968), giving individual language tuition to children, where the teacher works upon the child's responses and draws him into conversation about his activities while he is playing are in some ways reminiscent of the methods used by Joan Tough (1973) in the ordinary classroom. These programmes have had varying degrees of success but naturally enough have not escaped criticism, particularly because of the teaching methods employed.

Parry and Archer (1975) in this country express concern about the USA language programmes because of the heavy emphasis on language tests and on repetition and drill of linguistic patterns. The 'Talk Reform' programme (Gahagan and Gahagan, 1970) was begun in 1964 in infant classrooms in East London and was carried out under normal classroom conditions. The schools selected had large numbers of immigrant children in need of help in language development. This programme was based on peer interaction and aimed to extend children's vocabulary, encourage a variety of speech structures, and improve auditory discrimination. It was the Schools Council Pre-School Education project (Parry and Archer, 1975; Parry, 1975), set up to identify the needs of preschool children likely to suffer from language difficulties, which led to the establishment of Joan Tough's project, already discussed.

What emerged from all these studies was a picture of working-class children who were either language-less (*cf.* Bereiter and Engelmann, 1966) or linguistically deprived, and thus likely to encounter difficulties of comprehension in school. But to acknowledge that children use language in different ways does not mean that they fail to understand the language of their teachers.

Of interest at this point is the distinction made by Chomsky between linguistic competence and performance. Competence refers to our understanding of language, while performance is reflected in the way in which we use it. As everyone who has tried to converse with a foreigner in his own language knows, we understand far more than we actually put into words ourselves. The same holds good for the learning of the mother tongue, in Chomsky's view. To infer that children's understanding of language is necessarily impeded because their performance is limited is probably misguided. This distinction is a useful one for teachers to remember when they express concern about the way in which their pupils use language. Perhaps the distinction might help to demolish the notion that some children whose performance is limited are necessarily linguistically deprived or even nonverbal.

One of the most virulent critics of the notion of linguistic deprivation was Labov who, working within a linguistic rather than a sociological or psychological framework, wrote an impassioned argument declaiming verbal deprivation as a myth (1969). He defends the nonstandard English spoken by Negro *(his usage)* ghetto children, but some of his comments might well be applied to other nonstandard English speakers. The myth in Labov's view has arisen partly because speech data gathered from different social groups have been collected in very artificial situations. It is not surprising if a child, sitting in a strange room with an unfamiliar adult at the other side of a desk, fails to reply to his questions, thus appearing to be nonverbal. Labov's methods instead were to use Negro investigators who entered into conversation with Negro children in a relaxed situation. He describes the interviewer sitting on the floor, sharing a packet of crisps with an eight-year-old boy who has brought a friend along with him. This more natural context is conducive to conversation in a way that a more conventional interview technique fails to be. Labov's article is based on studies carried out with Negro boys of ten to seventeen during the period 1965-1967. Apart from suggested improvements in methodology, he examines the grammatical structure of Negro nonstandard English to see whether it does in fact have rules of its own or is merely randomly inaccurate as is frequently claimed, and to consider whether it does impede logical thinking. His findings were that Negro nonstandard English does not differ basically in syntax from standard English, having its own consistent rules, and that it does not prevent logical thinking. Samples of speech such as that of Larry, a fifteen-year-old school failure, talking about the nature of God, do show logical clarity but are clothed in a speech form which many teachers would reject and which most would have difficulty in understanding. In Labov's view then, no child is nonverbal or verbally deprived. His vernacular may be different from standard English but this in itself would not impede logical thinking or retard him in school learning. It is rather teachers' refusal to accept this vernacular and reluctance to learn to understand it that does make school learning problematic and unpalatable and eventually leads to school rejection.

Although the concept of linguistic deprivation has not met such stringent criticism in this country, probably because the term itself never became so powerful as in the USA, Rosen (1972) writes strongly against the idea of working-class speech being second-rate and inappropriate for school learning. He too questions the methods used in attempts to elicit speech from children in artificial situations, and hotly criticizes Bernstein's attempts to defend the value of working-class speech. Such remarks as 'A restricted code gives access to a vast potential of meanings of delicacy, subtlety, and diversity of cultural forms, to a unique aesthetic', are considered purely parenthetic and therefore of limited conviction, since Bernstein never goes on to examine working-class speech in detail or to investigate what a restricted code cannot do. This in Rosen's view is one of the large gaps in our knowledge of language. No one has hitherto examined in detail the strengths, richness, and potential of working-class language. Indeed only recently have attempts been made to investigate how language is actually used in school.

Wells (1981) refutes the notion of linguistic incompatibility between the home and the school and doubts whether this is the main contributory factor in the educational under-achievement particularly of working-class children. He suggests rather that we should examine not only the quality of linguistic interaction in the preschool years but also the importance attached to literacy in the home. His observations of children's literacy experiences indicate that those children whose parents read to them, tell them stories, look at books with them and who themselves are seen reading, are likely to be at an advantage in school. They have already become familiar with context-independent uses of language even before they themselves have begun to learn to read. The young child's first experiences with books and stories are therefore crucial for his or her literary enjoyment, as well as for his general progress in school. Marian Whitehead (1983) writes of the importance of books and story-telling with young children in school, and stresses the importance of an enthusiastic adult with whom the child can share his pleasure.

Multilingual contexts

The arrival in British schools in the 1960s and early 1970s of children with no English and of those speaking their own dialect version of English posed severe problems for an education system which was largely monolingual and monocultural. Although central government formulated no general policy or guidelines, most of the LEAs in whose schools large numbers of these children were to be found responded with an emphasis on teaching English as a foreign language. The assumption was that until children had mastered the tongue of the host nation they could not benefit from their schooling (Edwards, 1983). However, recent years have seen a shift towards the positive benefits of encouraging the use of the children's mother tongue alongside the use of English. But accurate information about the linguistic composition of ethnic minorities has until recently been sadly lacking. Rosen and Burgess (1980) have now collected information about linguistic diversity from 4,600 first-year pupils in 28 London secondary schools. Their survey established that no fewer than 55 languages apart from English and 65 dialect variations of English are spoken in their sample of schools. At one school alone 28 languages are spoken by a first-year intake of 300 children. For other parts of the country the Linguistic Minorities Project (1983) aimed to establish the range of diversity in secondary schools in selected LEAs, including Bradford, Coventry and Cambridgeshire.

While not denying the practical difficulties faced by teachers in multicultural and multilinguistic classrooms, many of those concerned with research and planning in this area see such problems as a positive challenge.

Miller (1983) urges teachers to make use of language diversity in order to encourage reflective awareness of language in all children. She reports discussions she had with twelve bilingual speakers and shows how children and teachers learn about the nature of language and the implications of linguistic and cultural diversity. Children whose mother tongue is not English and who have to learn to express themselves in at least two modes she finds are usually more aware than monolingual speakers of the appropriateness of their speech and of the effect it produces on their audience. In her view, this sensitivity could with benefit be nurtured in all children; teachers in multicultural classrooms are particularly fortunate in having such valuable human resources at their disposal.

As a result of the Rosen and Burgess survey (1980), examples of languages and dialects spoken in class were collected by the children themselves and this material was developed into a multidisciplinary project, published by the ILEA as *The Languages Book* (Raleigh and Miller, 1981). Its aim was to increase children's awareness of the language they use, of the power that it can exert and of the relationship of their own dialects to versions of Standard English.

Mother-tongue teaching has so far proved controversial. Many parents whose command of English is limited would like their children to maintain their native language and also to be taught in that language in school, in order to provide a feeling of cultural identity. Although such demands were initially met with incredulity on the part of many teachers, there have been several moves towards mother-tongue teaching (MTT). The Bedford Mother-Tongue Project (1976-1980) was designed to examine the educational implications of teaching children of Italian and Punjabi backgrounds the language, history and geography of their own ethnic origins. The Schools Council Mother-Tongue Project aims to develop curriculum materials for use with children speaking Greek and Bengali, while the ILEA has developed sets of bilingual material for classroom use, in addition to providing resources for ten schemes to teach mother-tongue languages outside school hours. Apart from the practical difficulties (including resources and appropriately qualified teachers), certain misgivings have been voiced about the desirability of MTT in schools. Brook (1980) fears that it might operate more as a means of social control than of promoting cultural diversity. Furthermore, special arrangements made for children to learn their own native tongue in school or to be taught in that language are bound to lead to segregation and divisiveness which can have an adverse social effect on all children. Nevertheless, so strong is the pressure on the part of some parents to maintain the mother-tongue in their children, that many voluntary groups have sprung up to teach minority languages. Edwards (1983) discusses fully many issues relating to MTT, language diversity and bilingualism and their implications for children learning to talk, read and write, both in English and in the language of their country of origin.

Accent and dialect

When we make judgements of other people, we use as one of our sources of information about them the way in which they speak. We recognize accents that are different from our own and can sometimes identify the speaker's region of origin by the dialect he speaks. Indeed as a nation we are particularly sensitive to accent and dialect differences, and often react more favourably to speakers using a preferred accent. Giles (1971) showed that speakers of Received Pronunciation were rated as more prestigious, competent and intelligent than speakers with South Welsh and Somerset accents, but were rated less favourably on social traits. Regional speakers were judged to have greater personal integrity, social attractiveness and a better sense of humour. Trudgill and Giles (1983) found aesthetic preferences for certain accents amongst English speakers who generally judge Received Pronunciation to be the most pleasant, and the accents of London and West Midlands speakers to be the ugliest. But how does all this relate to classroom practice? First of all, we need to be clear that accent refers to pronunciation only, while dialect includes syntax, morphology and vocabulary. Thus Standard English (a dialect) can be spoken with a nonstandard accent. Many teachers still argue cogently for the use of Standard English in school, not only in written English, but also in speech. Trudgill (1983), in an examination of the case for continuing to encourage the use of Standard English in schools, discounts many of the arguments hitherto advanced. Children do not have to learn to speak Standard English in order to understand it, since we are all capable of understanding a greater range of speech varieties than we use (*cf.* Chomsky's competence-performance distinction). And since English spelling is so different from pronunciation in any case, no one accent or dialect is superior when it comes to learning to read or write. Likewise claims that non-Standard English speakers will not be understood are usually rationalizations for an unfavourable attitude towards low-status accents. Labov (1969) had already demonstrated that Negro non-Standard English could be just as effective for logical argument, thus the case is not strong in relation to clarity or logicality. The only argument that really is valid, is that it is socially and economically advantageous to use Standard English. However irrational, it is an acknowledged fact that employers look more favourably upon Standard English speakers, thus non-Standard English school leavers are likely to be at a disadvantage when seeking employment. Standard English is a dialect which has long been associated with a particular high-status social group and is therefore symbolic of it. Children who have not grown up to speak Standard English will often learn to speak it only if they wish to be identified with that group. In practice, however, most children if not most adults become 'code switchers', speaking one dialect in the home or with their peers and another in school. Cheshire (1984) suggests that whether children do switch or not depends on whether they wish to show respect for the school or allegiance to their peer group. In her study of the speech of working-class adolescents in the Reading area (1982), she found that although most children consciously switched to Standard English in school, one persistent truant used more nonstandard forms in school than with his peers in order to demonstrate his hostility and anti-school attitudes.

However, whereas accent tolerance is increasing, there are still many teachers who are reluctant to accept dialect variations in school. They frown upon such features as the double negative or irregular uses of the singular and plural ('I haven't got none'; 'we was going') which are part of the grammatical structure of many dialects, albeit low-status ones. Trudgill's arguments for a change of attitudes on the part of teachers rather than a change of dialect on the part of pupils, were met with harsh criticism by those who condemned the kind of flexibility in spoken English that he supported. But whatever our own preferences or prejudices, we should be aware that there is a danger that those teachers who hold unfavourable attitudes towards low-status dialects often come, perhaps unwittingly, to evaluate speakers of these dialects less favourably than those who speak Standard English and to rate them as intellectually less able, thus setting in motion the familiar self-fulfilling prophecy about under-achievement.

Language and thought

For most practical purposes we are concerned with thought as it is conveyed to others either symbolically through language or through overt behaviour. Language is so obviously and inextricably linked with thought that in order to begin to appreciate their interdependence and complexity, teachers should have some understanding of the theoretical background within which observations of children's thinking have been made.

To consider the origins of thought and language, we turn to the work of Vigotsky and Piaget to examine two different theoretical explanations of the interrelationship. In Vigotsky's view, 'thought development is determined by language . . . the child's intellectual growth is contingent on his mastering the social means of thought, that is, language' (1962). Drawing on comparative data (the sounds produced by animals and human infants, together with their attempts at problem solving), Vigotsky recognized that speech and thought initially develop along different lines, independently of each other. Speech at this stage is preintellectual and is largely emotional in nature, for example babbling, calling, or crying. Similarly there is a prelinguistic phase in the development of thought when the infant will perform simple actions, solve simple problems, and clearly has some simple concept based mainly on recognition of the familiar, but has to accomplish all this without any attempt at speech.

In the human infant these two lines cross, according to Vigotsky, during the child's second year when he begins to learn to speak and to use his rudimentary language to help his problem-solving activities. Speech is beginning to become rational rather than just emotional and 'thought' becomes verbal. This stage is marked by a sudden increase in the child's vocabulary and attempts to use language and also a certain curiosity about words. The child's activities are now almost invariably accompanied by speech. His actions appear to be guided by his own autonomous speech which at first is overt but later on appears to die away. Everyone familiar with young children at play knows how they talk to themselves, giving a running commentary on what they are doing, regardless of whether there is anybody present. Vigotsky suggests that even when children cease to talk aloud when playing, this now inner or silent speech still plays an important function in regulating and directing activities. If the child's activities are frustrated or he encounters problems he cannot surmount in play, speech reappears at a remarkable rate, apparently to help him solve the problem.

The notion of language acting as a regulatory mechanism receives support from Luria's work. In his clinical study (1956) of five-year-old twins, retarded in all aspects of intellectual growth, he showed that when better opportunities were provided to promote language development, their behaviour generally showed signs of catching up with that of their age group. Play, which previously had been random, nonproductive, and nondirective, became far more advanced with the use of language, in that the boys could now plan activities and follow them through without abandoning whatever they had been doing after only a few minutes. Further experimental work conducted by Luria (1959; 1961) supported the view that one important function of language is to guide and regulate behaviour which otherwise becomes random and inconsequential. On this view then language is seen to be a necessary condition of thought and of the development of intelligence.

Piaget's emphasis is rather different. Although ready to admit that language is necessary for thought to develop, he does not regard it as a sufficient condition (1959). Rational or intelligent activities he sees as rooted in action, which is considered important at three stages of development: the sensory-motor stage, the level of concrete operations, and that of formal operations. At the sensory motor stage, the infant learns about his world through direct sensory experience, mainly by touching, tasting, and smelling. At the early stage of concrete operations, he begins to be able to classify and to form categories, which he can best do manually before working out the problem symbolically, that is, in words. Finally, at the stage of formal operations, he begins to think logically and hypothetically. Action however, according to Piaget, is at the roots of even propositional logic.

In these three areas Piaget suggests that language alone is not enough to explain thought because operations that characterize it nevertheless must be rooted in action. Without language, however, operations would necessarily remain at the stage of successive actions which could be performed only one after the other and not simultaneously. This in fact is what language allows us to do, namely to be released from the here-and-now world of action to a level where future, past, and present can be combined and where the purely hypothetical is possible.

Partly because of the influence of Piaget's work on operational thinking and the notion of a stage theory of development, it has been common until recently to emphasize the intellectual limitations of young children. However, as we saw in Chapter 3, recent work on language and thinking has concentrated on establishing children's strengths rather than revealing their weaknesses. Such studies (Donaldson, 1978; 1982) have drawn our attention to children's sensitivity to contextual cues in problem solving. Donaldson explains some of the difficulties encountered by children in standard Piagetian tests in terms of their sensitivity not only to the words of the questions, but also the context in which they are posed. Her studies show that preschool children can to some extent classify, measure, reason and appreciate perspectives other than their own, even though their thinking is still context-bound. Research has shown that preschool children have certain skills demonstrating their ability to think in a nonegocentric way, but that they use these skills largely in context-dependent situations, and not in the sort of context-free ones they encounter in school (Donaldson *et al.*, 1980). Similarly McGarrigle *et al.* and Gelman and Gallistrel (1983) have shown that children younger tharr seven can solve inclusion problems and are not ignorant of counting procedures once they grasp the significance of the language the adult uses in his questions. Once they begin to learn to read, their awareness of context-free language is increased and with it, context-free thinking.

Language and concepts

Having considered the origins and interrelationship of language and thought in a general way, we now turn to a consideration of the part played by language in concept learning. Basically, to learn a concept means to recognize an object or event as belonging to a category or to recognize something already familiar. Early concepts then clearly do not depend upon the use of language. A baby learns to recognize his mother as the one who feeds and protects him long before the concept 'mother' is learned. Animals too can be said to have acquired a concept when they distinguish between different objects. In food-seeking experiments, for example, rats can learn to distinguish between different shapes; chicks have been shown to learn a relationship concept when they seek food from the brighter of two squares (black or grey; dark or light grey; grey or white). But clearly an adult human being develops far more sophisticated concepts than these and it is useful for us to examine what kinds of concept adults do use, in order to understand how they are developed in children.

Dearden offers a useful but simple account of the main kinds of concept we use. He distinguishes three important categories, though, as noted, this is a simplified scheme and not all concepts fit neatly into one of the categories, while some categories can be further subdivided. *Perceptual* concepts include physical objects such as cat, flower, earth, blue, straight, that is, concepts which share certain manifest characteristics with other members of the same category. Young infants begin to acquire this kind of concept before they have a grasp of language, during the normal course of their random exploration of the environment. *Practical* concepts in Dearden's classification are those which are best understood by reference to their function, such as chair, post office, book, door. *Theoretical* concepts include the far more abstract ones such as wisdom, truth, freedom, mass, weight. When we come to examine how these various types of concept are learned, we shall see the rather different function of language and the implications for the ways in which teachers might help children to learn concepts of different kinds.

Children explore practical concepts by direct experience, by looking at objects, tasting them, touching and feeling them. There is no doubt that some sort of recognition goes on, but it is difficult to know whether the concept they 'discover' is the same as the one an adult has when he uses the publicly accepted symbol, its name, to denote it. If an adult points to an animal, telling the child it is a cat, how can the child know what is being pointed to unless he already has a concept of what a cat is and already understands the social convention of pointing? As far as he is concerned pointing could mean the finger used, the animal's fur, its colour, its tail, and so on. This explanation of how children learn the names of objects is clearly not very satisfactory any more than is the abstractionist model whereby a child is supposed to abstract the attributes common to the class of objects denoted by a specific label (attributes such as fur, four legs, tail) and to understand that the label denotes a cat. Simple though it may seem, learning the names of objects is highly complex to explain theoretically. Wittgenstein (1953) suggests that children learn to use language by participating in 'language games' and that they learn these rules by playing games. And before a child starts using words himself, he has had plenty of language preparation. He has handled objects, heard an adult refer to them by name, and can recognize them. It is only when a child uses language to denote objects in the same way as adults that we can even suspect that he shares the same concepts. Yet to use words correctly as labels does not necessarily mean that the child fully understands the underlying concepts. Jahoda (1963) shows how six-year-olds use geographical terms like 'town', 'city', 'capital' correctly in some contexts (for example 'London is the capital of England') but in other contexts reveal incomplete understanding.

Learning to play language games is then a continuous process, and indeed a social process. To make themselves intelligible children must learn the public rules governing the use of words. Without these rules, which are of course not explicitly taught, there would be no common understanding and no language as we know it. This notion of public rules governing the use of language is clearly applicable to the learning of practical concepts. Children learn the uses and functions of concepts not only by observing adults using them, but by talking about them themselves. Language has gone beyond the mere labelling stage. They might learn the use of a spoon by observation, but it would be difficult to learn the use of a post office or a bank merely by observing what people are doing in them. Without language none of the activities that go on in these places would make any sense at all, so that the concepts could never evolve.

Theoretical concepts, those we aim to introduce children to in school in various forms of knowledge and understanding, would be quite impossible without using language in its widest sense. Labelling would be far too limited. How could the label 'truth' tell us anything about the concept behind it? Even when specific theoretical concepts are labelled by the same word — fish, mammal, bird — (Natadze, 1963), real understanding develops only by reference to theoretical insight gained by symbolic means, that is, the use of publicly shared language.

Vigotsky (1962) refers to spontaneous and scientific concepts. The former are similar to Dearden's perceptual category, in that they are learned incidentally and are not necessarily dependent upon language. Scientific concepts are those which depend upon language, which need to be taught, and which provide systematic, generalized structures for thinking. The implications of this distinction for classroom practice are interesting. Such scientific concepts are not learned simply by learning to label correctly, but are based upon direct first-hand experience. For example, learning definitions for concepts such as 'mass', 'gravity', 'buoyancy' would result in nothing more than rote memorization, if children had not had first-hand experience of objects falling, floating or sinking and had not had the opportunity to talk about their observations using their own everyday language to explore new ideas. Likewise learning such concepts as 'fairness' and 'justice' depends on the experience of sharing and cooperating with others.

The classroom as a context for language learning: the current situation

We turn now to a more detailed examination of some of the implications of research findings already discussed for classroom and curriculum practice. It is now accepted by most teachers, whatever their specialism in subject or age-range, that language development is every teacher's responsibility. One of the main recommendations of the Bullock Report (1975) was that all schools should develop a unified language policy to promote and extend pupils' use of language in a wide range of different situations. Most primary schools have a language consultant with a particular interest and expertise, whose task is to construct a language policy in the school and to initiate language work as part of curriculum development. The consultant himself usually remains a class teacher. Marland and others (1977) have taken the main challenge of Bullock and tried to help secondary teachers to formulate and implement such a policy. Their central tenet is that learning is not merely through, but with language, so that the teacher's task is to guide children 'into language rather than round it'. Several other publications which followed the Bullock Report were designed to initiate amongst teachers discussion of school-based language programmes and to highlight the importance of language across the curriculum. Torbe (1976) issued guidelines for schools and later edited a collection of discussion papers on language policies, written by practising teachers in Coventry (1980). The Schools Council Working Paper No. 67 (Robertson, 1980) presents and discusses case studies of investigations carried out in four schools where some progress had been made in developing language policies.

The Schools Council indeed was responsible for stimulating discussion of language issues in its many working papers and research studies published during the 1970s and early 1980s. For example, Working Paper No. 59 *Talking, Writing and Learning* (1977) explored theoretical and practical issues relating to the eight to thirteen age range; No. 64 *Learning through Talking* (1979), published in collaboration with Avon Education Authority, examined the possibilities for small-group discussion with pupils of eleven to sixteen. This is an interesting example of school-based curriculum development, initiated by one teacher, setting out to study the place of English in the curriculum of third-year secondary pupils. It subsequently developed into a group study of the importance of talk across subjects and all secondary age groups.

Schools Council research studies include *The Language of Primary School Children* (H. and C. Rosen, 1973); the Communication Skills in Early Childhood Project (Tough, 1971-1976); *A Development of Writing Abilities* (Britton, 1976) and many others.

This surge of interest in language work in schools, together with the important findings in the research studies by Wells and Tizard amongst others on early childhood language, seem to form a promising and supportive background for practising teachers. But what in fact is happening in schools? Flanders' studies in the early 1970s suggested that teachers did most of the talking: has practice changed under such widespread professional interest in language? Edwards and Furlong (1978) present an empirical study of language used by teachers and pupils in open-type classrooms which are supposed to offer more active roles to pupils. They found, however, surprisingly little evidence of successful learning through talk. As in traditional classrooms where the pupils' main role is to listen, most teachers still told pupils 'when to talk, what to talk about, when to stop talking and how well they talked'. Pupils' language is very much 'talk as performance', where they typically rely on the clues teachers provide to achieve the right answer. Stubbs (1976a) comments on the 'conversational control' exerted by teachers over the relevance or correctness of what pupils say and indeed when they may speak.

Barnes (1976) makes an interesting distinction between exploratory talk and final draft language. Pupils using the former are using language creatively and experimentally to explore new concepts and clarify familiar ones. They do not expect to be criticized, corrected, or censured for what they say or the way they express themselves. Final draft language, on the other hand, does not reveal detours or processes of thought, but presents only a finished product for assessment. The kind of style used will depend on the audience. If children know that the teacher is asking questions to which he clearly knows the answers and is interrogating or cross-questioning them, they will use a final draft or performance style. Exploratory talk is used in a collaborative relationship, whether it is with peers or adults. This distinction is paralleled by the one Bruner (1961) makes between expository and hypothetical modes of teaching. A move away from the expository mode, to meet the needs of some recent curriculum projects relying largely on discussion techniques, requires a change in relationship between teacher and taught, accompanied by a change in the style of language used by both.

Official surveys of primary and secondary schools (DES, 1978; 1979; 1982) have also shown that in the sample of schools observed much of the language work was on formal writing and the mechanics of language. Talking and active listening were still not fully exploited in infant, junior or secondary schools. Even in nursery schools and classes, as we discussed earlier, teachers were to be observed asking children closed questions as if to test them, and effectively stemming the flow of genuine conversation (Wells, 1982b; Tizard and Hughes, 1984).

Fears have been voiced that the sampling programme set up by the Assessment of Performance Unit (APU) to monitor standards will discourage teachers from attempting the kind of exploratory work in language that is difficult to evaluate. Rosen (1982) was highly critical of the APU's Primary Survey Report No. 1, pointing out that rather than contributing towards a national picture of language development, as it claims to do, it in practice deals largely with performance on a series of tests of reading and writing and says nothing about what children can do with language. Recommendations of the HMI document *Bullock Revisited* (DES, 1982) seem inconsistent or perhaps confused: the Committee recommends that there is still room for vast improvement in the use of spoken language in the classroom, but at the same time they advise teachers responsible for language work to consider the test result and assessment procedures used by the APU and to relate them to their own practice. Surely to begin with testing and assessment lays an emphasis mistakenly on the outcome, on final draft language, thus clouding the issues of the processes of learning and using language, and indeed shifting attention from the dynamic growth and development of language that so many teachers have been striving to achieve.

In order not to conclude this discussion on a rather despondent note, let us remind ourselves of some of the areas that research and observation highlight as important and useful starting points. At the stage of early childhood education, Tizard and Hughes suggest that teachers have much to learn from mothers and their young children in the home, where conversation is observed to be highly educational and children are constantly extending their knowledge of the world and being stretched intellectually by talking, arguing and asking endless questions. The school's task is to build on this early intellectual achievement by providing more time to extend children's general knowledge and opportunities for verbal exploration of their environment. Wells (1983b) likewise suggests that teachers of young children devote more time to encouraging them to talk in the more spontaneous ways with which they are familiar at home and suggests domestic-type situations as useful starting points for this.

Barnes and Todd (1977) are strong supporters of small-group learning at the secondary level and point out that spoken language is the crucial mediator between children's own common sense knowledge expressed in everyday language, and specialist subject knowledge expressed in a more theoretical register. Working within a small group, they claim, affords pupils the opportunity to explore new concepts and to contribute to the discussion without having to formulate ideas in a polished form for the teacher. In such a set-up, group members are thrown back on their own resources and since they cannot rely on the teacher to give them answers, they are forced to think and use language in an exploratory way.

Let us conclude with a quotation from C. Rosen (1973), which although a reflection on primary school practice, sums up the thinking of many teachers of all age ranges:

Children have available much more linguistic competence than usually finds its way into their speech. We need to create those situations which exert the greatest pressure on them to use their latent resources, to provide these experiences which urge them towards the widest range of language use. (1973, p. 256).

Summary and conclusions

In this chapter we have discussed briefly the nature and functions of language, then examined three theoretical approaches to early language acquisition, that of SR psychology, the nativist approach, and the more recent work by those taking an interactionist stance. Implications of this work for classroom practice were then noted.

We have continued by looking at some types of language variation including social class differences, accent and dialect diversity. The relationship between language, thinking and learning of concepts was then considered and some of the recent challenges to Piaget's work noted.

Finally we have looked at current practices, drawing attention to recent official publications and to the work of the Schools Council.

CHAPTER 5

AUTHORITY

The progress that children make at school will not depend only on the views that teachers hold about such things as intelligence, motivation, and language, and the judgements that they are thus led to make of their pupils. That progress, and indeed those judgements themselves, will depend equally, if not more conclusively, on the kinds of relationship the teacher develops with his or her pupils, the approach he or she takes to classroom control, and the kind of atmosphere that is generated by the view he or she takes of the competing demands of freedom and authority. It is to this question of the teacher's authority, therefore, that we must next turn our attention.

Questions about authority cause teachers concern at the levels of both theory and practice. Whether they will in fact have the authority to control their pupils is a question that worries all trainee teachers and new entrants to the profession and it is a question that continues to concern most teachers throughout their careers. Nowadays, however, many teachers are also uncertain about whether they should be exercising authority over their pupils at all or at least to what extent such control can be justified. There is a feeling abroad, strengthened by developments such as the 'free school' and increased demands for participation by pupils in decision making of all kinds, that any exercise of authority is an infringement of the freedom and rights of the child, so that a certain uneasiness results for those teachers who regard these things as important yet find themselves required by the exigencies of the school situation to place restraints on children's behaviour in many different contexts. Nor again are the practical and theoretical aspects of the problem readily separable, since to a large degree the extent to which one is able to exercise authority will depend on how clear one is about the justification of it, since confidence is needed here perhaps more than anywhere else in education and confidence can only come from a conviction that what one is doing is right. Conversely, much that can only be described as arrant nonsense has been said and written about the freedom of children by those whose view of the issues involved has not been tempered by experience of the realities of the teaching situation. Again, therefore, theory and practice need to be interwoven if we are to achieve a view of the place of authority in education that is both clear and constructive. Again, too, we must begin by attempting to sort out the different issues that are involved.

In doing this we must consider two main kinds of question, firstly, that concerning the justification of the exercise of any kind of authority by teachers and, secondly, a number of related questions concerning the nature of authority, the ways in which teachers can and do come to exercise it, especially in the context of a democratic society, and the repercussions that different approaches to control in the school and in the classroom may have on the development of pupils. These two kinds of question are not, of course, entirely independent of each other, since any discussion of the ways in which a teacher can acquire authority, and especially of the kind of authority that is appropriate to education, must presuppose and, indeed, depend for its substance on some view about its justification, but it will be in the interests of clarity to discuss the two issues separately and most useful to begin with the problem of justification.

Freedom and authority

We must begin our discussion in this field once again by attempting to clarify the concepts we are concerned with and, in particular, by trying to achieve some clarity over the notion of 'freedom' and the use of the adjective 'free'.

In its purely descriptive uses, the word 'free' denotes the absence of some hindrance or restraint. Thus to describe a piece of mechanism as 'free' is to suggest that it has been jammed or blocked in some way, while to describe a person as 'free' is to imply that he or she has been under some kind of restraint, in prison, for example, or with a full engagement book, or even merely married (Benn and Peters, 1959). In its most common use too, the word indicates the absence of a fee or charge that might act as a hindrance to the acquisition or possession of some object, commodity or service. Furthermore, in all of these uses of 'free' there seems to be the added implication that the hindrance or restraint that is absent is an undesirable hindrance or restraint. As evidence of this, it is interesting to note and compare the use of the suffixes '-free' and '-less'. In most, if not all, cases the use of '-free' suggests 'good riddance' and the use of '-less' expresses regret at what is missing. What is meat-free to the vegetarian is meat-less to the carnivore and the same can be seen in the contrasting notions of carefree and careless driving (Ryan, 1965). Even in its largely descriptive sense, therefore, and in contexts that might be felt to be largely neutral, politically speaking, freedom is generally regarded as something worth having.

However, all of this does point to the need for some qualification to be made, for some specification of the hindrance that has been removed or that might have been there. In many contexts it is, of course, possible to understand or to supply the appropriate qualification. If an AA patrolman tells me the engine of my car is now free, I can assume that he has found it to be clogged up with some kind of foreign substance which he has been able to remove, but if he tells me that he himself is now free, I will need to know something of his history to be able to find some clues on the basis of which I can supply the necessary qualification to understand what he is talking about. It is this consideration that has given rise to a distinction that has been made between the two kinds of freedom, between the negative and positive views of freedom, between 'freedom from' and 'freedom to', but it is surely the case that in all contexts both of these elements are present and we emphasize that aspect that seems the more significant. It is only meaningful to speak of the freedom to do something if we are conscious that we are free from a restraint that has or might have denied us that freedom or to speak of freedom from something if we are conscious of that thing as having prevented us from being free to achieve some desirable goal or activity (Ryan, 1965).

Freedom, therefore, implies the absence of a restraint that has acted or might have acted as a hindrance to action of some kind.

Often, however, the emotive implications of the term come to the fore and we find it is being used prescriptively, not to describe a state of freedom so much as to demand that such a state be created. This is the kind of meaning the term usually has in social contexts. When Rousseau began *The Social Contract* with the words, 'Man is born free; but everywhere he is in chains', he was not describing men as he might have been if he had said, 'Man is born naked; but everywhere he is in clothes'; he was in fact prescribing or demanding that men should be treated in certain ways and similar demands have been made in much the same form in many other contexts. It is not always entirely clear, however, what such demands amount to. Again some kind of qualification brings clarification, so that discussion of freedom of speech or freedom of opinion or freedom of association or freedom of worship will be more meaningful than discussion of freedom in an unqualified sense. To speak of freedom in this kind of unqualified way cannot be to demand the removal of all restraints. To demand this would be to demand licence rather than freedom, a distinction which is very important since it suggests that the existence of some restraints is not incompatible with the notion of social freedom. It is, therefore, a demand not that all restraints be removed but that their existence in all cases be justified.

If this is a correct analysis of the notion of freedom, then it provides us with a negative point that will contribute towards the justification of the exercise of authority, namely that the idea of an authority used to apply justifiable restraints is not incompatible with the notion of freedom. Furthermore, we must note that every human society must have rules and those rules must be enforced by someone if they are to have any meaning at all. As Thomas Hobbes said, 'covenants, without the sword, are but words, and of no strength to secure a man at all' (*Leviathan*, Ch. XVII). And so we have a further, if again negative, point that authority is a necessary part of any rule-governed society. Neither of these points, of course, offers us any positive clues as to what particular restraints can be justified. It is, however, no small thing to have established that some justification is possible in view of the doubts about this that often exist in people's minds. We must, however, turn to a consideration of more positive arguments for the exercise of authority and in particular those that may indicate the kinds of situation in which it might be argued to be appropriate.

The classical argument for social freedom is undoubtedly that set out in J. S. Mill's essay, 'On Liberty'. The position Mill takes here is uncompromising. 'All restraint *qua* restraint is an evil.' But he suggests one fundamental justification, 'one very simple principle', for the existence of restraints. 'That principle is, that the sole end for which mankind are warranted, individually or collectively, in interfering with the liberty of action of any of their number, is self-protection'. A person may be restrained from interfering with or causing harm to others. Authority exercised to apply restraint in such situations is justified. It is not justified if it is used to restrain him from doing those things which affect him only, those actions that can be called 'self-regarding' actions.

The argument here, then, is that freedom can only be reasonably demanded by anyone up to the point at which the behaviour of one individual or group in a society begins to act as a limitation on the freedom of other individuals or groups. As a judge once said to a man before him on a charge of assault and battery, 'Everyone's freedom is bounded by the position of the other man's nose.' Too much freedom for some people will lead to too little for others, and it is at the point where this begins to happen that the exercise of authority can be justified to ensure that freedom can be enjoyed by all rather than licence by some.

If we apply this to education, we will find that there is beginning to emerge a case at least for one type of school rule, for the exercise of authority by the teacher in the context of general behaviour and the maintenance of order. Where the enjoyment of 'freedom' by one pupil or group of pupils is resulting in a limitation of the freedom of others, through overuse of some facility, for example, the making of excessive noise, running in the corridors, or any other behaviour which is likely to endanger the safety of others or to create an atmosphere in which the ability of others to profit from the educational opportunities offered by the school is impaired, then the teacher must exercise his or her authority to apply restraints in order to promote a proper level of freedom for all. In the sphere of behaviour, then, a good case can be made for the teacher's authority. Schools, like all other rule-governed societies, must have rules that are framed for the protection of all members from each other's excesses and, provided that these rules do not go beyond what that consideration seems to justify, a good case can be made out for them.

No argument that we have adduced so far, however, justifies the use of authority to compel children to join this rule-governed society in the first place. For the law to require that children attend school between the ages of five and sixteen and for us as teachers to demand of them not only certain kinds of behaviour but also certain kinds of learning while they are there requires a different and more positive justification than we have given so far. This proved a difficult problem for Mill too since it goes well beyond what can be justified in the name of self-protection. Yet Mill was strongly committed to the value of education and the qualitative superiority of certain kinds of intellectual activity of the kind that he felt schools ought to promote (West, 1965). The justification of the exercise of authority by teachers in the area of the curriculum, however, is a much more difficult problem than that in the sphere of behaviour, although we must not lose sight of the fact that even in the realm of rules of conduct, learning of a moral and social kind will go on, as we shall see in Chapter 7, so that the distinction between behavioural and curricular problems cannot be pressed too far.

A more positive justification for the use of authority to require children's attendance at school and to direct their activities while they are there must be sought in the notion of education itself or ideas one has about the purposes of the school and the educational enterprise generally. However, we will see in our discussion on the curriculum in Chapter 7 how difficult it is to define education in terms that will be generally acceptable or to reach agreement on what the purposes of the schools should be or what kinds of learning we should be using our authority to require pupils to engage in. Many different views are held and, although they all need some kind of justification in themselves, each will give rise to a justification for the use of authority in the school in different areas. The view that schools should be concerned primarily to promote the development of the rational mind will result in different demands to be made of pupils, for example, from those that will be justified by the view that they should be more concerned with the social welfare of their pupils. Indeed, some views of education, such as those that have advocated non-interference and the current views of some sociologists about the dangers of imposing values on children, are such as to provide no justification for any exercise of authority at all in this area.

Once some kind of overall justification for education itself seems to have been established, however, we will have a basis for the exercise of authority in particular situations. Once we are committed to the value of a particular subject, for example, the 'discipline' of that subject will take over and provide us with our cues as to when authority can be justifiably exercised. The absence of any kind of consensus in this area, however, makes this kind of justification highly subjective and, as a result, less satisfactory a basis than perhaps we would wish to have for requiring a great deal of children and applying real and extensive restraints to their behaviour.

There is, however, one kind of argument that may reveal to us something like a lowest common denominator here, something that will offer some justification at a fundamental level for the exercise of authority in education. Whatever view one takes of the kind or selection of knowledge that should be presented to or even imposed upon children, it would be difficult to maintain that that knowledge should not be characterized by being true. In short, whether one believes that children should be introduced to physics or French, Byron or the 'Beano', Beethoven or the Beatles, the one common feature of the 'knowledge' to be presented to them that all would agree to would be that it should manifest a respect for truth, or at least for objectivity. We can say, then, that there is a conceptual connection between the notion of 'education' and that of 'truth' or 'objectivity'. Some justification for the exercise of authority by teachers may be found, therefore, in an appeal to this connection and a demonstration that in particular cases authority is being exercised in the cause of promoting truth and objectivity, by insisting, for example, that children explore all sides of an argument before reaching an opinion, rather than adhering to a prejudice acquired from their parents or elsewhere. If education is connected in this way, then, with the pursuit of truth and objectivity, the exercise of authority by educators can be shown to be justified if it has the purpose of assisting this process.

Paradoxically, however, this argument constitutes an equally strong if not a more compelling case for the promotion of freedom. This concern with truth necessitates academic freedom and academic autonomy, 'freedom of opinion' as it is more usually called. The classic arguments in support of this are again those of J. S. Mill's essay 'On Liberty' and we must briefly note them here.

Mill argues that truth cannot be pursued nor can human knowledge develop without freedom of opinion for those who seek after it. He gives several cogent reasons for this claim. Firstly, we cannot assume infallibility so that we must concede that any opinion may be true and, therefore, ought not to be suppressed. If anything, this is an argument that has more force today when it is perhaps clearer than it was in the nineteenth century just how hypothetical and consequently open to modification all our knowledge is. Secondly, Mill argues, even if a silenced opinion is wrong, it may contain some truth and, since the prevailing opinion on any issue is rarely wholly true, we need the clash of contrary opinions to help us towards the whole truth, a point supported by many philosophers who have seen the development of knowledge as an unending triadic dialectical process of thesis, antithesis, and synthesis. Thirdly, even if the opinion that is accepted and allowed is the whole truth and nothing but the truth, it can only be held as such by those who have been able to weigh it against contrary opinion. Without that it will be 'held in the manner of prejudice, with little comprehension or feeling of its rational grounds'. It will be dogma rather than real conviction and, as a result of this, truth will lose its essence.

This, then, for Mill is one aspect of that liberty which is essential to human progress. Liberty is necessary for 'the free development of individuality' and also without liberty 'there is wanting one of the principle ingredients of human happiness, and quite the chief ingredient of individual and social progress.' Unless there is freedom of opinion, unless people are free to disagree, human knowledge will not develop. These are the classic arguments for academic freedom and they lead us to recognize not only the hypothetical and evolving nature of human knowledge, which we have had reason to note elsewhere, but also that if there are conceptual connections between education and knowledge and education and truth, there must also be such a connection between education and autonomy.

However, they would seem equally to constitute an argument for the exercise of authority in the interests of the promotion of knowledge, truth, objectivity and autonomy, or, to put it differently and somewhat paradoxically, the exercise of authority to promote freedom, either by enhancing the range and scope of the choices open to the individual or by developing in him or her the ability to make choices by means other than either 'plumping' for something or acting according to prejudices, wherever and however acquired. We have noted elsewhere in this book how working from children's interests requires us also to give them opportunities to acquire interests and how 'discovery methods' are only effective if linked to careful preparatory work, if employed, as Bruner (1961) suggests, by the well-prepared mind. We now have a theoretical justification for this apparent infringement of freedom in so far as its main purpose can be to enhance freedom and to promote autonomy since, as Bruner also tells us, the freedom of the child is increased by approaches such as discovery learning. In this connection, it is also interesting to note that those psychologists, such as Piaget (1932) and Kohlberg (1966), who in considering the stages of the child's moral development have posited the existence of an autonomous stage at the end of the process, have not wanted to suggest that this stage is automatically reached by all children as a result of a purely developmental or maturational process; they believe, as we shall see in Chapter 6, that the attainment of autonomy can only be the result of education. This, then, is a task for the teacher which can only be accomplished by the exercise of authority.

If there is any substance to these arguments we have tried to set out, certain implications follow for the practice of education. In the first place, it becomes clear that the teacher must take whatever action he judges necessary to promote the progress of pupils towards autonomy, to enhance their freedom and their opportunities to use it, to create the conditions necessary for these developments to take place and, more controversially, as we will see when we consider the problems of curriculum content in Chapter 7, to introduce and extend those studies that he or she feels are justified on other grounds, whether for vocational reasons, because of the choices of the pupils themselves, or because of a conviction that they are 'intrinsically worthwhile activities'. There are no hard and fast answers to be given in practice to questions about when the exercise of authority by the teacher is justified in these areas, but these are the kinds of justification to be sought.

Secondly, some negative conclusions at least emerge from these arguments. For they imply that the exercise of authority by teachers cannot be justified in areas that cannot be shown to be connected in some way with the promotion of those qualities we have just discussed. It is difficult, for example, to justify its being exercised to ensure that all pupils travel to and from school with caps on their heads, unless it can be shown that a warm head will mean a warm brain and that a warm brain will reach its educational goals faster. Nor can we, without stretching our notion of education to breaking point, find a justification in it for any requirement that relates more to fashion than to education. Fashions are too ephemeral to constitute a basis for any learning of a permanent kind. One has only to look at those headmasters of today whose hair is of a length that they would not have permitted on their pupils a few years ago to realize how shifting this ground is. The spectacle of one headteacher forbidding entry to school to a child who insists on wearing blue rather than white socks and another sending a child home for precisely the opposite reason merely trivializes in the public eye the work of the schools and retards rather than advances the progress towards anything that can really be called education.

Thirdly, we must note that if the justification of the teacher's authority is to be found in his obligation to promote the freedom and ultimately the autonomy of pupils, it must follow that his or her authority is merely provisional, since if he is successful it will be progressively eroded until it disappears altogether. Certainly, university teachers have to get used to seeing their pupils draw level with and sometimes forge ahead of them, and, to some extent, this should be the experience of all successful teachers. If we are right, then the oddest thing about the teacher's authority is that it must contain within it the seeds of its own destruction, what the soap operas call a self-destruct mechanism.

This, then, is the kind of justification that can be found for the teacher's authority. In general, it leads us to the conclusion that the important question for the teacher is not that of authority and freedom, but of authority and authoritarianism, the use and the abuse of authority. The teacher's central concern in planning the work of his or her pupils should be not the rather naive question of whether he or she should direct their work or leave them to their own devices, but the rather more subtle issue of the kinds of authoritative action he or she is justified in taking. It is the abuse of authority not the attempt to exercise it properly that leads to resentment and progressive indiscipline in schools. Teachers often comment on the 'sense of fairness' of their pupils, especially in secondary schools; this phenomenon is no more and no less than their ability to recognize, intuitively and therefore sometimes more quickly than the theoreticians, when authority is being exercised properly over them and when it is being abused.

As every teacher knows only too well, however, it is one thing to be able to demonstrate the differences between the uses and the abuses of authority; it is quite another matter to ensure that in practice one has any kind of authority in the classroom. An understanding of its justification will be of some help, of course, but in addition to this it is necessary to have some understanding of its nature and its origins, of how we come to be able to exercise it, as this will indicate to us some of the ways in which we can work to improve it. It is to this aspect of authority that we must now turn.

Patterns of authority

There have been many discussions of the question of what authority is, whether, for example, it is the same as power or force, and it would not be appropriate or helpful for us to get ourselves too caught up in such debate here. It must be stressed, however, that authority is very difficult to define precisely. It is an ability that some people seem to have to get other people to obey them without recourse to the use of force or even sometimes to the giving of reasons. It is the quality of the well-known centurion of the New Testament who described his authority by saying, 'I say to this man "Go!" and he goeth.' At a more mundane level, it is that which makes us accept, often quite unquestioningly, the advice of anyone we regard as an authority on something, like, say, second-hand cars or coastal navigation. We do what such people instruct or advise without compulsion or compunction. If this is what authority is or if this is what it means for someone to have authority, then it is certainly not force, even though the threat of force may sometimes be there in the background. In fact, we tend to say, when we see people, teachers or parents, for example, having to use force, that they have lost their authority or that their authority has broken down. Authority, then, is this kind of ability to get things done without recourse to force or other methods of persuasion.

It is important to understand this, because it has crucial implications for the way in which we must tackle what is probably the most vital question in this area for the teacher, namely that of where he or she can get authority from or how he can be sure that he or she will have authority in the classroom. If we realize what a nebulous quality it is, we will immediately appreciate that it is not something 'given' and, therefore, not something we can look to someone else to provide. Many people in any society have authority besides teachers — policemen, referees, umpires, mayors, kings and so on — but it clearly does not make sense to ask where they get their authority from in the way in which one might ask where they get their helmets, whistles or blackboards from, even though in some cases visible trappings such as badges, white coats, academic gowns, chains of office, orbs, sceptres and the like may be worn to symbolize the possession of authority (Weldon, 1953). Nor does it even make sense to claim that authority, at least as we have defined it, has been conferred on them by the MCC, the FA, the DES, the Archbishop of Canterbury, or any other person or body. Such persons or bodies cannot confer authority on anyone, since they cannot ensure that people will do what such a person tells them to do without question. It is not as simple as that, as many teachers and football referees know to their cost. The most that a body of this kind can do is to promise to step in when one's authority has been challenged, questioned, or even defied, in other words when it is lost. Furthermore, if we ask where these bodies get their authority from, we see that we have only pushed the question back a stage. The real question, therefore, is not 'Where does authority come from?' but 'How do people come to exercise authority?' Once we put it that way, we begin to see both how to set about seeking an answer to it and that there may be several kinds of answer to be found. We can also see that from the teacher's point of view this kind of approach is likely to be more helpful because it should indicate some of the ways in which he or she can work at developing authority.

A number of different categories have been used in attempts to delineate the possible sources of authority and it will be worthwhile to look at these briefly. One major distinction that has been drawn is that between authority exercised *de jure* and that exercised *de facto*. If a person has authority *de jure*, that authority derives from a right to issue commands that goes with a position that he or she holds and stems from certain rules, a legal system of some kind, which authorizes him or her to issue commands and will back him or her or step in if those commands are challenged. Such a person is our referee and in the same way teachers may have some authority conferred upon them by the position they hold. On the other hand, to say that a person exercises authority *de facto* is not to say he or she holds any position or has any backing for his or her authority; it is to say merely that people do in fact obey him or her. The classic example of this is the ordinary member of the audience who takes charge when there is a fire at a theatre or a cinema and organizes an orderly exit. He or she is able to exercise authority perhaps because of certain personal qualities he or she has or a superior knowledge and experience that he or she is thought to possess, but not from any position or status that he or she holds.

This latter point brings us to a second distinction that has been emphasized, that between being *in* authority and being *an* authority, between positional and expert authority. Sometimes, as we have just seen, *de facto* authority will derive from the fact that someone is regarded as *an* authority in a particular area, that he or she has a relevant expertise. His or her injunctions are accepted because of this expertise, even though he or she does not hold a position that confers the right to issue commands. We have already referred to those people whose word on certain matters, the internal mysteries of the motor-car for example, are regarded as 'law'. It will be clear that if a person who is *in* authority is also accepted as *an* authority, his or her position will be considerably strengthened by the possession of such expertise.

A further distinction was made by Max Weber (1947) when he suggested that there might be three possible answers to the question of how people come to exercise authority, three different sources from which their ability to issue commands and have them accepted as legitimate might derive. Firstly, he suggests that the authority of some people may derive in part from *traditional* sources. Some people are obeyed because they are seen as representatives of a traditional and accepted system. A father or mother in a family, when he or she exercises authority, does so largely for this kind of reason. In some situations too, perhaps especially in schools for younger children, the authority of the teacher will derive in part from this source. A second source of authority that Weber posits is what he calls the *legal / rational* source. An increasing number of people in modern societies exercise authority because they have been elevated to it under a system of rules, the legality and rationality of which are accepted by those over whom the authority is being wielded. They have *de jure* authority within an accepted rule-governed situation like that of the football field, the cricket pitch, or the classroom, but that *de jure* authority derives from expert as well as positional sources, it is rational as well as legal, since they hold their position by virtue of proven expertise. Thirdly, Weber draws our attention to the *charismatic* type of authority exercised by some people because of their personal characteristics and outstanding qualities. He himself had in mind here outstanding historical figures like Christ and Napoleon, but the notion has relevance at less elevated levels too. We might perhaps, in the case of teachers in particular, distinguish two aspects of this concept, that of being *an* authority which we have already considered and that of the kind of personal flair or brilliance which can lead us to obey certain individuals without evidence of either their expertise or their legal rights to issue commands (Peters, 1966). In other words, this concept offers us a distinction between two kinds of *de facto* authority.

The authority of the teacher

With these categories in mind, let us now turn to a more detailed examination of the authority of the teacher and the factors that will affect both its nature and its extent. The most important thing to be stressed at the outset of this discussion is that our analysis so far indicates that it is something which can and should be worked at by teachers. The following discussion may indicate some of the ways in which teachers can work at the development of their authority but it will also reveal some of the external factors that will come into play and which must be taken into account by them. There are two main kinds of factor that we must note, those deriving from the school itself, its organizational structure, its goals, and the kinds of pupil it contains, and those deriving from the personal characteristics and qualities of the individual teacher. The kind of authority each teacher can exercise and the kind of authority he or she will in practice exercise will be a result of the interaction of these two forces.

One important factor here is the age of the pupils. It is dangerous to be too dogmatic about age differences in education since this has led to wide variations in our practices that are difficult to justify. However, it is worth noting that younger children are less likely to question the teacher's right to obedience than older ones and are more likely to need a firm authority and control to support them, so that teachers of younger children will find that they can place greater reliance on tradition, on position and on their personal qualities than can those whose pupils are older and more sophisticated. Bright pupils too will more readily challenge or at least question the authority of their teachers. Thus patterns of authority will differ quite widely between types of educational institution.

We saw earlier that authority is an essential part of any rule-governed society. The kind of authority that is appropriate or possible will depend also on the nature of the rule-governed society in question. Clearly a society that is tightly structured, highly cohesive, and has a clear view of its goals and purposes will require and will give rise to a different kind of authority structure from one which is much looser, more diffuse, and less clear-cut in its view of its essential purposes. No society of course is completely bureaucratic, but obviously there are different levels of bureaucracy and each will give rise to a different pattern of authority. Schools must inevitably be less clear-cut in their goals and purposes than many other institutions, but there will be great variations between schools themselves.

At one extreme we might picture a school which is based on a relatively fixed view of child nature and of knowledge, which regards children's abilities as readily measurable, and consequently streams its pupils according to their ability, which has a view of knowledge as something external to be acquired by pupils and as a result places its emphasis on class-teaching methods, on subject boundaries, on encouraging the kinds of stock response to questions we discussed in Chapter 4, and perhaps on regular examinations and tests, seeing its role in terms purely of the intellectual advancement of its pupils. In such a school, the relationships between teacher and pupil will tend to be distant and impersonal and the authority structure will tend to be relatively clear-cut, hierarchical, and for the most part positional, the emphasis being on the teacher as set in authority; where his expertise is relevant, it will be an expertise in a particular subject area. Tradition will also be of significance to the teacher in his attempts to establish his own individual authority in such a school (Hargreaves, 1972).

At the other end of the spectrum, we may imagine a school which sees children as having many facets to their development and their abilities too diffuse to be readily measurable, which as a consequence does not stream them by general ability, which has a broader view of knowledge and perhaps not too much regard for the sanctity of subject boundaries, and which as a result will often abandon class teaching in favour of other methods designed in one way or another to involve the children themselves more fully in their own education; in short, a school which takes a looser view of its own role and of the nature and purposes of education. In such a school the authority patterns will be very different. Teachers will be less distant from their pupils so that the relationships will be more interpersonal. The extent of their authority will depend far more on their expertise not only in a subject area or areas but in a wide range of pedagogical abilities. Position and tradition will be of relatively little help to teachers in such a school; the onus will be much more on personal qualities of a number of kinds.

Clearly, no real situation is quite as clear-cut as these we have described, but perhaps the caricatures we have drawn will serve to indicate the extent to which the type of authority a teacher can exercise will be affected by the kind of school he is in, by both the content of what he or she is teaching and the method or pedagogy he is using (Bernstein, 1971). Any occupational role is governed to some extent by the institutional structure within which it is practised and this structure in turn will be subject to pressures from the headteacher, the local authority, the governing body and all other outside agencies that wield authority over the teacher. But this is only one kind of factor that will determine the kind of authority the teacher will be able to exercise.

The nearer a school comes to the second of the types we have just pictured, the more onus there will be on the personal qualities of the individual teacher. We must remember too that while the organization of the school will determine to a large extent the kind of authority a teacher may exercise and will make it easy or difficult for him or her to achieve a proper control of his classes, no kind of school can confer authority on him or her or ensure that his or her authority is accepted by pupils. In all situations, this will depend on his or her own qualities and abilities.

What sorts of quality are important here? Obviously, the most important single factor is the individual teacher's expertise. Where a teacher cannot rely on tradition or position, on being *in* authority, to ensure that he or she is obeyed, he or she must depend on his or her skill and knowledge, on being *an* authority. It is important to remember, as we hinted just now, that there are two aspects to this. One of these is clearly expertise in one's subject, the ability to answer children's questions and provide them with knowledge in a given area of the curriculum. The other important aspect of this expertise, and one that becomes crucial as we move towards a looser and more open view of schools, of the curriculum, and of education, as we shall see in the next section, is pedagogical skill, the ability to organize pupil's work, to advise them on many aspects of it, to help them to frame their questions rather than merely to provide answers, to ensure that they are stretched while steering them away from work of a level that would be likely to defeat them, to develop the kinds of interpersonal relationship that will both forward their learning and establish one's right to direct it. The more interpersonal these relationships become, the more onus will fall on the teacher's ability to develop them.

This ability will in turn depend on a number of factors, such as the age and the sex of both teacher and pupils, the view taken of knowledge and of the purposes of education, and the extent to which the teacher is in sympathy with the ethos of the school. It will also depend on those wider personal qualities sometimes subsumed under the single title 'personality'. There is no doubt that the personality of the teacher will affect his or her ability to develop relationships and, therefore, to establish his or her authority with his or her pupils.

The significance of this should not be overstated, however. Many teachers are too ready to exaggerate the importance of personality and to take the view that you have either got it or you have not. There are two dangers in this. The first is that it leads to a defeatism on the part of those teachers who feel, rightly or wrongly, that their personal qualities are not strong and a resultant failure to appreciate that there are ways, such as those we have tried to describe, in which one's authority can be developed. Secondly, it can lead to too great a dependence by some teachers on a charismatic type of authority, which, while it may have certain short-term advantages, cannot in the long term lead to effective education, since it is based not on reason but on emotion and largely blind admiration. We all know what Napoleon did. As John Wilson once remarked in a similar context (1964), it is when the individual loves Big Brother that he or she really loses his freedom. 'Personality' is important in the development of relationships and of one's authority in the classroom, but it is not crucial and it can even be inimical to education if one comes to depend upon it to the exclusion of other, more important aspects of one's teaching.

We must finally note the changes that are taking place in the nature of the authority wielded in many areas of society and no less in our schools. These changes are due to changing attitudes in society as a whole, a growing unwillingness to be 'dictated to', and increasing demands that reasons should be given for any infringement of our liberties, a justification and a demonstration that what is being required is 'fair' and 'equal'. In this respect, it is worth remembering that Weber's main point was to stress the trend in society towards an increased bureaucratization and away from the traditional, unquestioned sources of authority towards those with some legal/rational basis. The development of the 'open society' is paralleled by that of the 'open school' (Bernstein, 1967), that school which has the looser organizational structure we were discussing just now.

Our earlier discussion of the justification for the exercise of authority led us to the conclusion that in education, as in society at large, it can only be justified as a device for enhancing and protecting freedom. Another way of expressing this is to say that in a democratic society we must have democratic schools and a democratic form of education. What is being suggested here is that this is something which it would be very difficult to avoid, since the patterns of authority existing in society at large must inevitably influence, and perhaps even determine, the patterns of authority which are not only desirable but also possible in schools. We must now consider this a little more fully.

Democracy and education

It was once argued very fully and compellingly by John Dewey (1916) that the only form of society which facilitates the continued evolution of the human species is a democratic form of society and, furthermore, that the development of such a democratic society is dependent to a large degree on the democratization of schools and schooling. Schools, he argued, must be democratic communities, with their own form of 'embryonic community life'. By this he did not mean merely the establishment of schools councils, the election of school officers and so on, any more than his concept of democracy in society was concerned with universal suffrage. Rather, for him, democracy was a way of life, a form of 'conjoint communicated experience', a matter of interpersonal collaboration, a climate or a context for the development of society, of individuals within society and also of human knowledge. In essence his concern was to create an open society, and open schools within it, as the *sine qua non* of continued evolution.

Dewey's theory, then, is an assertion of what he believes ought to be the case, how society and its schools ought to be organized. It has gained a good deal of support recently from certain sociological studies which have suggested that society, or at least some societies, are developing in this kind of way, that, where this is the case, similar changes can be detected within the schools in such societies, and that these kinds of social change have important implications for the inner workings of schools, and in particular for the kinds of authority relationships which are possible within those schools. In short, we have here a view which does not merely assert that schools ought to be organized democratically, but claims further that in a democratic society there is no other way in which it is possible to organize them.

The claim, then, is that significant changes have occurred in recent years in the fabric of society and that these have important implications for patterns of authority within society's schools. There are two major features of these changes that we must familiarize ourselves with if we are to understand the processes that we are part of and are to play our roles in them effectively.

The first of these features is a progressive shift towards a greater social and educational egalitarianism whose implications for educational practice we shall examine in some detail in Chapter 8. The second is the developing sense of freedom which has characterized many societies in the last few decades and which has led to an opening up of many areas of social living, of schools no less than of other social institutions. It is to a brief examination of some of the implications of this development for the practice of education that we must now turn.

The process we are concerned with is that progressive democratization of society which has resulted in a loosening and an opening up of many social structures. It is a process that educationists should welcome and embrace, since it might be argued, as we ourselves have from time to time argued, that education itself is essentially a democratic process which requires of us that we open up the minds of our pupils, so that freedom is an essential element in any educational process worthy of the name. Such developments within society, therefore, may be regarded as totally appropriate to true educational practice. Their precise implications, however, must be picked out.

But first we must consider what they have meant for society itself, since the change we have referred to as occurring in our schools is a reflection of a corresponding change in society. In broad terms, it is a shift from what Durkheim called 'mechanical solidarity' to what he referred to as 'organic solidarity' and its major features have been identified clearly by Basil Bernstein (1967). The concept of organic solidarity implies that the form of social integration within a society is one that emphasizes differences between individuals rather than similarities; these differences between individuals lead to their social roles being *achieved* rather than, as under mechanical solidarity, *ascribed;* and this in turn leads to the development of a differentiated or pluralist society in which not only are social roles diverse but there is a similar diversity of values, whereas 'mechanical solidarity refers to social integration at the level of shared beliefs' (Bernstein, 1967). Such societies, then, are characterized by a high level of individuality, diversity of values, and a greater sense of individual freedom, all of which lead in turn to different patterns of interpersonal relationships and authority structures. In short this represents a shift towards a more democratic and open society.

Such a shift has implications for all social institutions and schools are no exception to this. Its impact will not, of course, be felt equally in all schools; there may even be some that for a long time will escape it altogether; but in general most will experience a similar shift in their own forms of social integration which will represent the same kind of move from mechanical to organic solidarity, from purity to diversity. This will have many facets of which we shall try to pick out here the most important.

To begin with, certain changes in our approach to the curriculum which we shall explore in Chapter 7 are examples of this general change we are discussing. The move towards new combinations of subjects and various forms of curriculum integration, to a theme- or topic-based curriculum rather than a subject-centred one, reflects, as we shall suggest there, a freeing of the curriculum for continued development and is thus an especially good instance of the impact of this kind of change on the curriculum. It represents a new approach to curriculum planning in which the subject is no longer dominant but is expected to subserve the interests and the needs of the learner. It thus reflects a new concept of knowledge itself, since it recognizes, as Dewey suggests, that knowledge must change and develop and that it must be allowed to change and develop. At another level, it has also led to that emphasis on the development of creative abilities that we discussed in Chapter 3 and to a reduction in the level of insulation between pure and applied studies and thus to a weakening of the boundaries between 'high-status' and 'low-status' knowledge.

The same movement is also apparent in certain changes of method that can be seen in some schools and, especially, in the idea of 'learning by discovery'. 'There is a shift — from a pedagogy which, for the majority of secondary school pupils, was concerned with the learning of standard operations tied to specific contexts — to a pedagogy which emphasizes the exploration of principles; from schools which emphasize the teacher as a solution-giver to schools which emphasize the teacher as a problem-poser or creator' (Bernstein, 1967).

Such changes in the foundations of education must inevitably lead to changes in relationships of all kinds. From time to time throughout this book and especially in our discussion of equality in Chapter 4, we suggest that the barriers once erected between different 'types' of pupil, like those between subjects, have been slowly eroded by the introduction of such devices as comprehensive education and mixed-ability groupings. These have often led to a greater flexibility of groupings, in the same way as those methodological changes we have just considered. Again, this involves a greater mixing of pupils and entails new kinds of relationship between them, thus leading to that kind of unity in diversity that Basil Bernstein is claiming characterizes the organic solidarity of the open school. The unfortunate consequences of labelling pupils and of placing them in rigid categories were highlighted in Chapter 2 in our discussion of interpersonal judgements in education.

Relationships between teachers and pupils have also changed, as we discovered when we discussed the nature of classroom interaction in Chapter 1. New and less formal methods of working will require new, and also less formal, forms of authority and control. There is more to it than that, however, since the process of increased democratization that we are describing requires that in schools, as in society, the basis of our authority should be expert rather than positional, so that the teacher must be *an* authority rather than attempt to claim that he stands *in* authority. Again, we might also note with Basil Bernstein that the shift is 'to more personalized forms of control where teachers and taught confront each other as individuals. The forms of social control appeal less to shared values, group loyalties and involvements; they are based rather upon the recognition of differences between individuals' (1967).

There are also implications for relationships within the teaching profession, between teachers and others. Authority patterns there have also changed so that, for example, the headteacher is no longer the unquestioned autocrat he once was in many schools. Changes in the knowledge base of education have also led to a reduction of power for heads of subject departments in schools (Musgrove, 1973), since the subject is no longer sacrosanct and the introduction of some form of integration or new grouping of subjects will necessitate cooperation between departments and thus again will require different kinds of relationship. The change in pedagogy towards less formal methods that we mentioned earlier will require similar adjustments on the part of all teachers. Often such changes in method are accompanied by the introduction of schemes involving some kind of team-teaching; sometimes even the architecture of the school is changed to require that the learning that is to be promoted be tackled in an 'open-plan' way; but, even when this is not formally demanded, doors are opening and teachers are having to learn to work together more often and more closely than before.

We should also add that these developments are to be welcomed rather than deplored. There is no doubt that they make the teacher's task more complex, but they do so by requiring him or her to take a wider view of that task. We saw earlier that the only kind of justification that can be found for the exercise of authority in education is that derived from the central concern of the educative process with the development of individual autonomy. If this is what education is essentially concerned with, the only kind of authority that will forward this process is one which is rationally based on the expertise of the teacher. To expect or require pupils to obey their teachers merely because they are teachers, to rely on tradition, on status, or on personal qualities for one's authority is at root to deny the child the right to think for himself, and thus to erode the very foundations of democracy.

We mentioned earlier that these are sources of authority that are more readily available to the teacher of younger children and so it might be claimed that this makes his or her task easier. It is also true, however, that it makes his or her task a more complex and responsible one. For, while he or she can rely on these sources for his or her authority more effectively than the teacher of older pupils, he or she must also be aware of the threat that this may pose to the long-term educational interests of the pupils. He or she must, therefore, attempt the very difficult task of achieving the kind of authority that will lay the right foundations for the development of the ability to make rational appraisals of subsequent educational relationships. The more schools move towards unstreaming, integrated curricula, greater pupil involvement, freedom, and even participation in management, the more, as we have seen, the teacher's role becomes 'achieved' rather than 'ascribed' and the basis of his or her authority moves from the positional to the expert. Tradition and status are bent reeds now, as the current experience of many teachers and schools reveals, and increasingly the onus is on the teacher to establish his or her authority rather than to expect it to be conferred in some way by the job itself. The developments we have been considering make increasing demands on that authority that stems from the teacher's understanding of and skill in handling the many facets of present-day educational practices. These are the ways in which teachers can and should work at improving the nature and the extent of the authority they wield and these are the ways in which the trainers of teachers must help them.

However, while few teachers will want to quarrel with the desirability of the kind of rational basis for authority we have been recommending, all will know that in practice such an ideal is seldom to be attained. In fact, although we have singled out for the purposes of our discussion these different types of authority, the authority any individual teacher wields will be an amalgam of all of them and will vary from age group to age group, from class to class, even from day to day. All teachers will find it necessary to rely on sources of authority other than their own expertise quite frequently. How far they can do this will depend on many factors but particularly on the age of their pupils since, for example, as we have just suggested, the older the pupils, the less ready they are to accept authority that is not backed by expertise. However, all teachers will find themselves from time to time relying, or attempting to rely, on tradition, on position or, perhaps especially often, on charisma, on the force of their own personalities, on what might more honestly and realistically be described as sheer bluff. All will find too that from time to time they must recognize the important distinction between authority and control and the need to achieve or maintain control by the use of other devices such as punishment or the threat of punishment when their authority proves inadequate.

In this connection it is perhaps worth noting another useful distinction that sociologists have made between different bases of social control. They have suggested that our methods of getting people to obey us must be normative, calculative, or coercive (Etzioni, 1961). In other words, we can get people to do as we tell them either by persuading them that it is worth doing, that our norms are to be accepted, or by offering them incentives or inducements, or by resorting to force, whether overt or otherwise. In practice, teachers will find themselves using all of these measures or some mixture of all three, but the message of our discussion of both authority and democracy in education is that all teachers and schools should be aiming at some kind of normative order and endeavouring to avoid as far as possible the need for coercion or even for the dangling of carrots.

There are at least three good reasons for this. The first and most straightforward of these is that based on the relative ease with which this kind of order once achieved can be maintained. There is no doubt that life is easier and far more pleasant when one is working with pupils who want to learn than with those who have to be driven and threatened or cajoled, if they are even to remain in the room and behave themselves. In fact, it is sometimes suggested that some of the changes currently taking place in schools are prompted by an awareness that it is increasingly difficult to coerce pupils, especially older pupils, that calculative methods will not work with pupils who can see nothing of value for them in school work, and that if the establishment of a normative order necessitates changing the norms in a way that will make them more acceptable to such pupils, then this must be done. If you cannot beat them your only solution lies in joining them.

The second reason for preferring a normative order is more complex but absolutely crucial. A system of control that has this kind of basis is the only kind of system that is conducive to education in the full sense and to education in a democratic society. We have seen often enough that to be educated is to have come to value what one has been engaged in for its own sake. If this is not achieved, education has not taken place. Thus to force knowledge into unwilling pupils or to offer it to them purely as a means to some extrinsic reward will be positively counter-productive to truly educational ends. Furthermore, in discussing the relation of authority to freedom at the beginning of this chapter, we noted the arguments for freedom and autonomy in education and saw that the concept of education itself requires that our authority be progressively eroded in favour of the autonomy of the pupil. Again the only basis for this is a normative social order. The case for this has been further strengthened by our more recent discussion of democracy and education.

The third reason for preferring this kind of order derives from a consideration of the possible effects on pupils of different kinds of authority and methods of control. There are a number of facets to this and we must now turn to a detailed examination of them.

The effects of authority and freedom

We might first note how little is known about the effects on teachers of different patterns of authority and freedom in the classroom. Little research has been done in this area but it would seem to be a fruitful one since there are many things that one would like to know here. There is evidence that teachers achieve more success when they are in tune with or enthusiastic about the particular schemes they are engaged in. Teachers who believe in unstreaming, for example, have more success in teaching mixed-ability classes than those who are opposed to it (Barker-Lunn, 1970) and it also emerged in a study of the teaching of French in primary schools that more success was achieved by teachers who were enthusiastic about the experiment and pleased to be involved in it (Burstall, 1967). One would, of course, expect the teacher who is thus in harmony with what he or she is doing to be more successful and, indeed, to gain more satisfaction from his or her work. This would suggest in turn that teachers should be given the kind of flexibility that will enable each of them to develop their own pattern of working and of authority. As we have seen, however, there are factors which set limits on the extent of the variety that is possible.

What does seem a more reasonable conclusion is that teachers should choose their schools and schools their teachers with the need for this kind of 'match' in mind. It is not clear how important this factor is, as against considerations of such things as salary, location and general convenience when teachers are looking for a post. It is also apparent that a greater level of job satisfaction and success is achieved in schools where there is freedom for teachers to experiment with new curricula and new methods and where they are involved in planning and policy making, but again this is probably true only in the case of those teachers who want such freedom and involvement. Those who do not want it will not only fail to take advantage of it and will thus be less efficient; they have also been known to sabotage the efforts of more enthusiastic colleagues. We need to know a lot more than we do about the effects of different kinds of structure on different teacher personality types and the effects of the teachers on the structures.

There is more evidence, however, of the effects of different patterns of organization on the pupils and to this we must turn.

The first thing we must note here is the difficulties that can arise for all children, although for some more than others, from an excess of freedom given to them too soon. The work of Erich Fromm (1942) has indicated the dangers that can arise from man's 'fear of freedom' and this is an important consideration for teachers. Fromm was appalled at the limitations to the freedom of the individual that were part of the regime of Nazi Germany from which he had fled to the USA, but he was also struck by the inability of people to cope with freedom and their readiness to accept even extreme forms of authoritarianism. In looking at children in the USA, he draws our attention to the fact that, while they are gaining more and more freedom, this entails emancipation from a world that offered them security, so that they experience a conflict between the freedom that they want and the fear of losing the security that reliance on authoritarian figures can provide. The same phenomenon forms a major feature of the existentialist philosophy of Jean Paul Sartre (1957), who sees it as obligatory for every human being to choose for himself and to make his own decisions, but recognizes the constant temptation that besets everyone to abrogate this responsibility and to slip into a role which will make decisions for him.

Others have noticed the same tendencies in children. Some children reveal a real reluctance to take responsibility for their own work, for example (Musgrove and Taylor, 1969), and this has been noted also in higher education students who have asked for lectures to be made compulsory rather than attendance at them left to their own discretion (Dunham, 1964). In the realm of moral education, too, it is apparent that many children prefer to be told 'what is right and what is wrong' rather than being left to reach their own conclusions on these matters (McPhail et al., 1972).

An awareness of this is vital to the teacher. For if he or she does not take charge in such cases, often a leader will emerge from among the pupils themselves. Some guidance is needed and the teacher must realize that the development of autonomy and the ability to cope with freedom is a gradual process; children must have time to learn to welcome and to use their freedom. They are only potentially free and, as we saw earlier, it is the teacher's job to lead them to freedom rather than to hand it to them straightaway.

It must also be kept in mind that children will react in different ways to the demands of freedom. The most influential factor in deciding how they will react will be their own backgrounds, the ways in which they have themselves been handled both at home and at school. In this connection, it is particularly important to note what psychologists have told us about the 'authoritarian personality' (Adorno, 1960). Such a person tends to value obedience highly; he or she obeys rules for their own sake or from fear of punishment rather than from a concern with the reasons behind them; he or she may resent authority but will readily succumb to it and, conversely, he or she likes to wield power over others regarded as inferiors; he or she tends to be conformist rather than original and is consequently suspicious of change or of anything new; in relationships with others he or she is concerned more with status than with personality characteristics and tends, as we saw in Chapter 2, to hold stereotyped views of them; as a parent his or her affection for the children will be conditional on their good behaviour and obedience.

Children brought up against this kind of background by parents who reveal such traits or, to a lesser extent, by teachers of this kind, tend to acquire the same characteristics themselves quite early in their development. They will as a result prefer a fairly rigid system both at home and at school; they will prefer direction and control to any freer, more suggestive or cooperative approach to education; they will have more respect for the *de jure* or legal authority of the teacher than for that based on any expertise or personality characteristics he or she might show. This kind of background and the resultant personality development, therefore, will be crucial in determining the reaction of pupils to the authority patterns of the school and the degree of freedom they allow. However, it will equally be a product of certain kinds of authority pattern and we must now turn to a consideration of the effects on pupils of different kinds of school and classroom organization.

Quite the best known and most quoted research in this area is that of Lewin, Lippitt and White (1939) in examining the effects of three types of leadership style which they dubbed as autocratic, democratic, and *laissez-faire*. The results of this experiment have been questioned on the grounds that it took place in a voluntary youth club rather than a school and we must also remember that the reaction of the children was not uniform in each situation, as one would expect in view of their differing backgrounds, but most people have nevertheless seen some significance in these findings.

A number of tasks were set to each group and the role of the leader in each was clearly defined. The autocratic leader was to initiate and guide all the activities of his group; he or she was not to reveal to them the overall programme but rather to dictate each stage of the work for each individual member. In the *laissez-faire* group, members were to have complete freedom to decide what to do and how to do it; the leader was involved only when asked for information, advice, or materials by the group. The leader of the democratic group was to generate group discussion for the formulation of policy, to ensure that all members had an overview of the programme and that each shared responsibility for the work and the final achievement.

The main results of this experiment were that in the autocratic situation children worked well while the leader was present but when he was absent this stopped and was often replaced by misbehaviour of all kinds; little initiative was shown by individuals and no pleasure or satisfaction in what the group produced — in fact, in one case a mask they had made was destroyed. On the social plain, two kinds of reaction were detected: aggression between members of the group or a submissive reaction, involving little hostility between members but a good deal towards outsiders. There was little evidence of friendliness either between the children or towards the leader.

The *laissez-faire* climate resulted in haphazard work from the children which seemed little affected by the absence or presence of the leader. Less consistent application to the work was shown and there was a good deal of time wasting. No interest at all was shown in the products of their work.

In the democratic group, the work done did not reveal the same level of industry as that displayed by the autocratic group but it went on consistently even when the leader was absent. The children were more personally involved in what they were doing, wanting to discuss it with each other and with the leader, and far more friendly behaviour was shown between individual members of the group and towards the leader.

Further evidence of a similar kind comes from the work of Anderson and Brewer (1946) who studied two types of teacher behaviour among younger children. These types of behaviour they described, on the one hand, as 'dominative' or 'authoritarian', where the teacher tended to dominate by issuing orders and instructions, and, on the other hand, as 'integrative', where the teacher tended to accept children's suggestions and offer suggestions in return rather than giving orders. The effect seemed to be that the dominative behaviour was met with aggression on the part of the children, who showed rebellious and dominative behaviour themselves, while the integrative teachers gained the children's attention more often and the children showed more cooperation with one another and with the teacher and more spontaneity in what they were doing.

This latter point raises the question of the possible effects of different approaches on the kind of thinking that children learn to engage in. A rigid and authoritarian approach would seem to be unlikely to promote original or individual thought. Children who reveal this kind of divergent thinking are those who tend to challenge authority, to question traditional knowledge and the norms of the school, and such children are rated fairly low on behaviour and regarded as troublesome by their teachers (Getzels and Jackson, 1962). Convergent thinkers tend to express more authoritarian views than divergent thinkers, to value conformity, to respect rules and to think that obedience is important (Hudson, 1966). There are two aspects of this that seem relevant to teachers. Firstly, one of the problems of promoting 'creativity' in schools, as we saw in Chapter 3, is that 'creative' children tend to be less comfortable to work with than those who are more conformist and teachers must learn to live with this if such potential is to be developed. Secondly, it is pertinent to ask how far these characteristics of convergent thinkers are the product of the kind of approach to education and particularly the pattern of authority favoured by the teacher.

The kind of approach adopted by the individual teacher, then, will have considerable implications for the child's attitude to work, the kind of thinking he or she comes to favour, and his or her attitudes to other people, his or her social education. Similar effects can be discerned in the organizational structure of the school as a whole. We saw earlier that this will be a major factor in determining the kind of authority that the teacher can and must wield within it. It is clear now that it will also have its effect on the development of the pupils and the effects of the different patterns of authority generated by different kinds of organizational structure are clear, especially from studies of streaming (Barker-Lunn, 1970; Hargreaves, 1972; Kelly, 1975).

It is important, therefore, that all teachers should be aware of the impact that the methods they adopt in organizing their schools and their classes and in handling their pupils will have on many aspects of the development of these pupils. It is also important that they recognize that their central concern throughout as educators is to set about these tasks in such a way as to develop the kind of authority and the kinds of relationship that will lead their pupils at a proper pace towards the point where they can exercise self-control and self-discipline and take responsibility for their own behaviour and learning. Again, what is required is that teachers be sensitive to the changing balance of freedom and authority in the upbringing of each child at each stage and in every context. Education as we defined it in our earlier discussion requires a gradual movement towards the total erosion of authority in the interests of the freedom and autonomy of the individual and all that we have said subsequently would seem to confirm this. It also suggests that where authority is necessary, it should be a rational authority, that our methods of control should be normative as far as possible, and at the very least justifiable, and our relationships based on mutual trust and confidence. Only a climate of this kind is likely to be conducive to the attainment of freedom by our pupils or to the development of a truly democratic form of society.

Such an ideal is not easy to achieve and it is impossible even for the most highly skilled and gifted teacher to maintain this kind of authority all the time. Often, as we have said before, he or she will be reduced to other measures and sometimes, when authority of any kind deserts him or her, he or she will have to have recourse to punishment. We must conclude our discussions of authority in education, then, with an examination of what is involved in the use of punishment by teachers and of the place of punishment in education.

Punishment

We said earlier that rules must be backed by sanctions and it would be a mistake to imagine that we can forever avoid a situation in which these rules will be broken and the sanctions will need to be brought into play. Punishment becomes necessary, then, when a rule is broken and our authority is lost, when we say to this boy 'Go!' and he saith, 'Drop dead!', when the normative and even the calculative orders have broken down, the mere threat of coercion is not enough and the coercive measures themselves become necessary. The point of punishment, then, is to re-establish authority and respect for both the rule and whoever issued it. The aim is to re-establish control.

The first thing we need to get clear about in any discussion of punishment is what precisely it is; for we need to be able to distinguish it from other related notions like vengeance, deterrence, discipline, and so on. We need to know, if we are beating or beheading someone, how we can be sure we are punishing him or her, rather than working out our spite or indulging our sadistic propensities. It has been suggested that there are five criteria that must be satisfied if we are to use the word punishment appropriately of any act (Flew, 1954). The act must involve an unpleasantness for the victim; it must be related to a supposed offence; it must be the supposed offender who is being punished; it must be the work of personal agencies; and it must be imposed by virtue of some special authority conferred by the system of rules against which the offence has been committed.

It is one thing to say what punishment is; it is a very different matter to justify its use; yet it is to the question of its justification that we must next turn. Two kinds of answer have been offered here. Some philosophers have offered a justification of punishment based entirely on retributive grounds. They look back to the offence and answer the question, 'Why ought we to punish?' with a reason, telling us that it is because an offence has been committed. Others have offered a utilitarian justification, looking to the results, the consequences of the act of punishment, and answering the question by reference to the purposes, telling us that we must punish in order to achieve certain goals.

The retributive argument can really be summed up in the words of the Old Testament 'an eye for an eye and a tooth for a tooth' and there is a strange ring to many of the arguments produced in support of it. We are told, for example, that there is a deep-rooted retributive feeling in all of us and that this is a justification for acting retributively towards offenders, but the presence of a feeling, however deep-rooted, can never in itself constitute a justification for giving full rein to the expression of that feeling. Secondly, they claim that a moral imbalance has been created by the offence and that this must be corrected. Apart from the problem of making the punishment fit the crime, the difficulties of which have been well expounded by Gilbert and Sullivan, there is a problem here that derives from the fact that not all rules are moral rules and not all moral rules are backed by sanctions. In other words, punishment is not always a matter of moral imbalance nor does every such moral imbalance bring punishment on our heads. This does suggest, however, the need to distinguish the use of punishment in moral contexts from other uses of it. Thirdly, retributivists often speak of the offender's right to punishment and, although this is indeed 'an odd sort of right whose holders would strenuously resist its recognition' (Quinton, 1963), it does draw our attention to the difficulties of the alternative view that suggests that we should regard the commission of an offence as an excuse to manipulate someone, to try to turn him or her into a different person. These arguments are not entirely convincing, although they are certainly worthy of more elaborate discussion than we have been able to give them here. A number of interesting features do emerge, however, which we will take up in a moment when we come to consider the place of punishment in education.

The utilitarian view of punishment regards it not as retributive, but as preventive, deterrent or reformative. The view is well summed up in the words of Jeremy Bentham, 'All punishment is mischief, all punishment in itself is evil. Upon the principle of utility, if it ought at all to be admitted, it ought only to be admitted in so far as it promises to exclude some greater evil.' In other words, punishment involves pain and pain for the utilitarian is always bad and can only be justified if it can be shown to lead to pleasure, happiness or the avoidance of greater pain in the future. Only the consequences, therefore, can justify punishment.

Again this is a view that merits more detailed consideration than it can be given here. Its main difficulties, however, stem from the fact that, while it may offer us useful suggestions as to the most efficient methods of social control, it is not strictly a theory of punishment as we have defined it. For if the only criterion we are to take account of in dealing with offenders is a consideration of the likely consequences of our action, then there will be occasions when we will be led to take action that will involve no unpleasantness for the offender at all, or even action which is taken not against the offender himself or herself but against some other person. Action taken against the mother of a juvenile offender, for example, may be more effective in curbing his or her behaviour than action taken against the offender himself. If a calculation of likely consequences is all that need concern us then punishment as such will not always necessarily be the best solution.

It is this feature of the utilitarian view that has made it attractive to some educationists, who have felt that deliberate acts of nastiness should be no part of education and that it is better to have the freedom in which to decide what is best for the individual child in each situation. It has been noted that there are similarities between the notion of education and that of 'reform' (Peters, 1966) and that teachers should be concerned to make their pupils 'better' rather than to act as agents of retribution. It is suggested, therefore, that they should 'treat' offenders rather than punish them. When one puts it in these terms however, the difficulty with this line of reasoning becomes apparent. There is an equally cogent counter-argument which says that the notion of education requires us to respect every individual as a person, as a moral being, to regard him or her as responsible for his or her actions and as entitled to punishment if he or she commits an offence; that we cannot, without doing violence to the notion of education, justify reforming, moulding, shaping, or in any other way treating him or her like a thing rather than a person; that the only way to lead him or her to understanding and ultimately to autonomy is to enable him or her to learn the moral lessons that are implicit in acts of punishment (Wilson, 1971).

Both of these points of view seem to have some merit and some reconciliation may become possible if we make certain distinctions within the kinds of situation in which questions of the rights and wrongs of punishment arise. A distinction might be made, for example, between those offences which are committed against moral rules, where we must be aware of the morally educative dimensions of any action we take, and those where the rule broken has no real moral import, if there are such rules, and where it might as a result be possible to take appropriate action without the same kind of moral compunction. It might be important too to take account of the ages of the pupils concerned. For an act of punishment to have the kind of morally educative effect that is wanted, the child must be capable of understanding the reasons for it and appreciating its point; otherwise, it will be in his or her eyes an act of naked aggression.

This latter point draws our attention to the need to keep in mind the evidence of the possible psychological effects of punishment on children. There seem to be two main aspects of this. Firstly, it seems that in terms of getting pupils to learn effectively what you want them to learn, positive factors, such as encouragement, interest on the part of the adults, and rewards for successes seem to have more effect than 'negative reinforcements' such as punishment. It seems likely to be better, therefore, to reward good behaviour and success and thus to try to prevent bad behaviour than to wait until the bad behaviour occurs and punish it. Secondly, there is little doubt that if punishment is seen by children as an example of aggressive behaviour on the part of adults, as it will be in the case of children who do not understand its moral purport, the tendency will be for them to imitate it and to meet aggression with aggression. Nor is there any doubt of the adverse effects on the climate of a class or school of the widespread use of punishment, as we saw before when discussing the effects on pupils of authoritarian methods generally. In educational terms, it is likely to be counter-productive not only in the case of those pupils who are the recipients of it, but also in the case of all the others who have to live and work in the kind of atmosphere that it engenders.

Prevention is undoubtedly better than cure here. Punishment is a last resort that no teacher should welcome having recourse to. Rather than looking for a justification of it, whether moral or otherwise, we should be working at devising methods of control that will as far as possible obviate the need for it. There are several factors that should be kept in mind as we do this. We need a clearer view of how the rules of any classroom come to be agreed and of the extent to which they are the result of negotiation with the pupils, even when such negotiation is not made explicit; we need to be aware of the variations of structure and method that pupils will experience from teacher to teacher and from classroom to classroom; we need to remember that the fewer rules we have and the less explicit we are about them the more flexibility and room for manoeuvre we will have in our interpretation of them; in particular, where rules are not explicitly formulated, we can on occasion ignore breaches of them, a line that is sometimes far more effective in achieving the 'extinction' of particular forms of behaviour than the reinforcing process of recognizing the offence and punishing it, provided of course that it is not reinforced by the recognition of the other pupils. We will also find it helpful to distinguish those rules that are readily accepted and agreed by our pupils, those, for example, that relate very clearly to the agreed purposes and principles of the school or lesson, and those where their acceptance is less positive and their acquiescence less certain. Teachers and pupils may each define education differently and, clearly, where these definitions agree, the authority of the teacher will be more readily accepted.

This brings us back to a point we made early in this chapter, when we said that the exercise of authority by the teacher can only be justified when it can be shown to be conducive to the achievement of the purposes of education or the agreed purposes of both pupils and teachers. When this is not the case, it becomes authoritarianism, an abuse of authority, and in the current social climate this is unacceptable to pupils. It is here more often than not that direct head-on clashes occur of the kind that are always to be avoided, since they act to the ultimate detriment of the pupil, the teacher, the school and education itself. These are the situations in which punishment or restorative action of some kind comes to be required. It is always better to avoid them.

Since they cannot always be avoided, however, it is important to be clear about what such action is. It is action taken to restore lost authority. As such its justification is not to be sought in itself, since in itself punishment or any other such action has no merit and is at best a necessary evil. It is to be sought in the purposes and principles of the authority it is being used to support, sustain, or reestablish. Only in so far as that authority itself can be justified can we justify any reasonable attempts to maintain it.

Summary and conclusions

We have tried in this chapter to highlight some of the many facets of the exercise of authority in education. We began by considering the problem of its justification in relation to what appear *prima facie* to be conflicting claims for the freedom of the child. We then considered some of the different sources from which teachers might draw their authority and the ways in which they can work at developing it. We discussed some of the factors affecting the kind of authority the individual teacher can develop, in particular those factors deriving from the increasing democratization of society and its schools, and some of the effects of different kinds of authority on the development of the pupil. Finally, we examined the question of the justification of the use of punishment to regain control and restore authority when it has begun to break down.

Throughout our discussion of these issues one thread has run continuously and that is the central concern of any educative process with the developing freedom of the child. This was the only basis we could find upon which to build an argument to justify the use of authority of any kind. Consequently, it was this that led us to suggest that ultimately the only acceptable kind of authority for the teacher to exercise is that based on his own expertise, that the only defensible methods of class control are normative methods, that the use of punishment in education can only be justified if it leads to greater understanding and the restoration of a rational authority, and that, although the human realities of classroom interchange will often make it necessary for us to have recourse to other methods that fall far short of these ideals, we must be aware that these are unsatisfactory in a fundamental sense and can only be justified in so far as they may help us to attain the point at which we can employ methods that are conducive to the development of pupils towards freedom and autonomy.

What we have touched upon here, therefore, is the influence of our techniques of class management and patterns of authority on the personal, moral and social development of our pupils. It is to a fuller discussion of that aspect of education that we must now turn.

CHAPTER 6

PERSONAL, SOCIAL AND MORAL
EDUCATION

There is an important sense in which all education is moral education, since, as we have had cause to note on several occasions, education is essentially concerned with the development within the individual of a system of values. From the very beginning of both the theory and the practice of education a distinction has been drawn between those things that children are taught because of their utilitarian value and those whose purpose is the improvement of the life and character of the individual. Furthermore, only the latter have been seen as the legitimate concern of education as such. Thus in all those traditions, Greek, Judaic and Christian, that have contributed to the thinking of the Western world, the central concern of both the theory and the practice of education has been with moral development. This is a major feature of the work of all of those who have written about education from the time of Plato through to that of the 'great educators' of the nineteenth century, such as Pestalozzi, Herbart and Froebel, and it is the main explanation of the fact that, until the present century, the curriculum of schools and universities, especially in the United Kingdom, was dominated by subjects of a non-utilitarian kind, most notable among which was the study of the classics.

It was the advent of universal education that led to a more open approach to utilitarian aspects of schooling. Initially, the major intention was to provide every citizen with the basic skills of reading, writing, and elementary numeracy, to create a reasonably literate and numerate work force; and there is no doubt that a major justification of the expenditure of public money on the provision of schools has continued to be the purely economic consideration of the need to produce an ever more skilled body of workers to meet the demands of an ever more sophisticated and developing industry. At the same time, however, largely because this has been the kernel of traditional educational theory and practice, the concern with education for its own sake, with the moral and personal development of pupils, has continued. This has, therefore, created a conflict of aims for the educational system, a conflict that is reflected, although not recognized, in the demands that are made on schools from the outside. For many of those industrialists, politicians and others who are constantly demanding that schools cut out the 'frills' and concentrate on providing their charges with the basic skills that they believe industry needs are among the first to condemn the schools if they think they have failed in their duty to promote the development of character and to ensure what they would regard as an adequate standard of behaviour, in short, the very things that those 'frills' might be said to lead to. Thus the traditional concern of education with moral development has continued in spite of the fact that other kinds of demand have come to be made on the education system.

Recently, too, we have become more clearly aware of what this implies and have begun consciously to consider what should be done about it, as is apparent from the proliferation of curriculum projects in this area and the emergence of moral education as a subject on the timetable of many secondary schools. A major reason for this, as we shall see later, is the rapidity of social change that recent years have witnessed and the inability of traditional forms of morality or moral upbringing to meet these changes.

This tension is reflected in all of the many publications on the curriculum which have recently emerged from official sources in the United Kingdom. The main focus of these has been on those subjects deemed to be, although not always identified explicitly as, of utilitarian and economic value. Thus science, mathematics and Craft Design and Technology have usually taken centre stage and the Humanities subjects, those subjects which have traditionally been regarded as the major sources of moral education, have been given rather less prominence. However, there has also emerged a concept of personal, social and moral education — a phrase to be found increasingly both in documents of this kind and in the curricula of the schools themselves.

For some people, this concept embraces a number of quite trivial accomplishments. Thus one recent document from the Department of Education and Science (DES 1985, p.40) includes among the skills to be developed under the heading of 'personal and social', 'to meet personal needs such as dressing oneself, handling a knife and fork, using a telephone'. And most of these documents include careers guidance and preparation for the world of work under this kind of heading.

Our concern here, however, is with that dimension of schooling which consists of the development in pupils of values, attitudes and the ability to make moral judgments, and, if the term 'personal, social and moral education' is different from the more concise 'moral education', it is perhaps merely in the fact that it draws our attention to the breadth of what is involved here, to an awareness that the concern is not just with the ability to debate and to develop opinions on major moral issues, such as those of nuclear weaponry, race relations, questions of sexual morality and so on, but also with the day-to-day behaviour of individuals, especially at the interpersonal level, and with helping pupils to learn to live with others in a society which, as we suggested in the previous chapter, is increasingly diverse in its moral and social make-up. The concept of personal, social and moral education, then, is not in any fundamental sense different from the traditional notion of moral education. It does, however, stress the importance of taking the widest possible view of what moral education includes, and it draws attention to the recent increase of interest in this aspect of schooling.

With this increase of interest has also come a renewed awareness of some of those features of moral education that make it necessary to examine it separately from other areas of the curriculum. It is an area to which no clear body of knowledge can be assigned; it is an aspect of development in which the emotions play a particularly important role; it extends, like language learning, across every experience children have, both inside school and outside it; and it is thus the concern of every teacher, not only those who would lay claim to being educators also, since, as the Newsom Report told us, 'Teachers can only escape from their influence over the moral and spiritual development of their pupils by closing their schools' (1963, para. 160).

It is thus an area of educational theory and practice that we must look at in some detail and, since the increased interest in it that we have drawn attention to has led to certain important changes in our notion of what moral education is, as also has the awareness of these changes in society we discussed in Chapter 5, it will be as well for us to begin with a discussion of that question.

What is moral education?

There are three or four approaches that need to be made to this question. First of all, we need to ask what kind of moral upbringing children need if they are to be able to take their place in our society. Secondly, we must consider what is implied by the use of the term 'education' in this context, why people speak of moral education rather than of, say, moral training or moral instruction, and perhaps also examine the related question of what would constitute a moral education, who would be described as the morally educated person. Lastly, it will be useful if we adopt a negative stance and consider what moral education is not, since one of the major sources of difficulties in this area is that in the past we have tackled the moral upbringing of children wrongly or, rather, in a manner that would seem to be no longer suitable or acceptable, and we must be prepared to recognize this and to make appropriate changes in our provision.

The most striking feature of human societies during the last century or so is the rapidity and the extent of the change that has taken place within them. This has very great implications for all aspects of education, but especially for its central core of moral education. The most obvious features of that change, of course, are those that have affected the material circumstances of our lives, those technological developments that have transformed our styles of living — advances in communications, in facilities for rapid long-distance travel, in mechanical aids of all kinds in the home and at work, in industrial machinery, in medical and surgical devices and skills and so on.

What is less obvious and, therefore, less readily appreciated is the social and moral change that these technological developments have inevitably brought in their train. These have led to changes not only in the material but also in the social context of our lives. Ease of travel has resulted in all societies in an ever-increasing racial mix; industrial developments have led to a greater social mix; improvements in communications have led to a greater awareness of what is happening in other parts of the world, especially through the direct medium of television. These developments in turn have generated continuous changes in moral attitudes and values because of the altered circumstances not only of our social lives but also of our material lives. For, in both areas, new moral problems are posed for society as a whole and for every individual member of society by both kinds of development. No one can now side-step the moral issues presented by the greater racial mix that we find in society; equally no one can avoid making moral judgements in response to the totally new moral issues that he or she is faced with, often directly, as a result of technological advances which enable him or her, for example, to prevent birth, to abort birth, to transplant organs from one human body to another, or even, in some cases, to drop a bomb that will end the lives of hundreds of thousands of people and maim many more. Technological change, then, is constantly creating new moral problems to which new responses must be found. Traditional forms of morality cannot provide these answers because they were developed by people who were never aware of the questions.

However, we must go a good deal further than that. For it is equally clear that many different kinds of response are possible on most of these issues. There is no one, universally valid answer to any of the moral issues we have referred to nor, indeed, to any others. All shades of opinion can be observed in society on most issues and we are slowly coming to accept that it is quite right and proper that this should be so. Most advanced societies are now recognized to be pluralist, to contain within them and tolerate a wide variety of viewpoints on all questions. This is the essence of that notion of the 'open society', we explored in Chapter 5.

It is not, then, so much the changes themselves as the very fact of change that is of crucial importance to the educator. As John Dewey was endeavouring to persuade us half a century or more ago, we must recognize the evolutionary nature of all things, including knowledge itself, and prepare our children accordingly. In the moral sphere, as in any other, this would seem to mean that we should not, indeed that we cannot, prepare children only to meet what is immediately before them but we must prepare them also to adapt to what is coming, to cope with the changes they will see in their own lifetimes. The concept of a 'general mechanical ability', which the Crowther Report (1959) suggested should be central to the preparation of pupils to meet continuous technological change, must be extended to other aspects of their upbringing and especially to those moral aspects that are our concern here.

This brings us naturally to our second area of exploration. For it is precisely that need that makes it necessary for the moral upbringing we provide to be moral education in the full sense rather than moral training or instruction. The features which distinguish education from other activities which involve teaching are such things as the development of understanding, of critical awareness, of an appreciation of the value and importance of certain areas of human experience, of a respect for knowledge and truth and, above all, of the ability to think for oneself (Peters 1965, 1966). None of these is essential if we are training or instructing pupils; some of them, such as the ability to think for oneself, are positively to be excluded if we are indoctrinating them; all of them are vital when we are trying to offer them an education.

The significance of these general features of education for the provision of the kind of moral upbringing we have just suggested present-day society makes necessary will be clear. For it is precisely the development of understanding, of critical awareness, of the ability to think for oneself, and of those other qualities that are the concern of education that is needed in the kind of evolving social context we have briefly described. These are also among the qualities we would expect to find in a person we would describe as morally educated (Wilson et. al., 1967). For what we are claiming is that people need to be morally educated, rather than morally trained or instructed, in order to be able to make their own moral choices and reach their own moral conclusions in a society that will offer them new moral problems to solve and the opportunity to respond to them in a variety of ways. 'No school can, or should seek to conceal from its pupils the fact that there are moral questions on which people of equal integrity and thoughtfulness may reach quite different conclusions' (DES, 1985, p. 27).

It is worth noting here that this view of moral education is supported not only by a consideration of what we mean by 'education' but also by a similar examination of what we mean by 'morality'. For we do not normally accept that a person is behaving morally if we discover that he or she has not thought out and deliberately chosen the course of action adopted. The exploration of that kind of question forms a very important part of the process of law, since we think that, like praise, blame and punishment should be meted out in accordance with the level of responsibility of the individual for his actions. There is an important distinction that Aristotle drew our attention to between acting 'willingly' and acting 'not unwillingly', between doing something because we have thought it through and doing it without such careful consideration. And so, the notion of morality itself, like that of education, also suggests that our concern should be to develop the quality of our pupils' thinking about moral issues.

Another way of looking at this is to recognize that it involves taking a different view or model of man from that that has hitherto held sway. It involves seeing man not as a passive creature, an object acted upon by external forces, but as an active creature, an agent responsible at least in part for his own destiny and able to control some of those external forces for his own ends. It is only when we see man in this light that we can regard him as capable of moral action in the full sense. If we regard him as a passive object at the mercy of forces beyond his control, then he can be no more subjected to moral appraisal, to praise or blame, than a rock or a piece of wood.

One point needs to be stressed here, however, so that we can avoid falling for too simplistic a notion of moral autonomy. The juxtaposition of notions like understanding, critical awareness, and respect for truth with the notion of autonomy suggests that we must take a rather different view of moral autonomy than one that assumes that every moral opinion is equally acceptable and every moral position equally tenable. There is a sense in which we all have autonomy regardless of any educational provision we may or may not have enjoyed; we can certainly think and hold whatever opinions we like, even if in some circumstances we are justifiably restrained from acting on them. However, once we link the idea of autonomy with notions like understanding, critical awareness, and so on, we begin to see what the role of education is. For there is a difference between producing opinions on moral matters, as much as on any other, 'out of the top of one's head' and reaching informed, considered views as a result of having acquired a sound basis of knowledge and understanding upon which these views are built. It is the essence of moral education to help people to reach this qualitatively superior level in their thinking on moral issues, just as it is the goal of, say, scientific education to improve the quality of their thinking on scientific matters. The morally educated person, then, is, at least in part, the person who is well on his way to this kind of autonomous thinking on moral issues.

This analysis leads us in turn to a recognition of what moral education is not. It is not a matter of being instructed in the moral beliefs of someone else; it is not a matter of being trained to respond to moral issues in the way that someone else, whoever that may be, thinks we ought to respond to them. There are a number of implications of this point that we must note.

First of all, this suggests that we should not be concerned only with the content of moral education, with what children come to believe. For to concentrate on this, as many people do, is to offer them moral instruction or moral training rather than moral education. Such instruction and training do have their place in moral upbringing and we must not be interpreted as advocating that they be rejected entirely, but they are only a beginning and the essential point to grasp about moral education is that it must go far beyond this.

One most important way in which it must go beyond this kind of concentration on content is that it must concern itself with the *manner* in which such instruction is both offered and received and with the *manner* in which moral beliefs are reached and held. Its concern is with *how* we reach our moral positions rather than with *what* those moral positions are. In short, its concern is to ensure that our beliefs satisfy those criteria we have suggested are endemic to the notion of education itself and should thus be informed opinions of a superior quality to those that are reached by other means. They should, as we have just said, evince understanding, they should be the result of careful and critical appraisal, they should reveal a recognition of the importance of moral behaviour, they should display a respect for knowledge and truth, and they should be reached by personal choice, decision, and commitment. Moral opinions are not to be plucked from the air; they are not prejudices inherited from our parents or caught from our teachers or our peers; they must be the result of thinking as careful as that which supports views in any other field. If a person declares a dislike for the works of Shakespeare without ever having studied them, we do not take their opinion seriously. There is no reason why we should seriously entertain moral opinions that are similarly unfounded. Yet we constantly do so, as most so-called 'discussion' programmes on television and radio amply demonstrate.

It is important also to note that, if we are to ensure that children come to hold their moral opinions in the right way, their moral education must be offered them in the right way. In particular, we must recognize that an authoritarian approach will be counter-productive to our goals and intentions. We shall note soon in our discussion of moral development the problems this creates for the teacher of young children, who may not yet be able to engage in the kind of moral thinking we have described (although it might be safer to expect this to be true of most children of school age), but we must remember that at any age, if we offer moral precepts in an authoritarian manner, as beliefs or attitudes not to be questioned, they are likely to come to be held in a similar manner and to remain unquestioned for ever. It is also worth noting in passing that at all ages moral attitudes are likely to be offered in this form by teachers who themselves hold them in this manner. As in all aspects of education, a moral education in the full sense cannot be provided by a teacher who is not himself or herself morally educated.

Lastly, in considering what moral education is not, we must note one practical result of our discussion. If moral education is what we have claimed it to be and is not what we have claimed it is not, then it cannot be linked and must not be linked to religious education (O'Connor, 1957; Downey and Kelly, 1978). For a moral code that is based on any set of religious beliefs must of its very nature be authoritarian, centrally concerned with content, with what adherents of that religion believe, discouraging, and even intolerant of, questioning that might lead to rejection, and respecting the autonomy of the individual only up to the point at which he or she chooses the religious and moral 'package'. In short, the moral upbringing it offers is a moral training rather than a moral education. It is because we now recognize the need to encourage a questioning approach to morals, as well as because there is no longer any one religion that can be said to dominate our multi-ethnic society and, indeed, because many people have rejected institutionalized religion entirely, that religious education cannot be regarded any longer as a satisfactory basis for moral education so that something completely different is needed. This is another reason why moral education urgently requires the attention of teachers and educationists and why projects in this field are being spawned at both national and local level. Too many schools and teachers, however, still feel that they can leave it to the RE teacher and the RE lesson. For all the reasons we have set out here, we must get away from that approach before it is too late.

So far we have been painting an ideal picture, setting out what in principle moral education ought to be. The reality, of course, will fall far short of this, although that of itself is no reason for not being clear about our goals and principles. The reality will fall short for two reasons. First, as in all aspects of education, our practice will not be perfect and we must later in this chapter consider in some detail the practice of moral education and its place on the curriculum. But, secondly, there are a number of constraints within which the teacher must work as a moral educator, not all of which are equally significant in other areas of education.

Constraints are imposed by the process of moral development, since it would seem clear that children must pass through several preliminary stages of development before they can attain that level which Laurence Kohlberg has called 'the autonomous level of self-accepted moral principles' (1966). Secondly, this is an area of human experience in which the emotions play a more significant part than they do in most areas. Thirdly, this is an aspect of education to which no pupil comes absolutely fresh and ignorant, as he might be assumed to do to the learning of, say, French. A good deal of moral learning has gone on before the child comes to school and it goes on continually outside the school as well as within it. Furthermore, such learning is necessary because the making of moral choices cannot be delayed until the process of moral education is complete; such choices have to be made all the time. All of these factors place peculiar constraints on the teacher as a moral educator. All of them, therefore, we must now consider in turn.

Moral development

The process of moral development, like that of cognitive development generally, consists of a number of stages through which children must pass if they are to reach moral maturity and this presents teachers with problems comparable to those they must face in all areas of education.

These stages have been identified and elaborated by the major workers in this field, such as Jean Piaget and Laurence Kohlberg, as well as by others who have followed the line of thinking that they have opened up. Briefly, there is a general agreement that children begin at a stage of heteronomy, at which they take their principles and moral beliefs in a largely unquestioning way from others, especially their parents and teachers. Thus at the outset their approach to moral issues and their response to them is of an authoritarian kind. This stage Kohlberg calls the 'pre-moral' stage, a term that suggests that in his view too this kind of moral response is hardly worthy of being called morality at all. The second main stage is that of socionomy, a stage at which they have come to regard rules as emanating not from individuals in an arbitrary manner but from society. They have come to recognize that moral rules are concerned in some way with social cohesion and thus to realize that there are reasons for them. This stage Kohlberg describes as the stage of 'conventional morality' when children conform not out of blind unquestioning obedience, but in order to gain approval and because they have begun to see the point and purpose of the rules. The last main stage is that of autonomy which, as we noted above, Kohlberg calls the stage of 'self-accepted moral principles'. At this stage the individual has learned to think moral questions through for himself or herself and to adopt his or her own moral stances as a result of that thinking. It is this stage, therefore, that is the goal of moral education as we have defined it.

If this is an accurate description of the process towards moral maturity, there are several important things that teachers must learn from it. To begin with, we must note that, as in all aspects of learning, we will be wasting our time if we offer material to our pupils that requires of them a level of response too far beyond the stage that they have reached at that time. For if we do, they will not understand or absorb it. Our offerings and our approach must be suited to their particular stage of development. This, of course, has a special relevance to the teacher of young children, although, for reasons that should become apparent later, it is a mistake to assume that it does not also have significance for teachers of older pupils. However, it does create problems for us in that we may have to be largely authoritarian in our approach to the moral upbringing of young children precisely because they are unlikely to be able to think for themselves on moral matters. However, while in broad terms that might be true, there are at least two important factors that can or should take some of the sting out of it.

In the first place, if we are constantly aware of the nature of the process we are contributing to, we will appreciate that any offering or approach we make to the moral education of young children must be such as to help them on to the next stage of the route towards moral autonomy. For this reason, even when we are telliing them how to behave, we do not need to be, and indeed we must not be, completely authoritarian. We can and should give reasons for our precepts, since, even if those reasons are not in themselves understood, the children will begin in this way to learn that reasons are relevant (Hare, 1964). In this connection, it is worth noting what Kohlberg has told us of how individuals pass from one stage to the next. He draws on the notion of cognitive conflict and offers us the 'one stage above' principle. Its thesis is that if the child is offered arguments at the level of the stage immediately above the stage he is at, the conflict or mismatch of those arguments will require him to resolve the problem and in doing so he will begin to move towards the next stage. Conversely, if he is only offered material suited to the stage he is at, there will be nothing to stimulate or lead him or her beyond it. Thus moral education must be approached in such a way that at all points our main concern is to help children forward.

Secondly, we must note a related and perhaps even more important point. Moral development is like intellectual development in general and quite unlike physical development in that it is not a process that happens simply as a result of our living long enough to let it happen. We do not become morally autonomous just by living long enough, any more than we become brilliant intellectuals just by living long enough. As we have just suggested, we have to be helped if we are to pass through the preliminary stages and reach the stage of autonomous moral thinking. However, the converse is equally true. Just as progress through these stages will depend on our getting the right kind of experience, so the wrong kind of experience will cause us to become stuck or fixated at any one of these stages or perhaps in relation to one or several interconnected areas of experience. This is the important message of the psychoanalytical approach to the study of moral development. The wrong kinds of experience, especially in early childhood, can result in our being fixated at an early stage of development and can thus cut us off entirely from the final goal of moral autonomy. Here, as elsewhere, therefore, it may be more important for the teacher to be aware of the harm he or she can do than of the positive contributions he or she might make.

Thirdly, for this reason as much as for any other, we must not be too ready to link these stages to chronological ages and to assume either, on the one hand, that young children are all necessarily incapable of thinking coherently and constructively about moral questions or, on the other hand, that older pupils will all be capable of doing so. These are mistakes we are inclined to make in viewing intellectual development generally and they are particularly to be avoided here. We must not link the notion of stages too closely to ages.

We must avoid the dangers of seeing this scheme not merely in developmental or sequential terms, but also in chronological terms. Piaget was a philosopher and an epistemologist rather than a psychologist. What he is concerned with is not just a matter of stages of intellectual development; it is also a matter of qualitatively different levels of response to moral choices or dilemmas, different definitions of moral behaviour, all of which can be observed at all ages and in all people. It is thus similar to Bruner's notion of the different modes of thinking that we all employ. People, no matter how well educated they are morally nor how skilled in moral debate, will hold some of their moral principles in an uncritical manner, having accepted them without serious reflection from those who have exercised authority over them or from the society in which they live.

If we recognize the truth of this, we will cease to adopt the rather simplistic view of this kind of theory as being concerned with stages through which children pass and will realize that at all stages these different kinds of response can be expected and observed. Thus, at all stages and with pupils of all ages, teachers need to be concerned to promote an autonomous response to moral issues and to avoid reinforcing an authoritarian or a conventional response. Equally at all stages and ages they need to be aware that an autonomous response may not be forthcoming or even possible.

There are thus two main reasons why children can become stuck at an early stage of moral development or allowed to continue to respond to moral issues at a low level. First, they may not be provided with the right kind of help to get them on or to raise the level of their understanding and of thinking on these issues. That, of course, is a problem that moral education shares with all kinds of education. Secondly, however, they can become stuck at a low level because they have wrong experiences, experiences that are painful and, therefore, positively harmful to their moral education. One reason why this factor looms especially large in moral education is that the emotions play a larger part here than in most areas of education and it is to a consideration of the role of the emotions in moral education that we must now turn.

Moral education and the emotions

A moment's reflection will reveal the central role played by the emotions in the making of moral choices. In fact, it may well be the case that most of us respond to moral issues rather more often according to how we feel about them than as a result of a carefully thought-out intellectual appraisal. It might even be argued that such a response may in the long run be more satisfactory since, although philosophers throughout the ages have been inclined to see reason as paramount in morality and to regard the presence of human feelings as an unfortunate obstacle to the free exercise of reason, few of us are really happy to contemplate an action performed coldly and without feeling, no matter how closely it conforms to what appear to be the requirements of rationality. In short, there are those who would argue that this very capacity for feeling is one of the things that makes human beings human and that, rather than deploring it, we should welcome and embrace it (Downey and Kelly, 1978).

For this reason, it has been argued that we should take greater account of the role of feeling in all aspects of education (Jones, 1972), since in all fields our concern should be with the promotion of feelings of caring and valuing for the activities we offer as part of education in the full sense of the word (Peters, 1966) and with learning to understand and cope with our emotional reactions to experiences. The experience of the more sensitive of those teachers who have been involved in the project Man: A Course of Study (MACOS) has revealed the kinds of occasion on which such an approach by teachers appears to be desirable and possible (Jones, 1972) and this is an area that teachers would do well to explore.

Whatever our opinion of the role of feeling in education generally, however, there is no doubt of its centrality to moral education and one reason for the failure to achieve an adequate view either of moral education or of morality itself is that both educationists and philosophers over the years have failed to make or even to attempt a positive appraisal of the role of the emotions. For the most part they have taken the view, first expressed by the Greeks, that, while it may be true that the presence of feeling is one of the features that characterizes human beings, the aim is to transcend one's humanity and attain the god-like level of pure intellect (in spite of the fact that the behaviour of the gods in Greek mythology was far from free of emotional complications). Thus feelings are seen as obstacles to the achievement of this state so that they are to be 'tamed', brought under control, suppressed, in the interests of the full burgeoning of the intellect.

This view offers a caricature of moral education, since it suggests that this is the only approach one can adopt to the emotions in the moral upbringing of the young. As a result, the main thrust of what has passed for moral education in the schools has been this drive towards the suppression of those feelings that are felt to be undesirable, this being one of the reasons why the task has been gladly left to religion and the teaching of religion.

The most serious effect of this approach has been that it has led and must lead to those forms of repression the dangers of which have been amply demonstrated by many psychologists. Repression is the result of the introjection of the taboos of others, especially in our early and formative years. This is, of course, part of the development of conscience, of what Freud called the superego or ego-ideal, and of the growth of a self-image, and we must not be interpreted as asserting that this process is to be totally deplored. Everyone must develop some kind of ego-ideal or self-image and this must be recognized as part of the process of moral education.

However, the dangers of a wrong approach or of regarding this as the whole of moral education must be stressed. These dangers derive particularly from the fact that repression is an unconscious process; what is internalized affects our attitudes in ways that we are not conscious of and the emotions and feelings that are repressed continue to affect out attitudes and behaviour in one way or another without our being conscious of or recognizing that this is happening. It is thus a process that is opposed to moral education in the full sense we earlier tried to give it, since it militates against understanding, critical appraisal and autonomy rather than promoting them. In fact it is this that can lead to an individual's becoming fixated at an early stage of development — if only in relation to certain kinds of issue — and thus prevented from attaining in those areas the goal of moral autonomy. It can also lead to an odd, unreasonable and distorted sense of values and behaviour, of a kind best illustrated by the research of those whose questioning of young children on moral issues revealed that they thought that the worst crime one could commit was to kill someone and the second worst to run in the school corridors (Kellmer-Pringle and Edwards, 1964). In other words, it can lead to the overdevelopment of conscience in certain areas.

The converse is equally true and rather more serious. For it can lead to that absence of any kind of conscience that is a major characteristic of psychopathic behaviour. The behaviour of the psychopath is not so much immoral and antisocial as amoral and asocial, since he or she is completely indifferent to the effects of his or her behaviour on other people or on society (Wilson et al, 1967).

If we choose this road to moral education, then we will find ditches on both sides into which it will scarcely be possible not to fall. We will also find that if our concern is only to suppress emotions, it will be impossible to find a set of criteria by which we can distinguish between feelings, so that we will be unable to promote and encourage those that most would agree should be developed. In short, we will have cut ourselves off from a positive theory of the role of the emotions in moral education (Downey and Kelly, 1978).

Such a theory must begin by acknowledging that feelings are not always in conflict with the intellect. It is not the case that a moral dilemma always consists of a battle between reason on the one hand and feeling on the other, between rationality and irrationality. Sometimes our inclinations and reason are in agreement and this should not be a cause for worry as it has been for some of those philosophers who have clung very tightly to a conflict model. Secondly, often reason and feeling are to be found together on both sides of a dilemma. The essence of most moral dilemmas is that there are good reasons for all the choices open to us and, often too, feelings that pull us in all directions.

This suggests that the real mistake is to regard the emotions as irrational and not susceptible to any kind of reasoning. It is possible to speak of the 'rational passions' and this alerts us to the fact that the emotions should be seen as being responsive to some kind of education (Peters, 1973).

The first step towards a positive theory of the role of the emotions in moral education, then, is to recognize that they can be educated. The next step is to try to identify some of the ways in which this can be done.

First of all, we must recognize that some emotions are responsive to reason at what we might call a simple informational or factual level. Some feelings that we have are a result of what reason tells us about the world in which we live. When faced by a poisonous snake, I feel a fear that is the product of my knowledge of the capabilities of such a creature. Conversely, ignorance can have the opposite result, so that it can lead a child, for example, to have no fear of the same snake. It is also the case that fear is often the result of ignorance and can be dispelled if we are provided with the relevant knowledge. Thus our fear of snakes might not appear if we know that the snake we are confronted by is of a non-poisonous variety or has had its fangs effectively removed.

Secondly, not only may reason influence the kinds of feeling we have; it often also can affect the way in which we give expression to those feelings. It can help us to resolve conflicts between feelings; it can advise us on the most sensible way to give expression to our feelings, by steering us, for example, into socially acceptable ways of doing so. In short, it can provide us with a degree of understanding of our feelings and this is a more suitable starting point for moral education than mere repression. For it recognizes that the relation of feeling and reason in human experience is one of reciprocity rather than conflict (Downey and Kelly, 1978).

This in turn will lead to a proper kind of control of the emotions. We stressed earlier that our objection to the notion of suppression of the emotions was prompted not by a desire to remove all control but by a wish to see the development of a proper kind of control. We can perhaps now see how the control of the feelings that would come from a developed understanding of them would be a more suitable kind of control. For it would be a conscious form of control, thus avoiding the dangers of repression we referred to earlier, and it would be self-control and thus in keeping with the definition we have offered of moral education as a process leading to ultimate moral autonomy. Clearly, learning to control one's feelings is an important element in moral education, since it involves developing that facility for translating moral principles into action that John Wilson has called KRAT (1967) and identified as one of the main characteristics of the morally educated person. However, we must go beyond this and ensure that such control or discipline is self-control or self-discipline, since if it is a control that comes from without it cannot be part of moral education in the full sense.

One key element of the role of the emotions in moral education, then, is the promotion of the kind of understanding of our emotional lives that will lead to this kind of self-control and self-discipline. It will not be enough, however, if we learn only to understand our own feelings. It is also an important part of moral education to help us to develop an understanding of and a sensitivity to the feelings of others. This is one function, perhaps in some cases the major function, of several areas of the curriculum, such as drama, dance and the study of literature. It leads to the development of another characteristic of the morally educated person that John Wilson draws our attention to. 'EMP refers to awareness or insight into one's own and other people's feelings, i.e. the ability to know what these feelings are and describe them correctly. A distinction might be drawn between self-awareness (AUTEMP) and awareness of others (ALLEMP)' (1967, pp. 192-193). Thus understanding of our own feelings and sensitivity to those of others must go hand-in-hand and the development of both is a vital part of what we mean by moral education.

Finally, we must note that what this amounts to is a claim that some feelings should be positively promoted as a part of moral education. We earlier criticized the conflict model of the role of the emotions in moral education on the grounds that it does not enable us to distinguish between emotions but seems to suggest that they are all to be suppressed in the interests of rationality. We are now claiming that we must be able to distinguish among the emotions in this way so that we can pick out those that are to be encouraged and promoted. For we are arguing that we must accept rather than reject our emotional life, that we must not see it as something to be deplored but as a feature of what it means to be human that we should rather welcome and embrace. We are arguing too that it is this that provides the morality, indeed the beauty, of certain human actions, since what constitutes for most people a moral act is that it is done out of love rather than from a sense of duty. It is for this reason that John Wilson draws our attention to a third component of moral education, PHIL, which 'refers to the degree to which one can identify with other people, in the sense of being such that other people's feelings and interests actually count or weigh with one, or are accepted as of equal validity to one's own' (1967, p. 192).

Again, however, we must push this on a little further and take it beyond what appears to be the largely cognitive dimension he gives it. It is not only an intellectual recognition and acceptance of the feelings of others that we are arguing for here. It is the development of those affective qualities that will result in our behaving in certain ways not only because we understand the feelings of others, but because we sympathize with them, feel for them, even love them. We must not attempt to solve the problems of the education of the emotions or of the role of the emotions in moral education by intellectualizing them, by reducing them to some form of cognition. We must recognize them for what they are and look for a theory which also reflects that kind of recognition (Kelly, 1986).

This is the direction, then, in which there lies a proper, developed, human morality and our only way of achieving this as moral educators is to take a positive approach to the education of the emotions of our pupils, to help them to become people who not only recognize at the intellectual level what they ought to do but also acknowledge the importance of doing so because they understand and sympathize with the feelings of their fellows.

Thus, our programme of moral education must be so framed as to promote this kind of development in our pupils as well as the growth of those cognitive abilities we identified earlier. As we said before, however, our efforts in both of these directions will be affected, even inhibited, by the experiences our pupils have outside the school. We must now turn to a consideration of the constraints that this factor places on the teacher as a moral educator and of some of the ways in which he or she can respond to this problem.

Moral education and moral learning

We drew attention at the beginning of this chapter to the fact that the moral educator has to work within constraints similar to those that face the teacher in his or her concern with language development, since not only will a good deal of learning have gone on in this area before the child comes to school, it will also continue to go on throughout school life as a result of experiences outside the school as much, if not more than, those he or she has within it. For the growing child will be susceptible to many moral influences and he or she will be so mainly because from the earliest age he or she needs to act morally, to make choices, so that we cannot expect him or her to wait until he or she has reached a level of competence we would recognize before beginning to act as a moral being. Furthermore, as Aristotle said, we become moral by behaving morally. The two must run in parallel.

There are several obvious sources of this kind of learning. Firstly, children will from the earliest age absorb the attitudes and values of their parents and other adults, especially when they see these as emanating from a source of authority and are at the stage when they feel that that is the only reason there need be for acceptance of and obedience to such moral precepts. A good deal of racial prejudice, for example, probably begins this way. Secondly, the peer group will be an important source of moral learning. At certain ages and stages this will be the most powerful and, indeed, the dominant source of moral learning. Thirdly, perhaps the most important, certainly the most insidious, of these sources of moral learning are all forms of the mass media. So much uncritical and unreflective moral learning goes on simply as children, and adults too, watch television programmes of all kinds, listen to the radio, read their comics, newspapers and magazines and absorb the values that are concealed in everything that they are offered from these sources. Advertising may be one particularly obvious source of such influence and its importance must be recognized, but we must not forget that the same kind of persuasive processes are at work elsewhere in the media, whether by design or accident.

These, then, are the three most obvious and influential sources of that moral learning that goes on all the time. There are several important features of this kind of learning that need to be stressed. Firstly, we must note that the relative strengths of these sources will vary at different ages and stages of the child's growth. The influence of parents will probably be greater in the case of young children, for example, and that of the peer group at adolescence. Secondly, we must note that this is learning of a largely unconscious, certainly unreflective, kind. The attitudes and values that we pick up in this way certainly influence the way in which we respond to the world; they do not usually influence the way in which we think about it in the full sense of that term. Thirdly, as a direct result of this there is often confusion and a lack of coherence in the attitudes and values we thus acquire. This will reveal itself at a number of levels. At one level there is likely to be conflict between the values pupils absorb from their parents in this way and those they pick up from their peers, and this is one important point at which the sensitive help of the teacher or some other adult may be necessary. There will also often be conflict and confusion within the values that derive from any one of these sources, since usually they are no more clearly thought out by those who provide them than they are likely to be by those who receive them. And lastly, there will be enormous differences between pupils in this respect, since both the content of what they have thus learned and the manner in which they have learned it will vary very widely. Social class differences in child-rearing practices, for example, have been shown significantly to affect children's moral development (Kay, 1968; Bull, 1969) and the multi-ethnic nature of many classrooms will also contribute to the same wide variation of moral learning. The essential factor in all of this is that this kind of learning, because it is incidental, unnoticed, and to a large extent unconscious, is by definition uncritical and unreflective. It thus represents a response to moral issues at the level of heteronomy rather than autonomy. It is, therefore, to use a good old-fashioned word, prejudice, and these views are most likely to be held in this manner if they are learned from adults who themselves hold them in this manner.

Finally, we must note that this kind of learning is not confined to those experiences the child has outside the school. A good deal of similarly unreflective learning of attitudes and values goes on as a result of what happens within the school (Downey and Kelly, 1978); this is what is meant by the 'hidden curriculum'. Sometimes this will be the result of deliberate attempts on the part of teachers to ensure that pupils develop certain habits of behaviour or attitudes without concerning themselves too much with whether they develop these in a reflective or an unreflective manner. Nor must we too readily condemn this, since certain patterns of behaviour do need to be established before pupils are able to be reflective about them. More often however, such learning will be the result of those values that are implicit in the materials we use with children, the procedures we adopt, the way in which we handle those day-to-day situations that arise in every classroom and, indeed, the overall organizational structure that the school favours. All of these will both represent and display value positions and these will be absorbed, usually quite uncritically, by pupils. Thus the school may provide the same kind of unreflective moral learning as will the society outside the school. Issues of gender and sexual sterotyping are good examples of this process.

What are the implications of this for moral education? To begin with, we must again assert that this is not a process to be deplored. It is a natural process and one that provides pupils with that content to their moral development that they need from the earliest age. It must also be seen, however, as providing a basis for their moral education, since this kind of moral learning must be the starting point for moral debate and discussion. In other words, moral education must be seen as the process of converting this uncritical, unreflective moral learning into a fully conscious and reflective response to moral issues.

Two things follow from this. In the first place, we must try to ensure that the moral learning that we are responsible for is not of such a kind as to inhibit the development of our pupils' ability to consider it thoughtfully, even if this can only be done at a later date. This is perhaps of particular importance to the teacher of young children who, as we suggested earlier, may be as yet incapable of reflecting at a proper level on moral questions. Secondly, it means that we must recognize that all of our arrangements and provision in schools should be such as not only to avoid the dangers of inhibiting moral education but also to promote those qualities that we are suggesting are part of moral education. In particular, we should be concerned to raise the values which pupils have already absorbed to a conscious level, to encourage them to be reflective about them and to promote the kind of understanding necessary for a properly critical appraisal of moral issues in order to lead them to the ultimate goal of becoming fully autonomous moral beings.

If we are able to do this, it will only be as a result of a combined effort that not only goes across the curriculum but permeates all aspects of the life of the school. It is to a consideration of what this implies for the practical provision we make that we must turn in our next section.

Moral education and the curriculum

We suggested at the beginning of this chapter that there is an essential moral dimension to all education, that in a sense all education is moral education, and this must be the major theme of any discussion of the practice of moral education. For it is probable that the moral education we offer pupils will only be fully effective if it is the result of a concerted effort to ensure that all the experiences that pupils have in school have a morally educative effect.

This means that we must begin by acknowledging that, like language education, moral education goes right across the curriculum. It would be difficult to substantiate the claim that any curriculum subject does not have a moral import. In some areas, such as literature and history, the moral dimension is easy to identify, since there can be no real examination or discussion of any historical event or literary work that ignores its moral implications. In other areas, these implications may be less readily identified but it would be difficult to argue that they do not exist. Nor must we forget the contribution of many areas of the curriculum to the emotional and affective components of morality, to the understanding and the development of feeling that we referred to earlier. A good deal of what is done in drama, in dance and in physical education, especially when this takes the form of outdoor pursuits, has a major influence on this aspect of development.

Secondly, we must recognize the role that the total organization of the school has to play in promoting moral education. We have already referred to the hidden effects that such factors can have on the moral development of pupils, and the first thing we must do is to try to organize the school in such a way as to ensure that these effects forward that purpose of moral education. In other words, we must try to create a climate in the school of such a kind as to ensure not only that it does not hinder but that it actually contributes to the moral education of the pupils (Sugarman, 1973). This means that we must look very closely at such features of the organization of the school as the ways in which pupils are grouped, the teacher-pupil relationships, the system of rules and patterns of authority within the school, the form and purposes of any school council we might set up for the discussion of problems, and many other things, and recognize that these are not just administrative devices but parts of the total programme of moral education. For the same reason, it has been suggested that counselling should be seen not just as a mechanism for dealing with individual problems but again as part of the moral education of all pupils (Schofield, 1977).

This is why a number of the projects in moral education which have emerged in recent years, such as the Lifeline project (McPhail, 1972) and that of the Farmington Trust (Wilson, 1973), have stressed the need for the introduction into the school of a structure which will support what they are endeavouring to achieve.

Many of them have also stressed the need for the curriculum to include specific lessons in moral education and have offered advice on what such lessons might contain. There would seem to be little doubt that some such direct examination of moral issues is desirable and likely to be extremely helpful in developing those abilities we described earlier. The kind of discussion of moral questions advocated, for example, by the Humanities Curriculum Project (Schools Council, 1970) is clearly likely, if properly carried out, to be of great value both in encouraging critical thinking and in raising the quality of such thinking.

Much that has been done in this area, however, leaves a lot to be desired and falls far short of the principles we have been endeavouring to set out. We must devote a little time, therefore, to a consideration of some of the developments which have taken place in this area of the curriculum.

The content of personal, social and moral education

The developing interest in personal, social and moral education has been reflected in a proliferation of courses in schools which have covered a very wide range. These include the various Humanities programmes designed in the 1960s to provide interest and relevance for those pupils who were about to be required to remain at school for an extra year when the legal age of leaving was raised (Schools Council, 1965; 1967); environmental studies courses to provide opportunities for pupils to learn about the social world outside the school (Schools Council, 1974); community education projects of the kind planned by Eric Midwinter in Liverpool (1972); social studies courses to introduce pupils to basic sociological concepts; and broad programmes of moral education such as those proposed by the Humanities Curriculum Project (Schools Council, 1970). Closer examination of even a few examples of these programmes will reveal two disturbing features. First, for the most part these courses have been aimed mainly at the less able pupil and have thus too often been regarded as 'low status subjects taught to low status pupils by low status teachers' (Gleeson and Whitty, 1976). Secondly, they have lacked any kind of clear or common rationale, any kind of clearly conceived notion of what personal, social and moral education might or should be. This has been particularly true of those courses described as 'social studies', that is those courses which have stressed the social aspect of this area of education often to the exclusion of the personal and moral. And, since it is social studies courses which have tended to proliferate, especially in secondary schools in recent years, it will be worthwhile for us to explore briefly the ways in which many of these have actually been counter-productive to rather than supportive of personal, social and moral education.

A brief examination of the ways in which schools have attempted to provide some kind of social education over the past two decades will help to show how the concept has been interpreted and how and why it has come to be reinterpreted.

It was not until after the Second World War that the newly formed secondary modern schools began to introduce courses in environmental studies, civics, current affairs, and so on, designed mainly to show pupils how man adapts to the problems of his environment and, implicitly if not directly, teaching pupils how to conform to the society in which they live. Few such courses, if any, were provided for pupils in selective schools, who were considered capable of traditional academic subjects, or who at any rate accepted them unquestioningly, having been successfully socialized into the ethos of their school. Public attention was drawn to the importance of social studies for adolescents by the Crowther Report (1959), which recommended such courses for the fifteen to eighteen age group, to help them to find their way around the world. Four years later the Newsom Committee (1963) strongly supported the introduction of some kind of social studies for the less able, who, it was hoped, could be more easily contained in school by studies with a less academic flavour, deemed to be more practical and relevant to their needs. It was in response to demands such as these that the Schools Council published among others its Working Paper No. 11, *Society and the Young School Leaver* (1967), setting out suggestions for Humanities programmes designed to give the pupil 'a chance to learn more about himself and more about the community in which he is to live'. This working paper, in its attempt to provide some kind of social education for pupils of average and below average ability by sending them out into their own locality to explore, for example, the 97 bus, the press, shops and shopping, has subsequently been most stringently criticized on the grounds that this approach encourages pupils to accept their unfortunate lot unquestioningly rather than challenging them to think for themselves and reach their own conclusions.

John White's pithy comment (1968) that pupils were merely being instructed in obedience by 'interest-based indoctrination' has been echoed by other writers since then. It is this of course that has caused such studies to become low-status studies. They are also, however, more importantly a denial of moral education as we have defined it.

In the mid-1960s, social studies and social education took on a new look, partly as a reaction to the kind of programme that we have been describing and partly because of the influx of sociology graduates into schools for the first time. This movement, supported by influential sociologists at the London Institute of Education, became concerned with the planning and teaching of sociology-based social studies courses. This was an attempt to introduce a greater degree of academic rigour and to help secondary school pupils to pursue a more structured study of society based upon an understanding of the concepts and evidence from social science. Courses were no longer to be aimed at the less able pupils, most of whom were already labelled as academic failures, but instead set out to promote the social awareness of all pupils by developing in them an understanding of the society in which they lived. Lawton (1968a) called for social studies courses that were not only socially relevant and academically rigorous but also fostered discovery and problem solving rather than mere memorization of facts.

However, such ideals were in practice difficult to achieve. Academic sterility replaced academic rigour, in that brighter pupils tended to learn whatever the teacher offered, while less able ones still questioned the relevance of the material, as Keddie (1971) describes. Social awareness and social understanding were still not being developed, it seemed, still less moral education; pupils continued either to take for granted what their teachers offered or to reject it out of hand. Whichever it was, it was clear that the new social studies had failed to engender a questioning, critical attitude in pupils.

More recent approaches to social education and the teaching of social studies set out specifically to help pupils to think critically about their own assumptions and about the world in which they live, so that they are no longer content to accept their lot blindly but can learn ways of contributing towards change. Such is the aim behind some of the community education programmes set within the context of compensatory education. Midwinter's Liverpool project (1972), for example, was designed to forge links between the school and the community at all age levels and thus to enable pupils to see themselves as active members of their own community. As such they need to develop the social skills that will equip them not only to look critically at their immediate environment but also to take positive action where this is needed to make changes for the good of all. Within this framework, Halsey (1974) talks of arousing 'constructive discontent' in young people.

This brief outline of ways in which schools have attempted to make provision for some kind of social education since 1945 reveals many of the dangers and pitfalls associated with this area of the curriculum and shows quite clearly the need for a thoroughly thought-out concept of social education. In the early years, courses seemed to be largely instrumental in nature: they helped pupils to find their way about in the world by learning about local amenities, the kinds of job they would be able to do, and perhaps something about the workings of the local council and the provisions of the welfare state. However, as we have already remarked, critics were quick to attack these courses for teaching pupils to accept their position in life, thus maintaining the status quo (White, 1968; Ball and Ball, 1973; Pring, 1975). Working on a project on the police force, for example, was more likely to teach pupils the sort of attitude towards authority that adults thought they ought to have, than to help them understand the nature of authority, of personal relations, or even of working conditions within the police force. In other words many of these earlier approaches aimed implicitly to socialize pupils so that they learned to conform to the norms and conventions of society. The term 'socialization' nowadays for some people has unpleasant overtones, smacking of indoctrination and always conjuring up a picture of pupils being conditioned or trained in a machine-like manner, reminding us of Skinnerian reinforcement techniques more appropriate to the training of animals than the education of man.

The New Social Studies movement brought an ostensible change of concept in rejecting the ideal of socializing only the less able and, instead, introducing the notion of developing social awareness in all pupils. At first, this seemed a welcome aim. However, again, what was entailed by this concept was not made clear enough. Learning about the structure of society through sociological concepts seemed to imply that social awareness meant understanding what society is like and how it works, and that largely from a sociologist's point of view. Knowing what society is like can possibly mean little more to the individual than learning where his or her place is in it, in other words, being socialized.

We have so far explored several different ways in which schools have tried to provide some sort of social education for their pupils, by examining different approaches to social studies in secondary schools over the past twenty-five years or so. We have suggested that a major weakness which becomes apparent from this kind of review is the lack of a clear concept of social education and, in particular, the loss of the dimension of moral education which is a feature of many of these programmes. It will now perhaps be worthwhile looking briefly at two projects which seem to reflect more effectively the principles of personal, social and moral education which we enunciated earlier — Bruner's 'Man: A Course of Study' (MACOS) and the Schools Council Social Education Project (Schools Council, 1974).

Bruner's MACOS (1960) provides an example of a social studies programme for children in the middle years of schooling and in this country is used mainly with the ten to thirteen age range. It is in essence an enquiry-based project, drawing upon evidence from the social and behavioural sciences, particularly anthropology and ethology. The course structure is based upon Bruner's notion of a spiral curriculum, so that pupils can explore and examine basic and universal concepts of social life, such as communi-cation, aggression, and adaptation, in a variety of social contexts. These begin with the life-cycle of the salmon, the herring gull, the chimpanzee/baboon family, then proceed to the human level, taking the Netsilik Eskimo as an example of a culture very different from that of Western man. By comparing and contrasting life-styles at these various levels, using film material as the main learning resources, pupils are encouraged to pursue three basic questions: What is human about human beings? How did they get that way? How can they be made more so? Social awareness is interpreted as the ability to understand man's nature, to reflect critically upon and analyse the human condition and to understand and respect man's capacities, emotions, and shortcomings. Not only do pupils have the opportunity to observe and discuss how different species and different cultures cope with their basic needs, survival mechanisms, and emotional forces, but they also have the chance to express and reflect upon their own emotional responses to forms of behaviour that are totally alien to Western man. Thus social awareness is enhanced by understanding others and also coming to terms with oneself.

MACOS uses the concepts, evidence, and insights drawn from the social sciences to help younger pupils towards an understanding of what society is like, thus putting into practice the principles advocated by Lawton (1968a). It attempts to prepare pupils for participation in social life, without trying to equip them with specific social skills or to teach them to adhere to the norms and conventions of their own society. On the contrary, it gives them insights into ways in which very different communities organize their social world. Rather than atttempting, even implicitly, to inculcate certain attitudes or values into pupils, the programme leaves important social and moral questions open to pupils, thus allowing them the opportunity of forming some kind of moral judgement of their own. Thus, as a course in social education, MACOS meets many of the criticisms levelled against other projects. Its potential as a vehicle for personal, social and moral education in the full sense is clear from the use which has been made of it by some teachers and especially from the ways in which some teachers have been able to develop its basic principles (Edwards, 1983).

Clearly, however, its success depends upon the teacher's skill in handling the materials and the pupils' responses to them. It would be easy to use didactic methods and simply present children with unrelated chunks of predigested knowledge, though official attempts are made in this country to equip teachers with appropriate skills before they are permitted to use the resources. Similarly a teacher, unskilled in handling children's responses to such incidents as the killing of baby seals, the attacking of their young by gulls, or the practice of urinating on burning sand so that it might be strewn over the body to cool it, might suppress children's emotions rather than help them to understand their own feelings. And although, as we have pointed out, there is no attempt to persuade children to adopt any particular attitudes, there remains the danger that teachers and pupils might take Westerners as their ideal concept of man, by contrast with another apparently less civilized culture.

The Schools Council Working Paper No. 51 (1974) offers a very different programme of social education. It is designed for use with less able pupils in the fourteen to fifteen age range and aims to equip them to play a fuller part in the affairs of their own community, to be willing and able to engage in cooperative activity, to challenge and change their world, thus helping themselves and others towards a more satisfying mode of social living. Williams and Rennie (1972) see social education not as a variation on social and liberal studies, but as a means of equipping pupils to contribute towards much needed social change by seeing themselves in school as part of the wider community. The aims of the Schools Council Project are expressed in its definition of what social education is, namely 'an enabling process through which children will receive a sense of identification with their community, become sensitive to its shortcomings and develop methods of participation in those activities needed for the solution of its social problems'. Thus in implementing the project, the team members, led by Rennie, were attempting to involve pupils in specific activities rather than simply adding yet another subject to the curriculum. After an experimental trial period in 1968-1969, when an attempt was made to introduce social education programmes into ten schools in the Nottingham area, the main study (1969-1971) was concentrated in four schools.

To prepare pupils for the main part of the work, time was spent initially in building up communication skills by means of mime, simple group drama, group discussion of practical problems, and later of issues involving moral elements. In the fourth year pupils were ready to study in depth the structure of some of the groups that had a direct impact on them, in preparation for an examination of a specific aspect of the area in which they lived, such as play facilities, living conditions, emergency services, and so on. The aim was that eventually pupils would reach the final step in the sense of belonging to the community, by carrying out a survey to identify and possibly help to solve a problem they considered in need of attention and action.

One low-ability class, for example, who had been following a social education programme for two years and had compiled profiles of the groups they belonged to in school, embarked on a project involving problems of redevelopment in their area. They discovered during the course of their survey that about two-thirds of the population were going to be rehoused against their will and that the move would result in increased deficiencies in public services. What particularly distressed the pupils was that the adults concerned were apparently completely fatalistic about what was to happen to them and made no attempt to express their dissatisfaction publicly or to initiate any action to avert the move. The indignation of the pupils was so strong that they made plans to take action themselves, suggesting building a mobile exhibition for use in shops, launderettes, and waiting rooms; running a poster campaign to rouse adults from their resignation and apathy; and contributing articles to the local newspaper on the implications of the redevelopment scheme.

An initial evaluation of the project suggested that it had had some success in developing pupils' self-awareness and creating in them a sensitivity towards the needs of their community and a willingness to involve themselves in community problems. Clearly this kind of programme makes more demands on the social and intellectual resources of pupils than community service projects where pupils are presented with a practical task such as shopping for the elderly or looking after small children. As C. and M. Ball (1973) point out, pupils often have no idea why they are papering an old person's walls, let alone why problems of poor housing exist. Gleeson and Whitty (1976) scathingly remark that it often amounts to nothing more than 'papering over a few cracks in the welfare state'. We might add that such schemes successfully conceal the cracks in pupils' social understanding and awareness. The Schools Council type of project, on the other hand, does enable pupils to take a more active part, in that they themselves identify the problem, take action on their own initiative, and seek adult advice and guidance rather than merely accepting teacher direction.

Although this particular project was necessarily limited in scope, it clearly shows possibilities for development. Like the Humanities Curriculum Project, it involves considerable role changes on the part of pupils and teachers who are now both seeking answers together. Teachers are no longer problem-posers and answer-givers. Likewise, it necessarily entails a move away from didactic teaching methods since pupils must be involved in formulating their own problems, in decision making, and in taking responsibility and initiative.

What we need to ask now is whether a programme of this kind is appropriate and worthwhile for all pupils in all kinds of school. If such projects are restricted to pupils of lower ability in so-called deprived areas, yet again a divisive curriculum is created against which we have argued elsewhere. Moreover, if social education is important, surely it must feature on the curriculum of all pupils? The crux of the issue lies in an understanding of what social education entails. It is rather disconcerting to find within a project entitled social education several references to 'training children in school . . . in the skills required to work as groups' or to children being 'trained to act as agents of change within their community' (Williams and Rennie, 1972).

One final point needs to be made concerning the introduction of any form of personal, social and moral education as a separate subject on the timetable. Its inclusion as a separate area in this way may encourage other teachers in the school to assume that they have no responsibility for it, just as many did, and still do, when it is left to the teacher of religion. This could result in the loss of all those advantages that we are arguing will accrue only if every teacher acknowledges his or her responsibility in this area. We must finally turn, therefore, to a consideration of what all of this means for the individual teacher in his or her own classroom. In doing so, we may also regain the interest and attention of the primary teacher to whom all of our recent discussion of subjects and timetables may seem somewhat remote.

Moral education and the individual teacher

The first problem facing the teacher in this area is that of providing pupils with a continuously developing moral code which will govern their day-to-day behaviour, in short to provide a content for their moral development, since, as we said earlier, we cannot expect them not to act morally until their moral education is deemed to have been completed. Positive moral guidance is necessary, therefore, from the earliest age. What such guidance should consist of is probably the most intractable problem to be solved, since, as we have already stressed, on most issues there is a wide spectrum of opinion which must be allowed and there is no longer any point in seeking after some objective basis for any one particular moral position or set of values.

However, although guidance is necessary and content of some kind is needed for moral education, it is not too much of a problem to decide what that content should be if we pay proper attention to the manner in which it is presented and bear in mind throughout the goals and principles of moral education as we have defined it. Moral guidance does not have to be an imposition of our values on our pupils if it is offered in a spirit and in a manner that will ensure that in the end the pupil will be able to think for himself or herself and reach his or her own moral conclusions.

There are pitfalls here, however, that we need to be familiar with. In general, we need to be quite meticulous in our efforts to ensure that the guidance we offer is offered in this way. In particular, we need to be aware of the influence our own values are likely to have on the moral development of our pupils. Moral values are as readily caught from teachers as they are from other sources, so that we must be constantly alive to the risks we run, or rather which our pupils run, in this respect. This is one reason why moral disagreement among the teachers of any school is to be applauded rather than, as some seem to think, deplored. For if teachers themselves display to their pupils a wide spectrum of opinion, it is less likely that those pupils will uncritically accept any one viewpoint on any issue.

However, again we must stress that it is the manner rather than the matter that is important. A lack of consensus on matter may be an advantage; a lack of consensus on manner will be quite the opposite. For, not only will pupils catch particular moral values from teachers, they will also catch from them the manner in which they are held. If the teacher himself or herself holds a particular view in an authoritarian, heteronomous manner, the pupil who absorbs it will come to hold it in a similar manner and it is that rather than the temporary adoption of a particular value position that puts his moral education really at risk. The message here is brief but vital. If the teacher himself or herself is not a morally educated person, not only will he or she never become a moral educator, he or she is likely to have a positively inhibiting effect on the moral education of the pupils. No one should expect to be able to contribute to the moral education of children who is not morally educated himself or herself, just as no one can promote education in any field in which he or she is not a fully educated person.

In brief, it is more important that teachers should know what they should not do in the field of moral education than what they should do. It is important that they be fully alive to the dangers, to the harm they can do. As in all areas of education, teachers must recognize the importance and the complexities of the job they have to do and realize how much damage they can do if they do not do it properly.

Whatever formal provision we make, the first and most lasting moral education is that which grows out of the day-to-day interaction between teacher and pupil and the guidance that the individual receives in relation to those moral problems, however trivial, he finds himself faced with. The worldwide issues are important and opportunities to discuss them must be provided, but in the last analysis the real stuff of moral education is the everyday experience of the individual. In this area in particular, the only true education is that which is developed from the first-hand experience of each child, since it is here that he or she is sorting out his or her own life-style, structuring his or her own world, building up his or her self-confidence, and developing his capacity for responsibility. All of this is essentially a first-hand matter. This is why, although the other kinds of provision we have discussed must have their place, in the end the quality of the moral education any child receives will depend on the quality of the teachers with whom he or she finds himself or herself working at any and every stage of education. In this again moral education is no different from education itself.

Summary and conclusions

We have tried in this chapter to argue that an analysis of what we mean both by 'education' and by 'morality' requires us to see moral education as the development not of particular habits of behaviour or attitudes of mind but of the ability to think for oneself critically, sensibly and productively on moral issues. We further claimed that the same approach to moral education is indicated by an examination of the nature of the society in which we live, since the social change that we are constantly witnessing makes it necessary to help children to attain a flexibility and an adaptability in their moral outlook, while its pluralism requires that we be tolerant of many shades of opinion on most issues.

We then considered some of the major constraints that teachers must work within when endeavouring to bring about this kind of development in their pupils. First of all, they must take full account of the stages that the individual must pass through on his way to moral maturity. Secondly, they must recognize that the emotions play a major role in our moral lives and that this is a source of particular difficulties for the moral educator. Thirdly, we noted the volume of largely unconscious moral learning that goes on outside the school and, indeed, inside the school as well, that must be seen as providing the basic material with which and within which the teacher must work in this area.

Next, we considered some of the implications of this for the practice of personal, social and moral education within the school. We suggested that there is a place for the moral or social education lesson, for the provision of opportunities for pupils to discuss, debate and ponder on moral and social questions as such, and to learn more about the problems of social living. We drew attention, however, to the fact that this needs to be handled carefully if it is not to be actually counter-productive to moral education as we have defined it. We also stressed that such provision should not be allowed to encourage other teachers to ignore the moral dimension of every aspect of their work with children, but that they should be aware of that dimension and make proper use of it in all areas of the curriculum and of their work as teachers. We also emphasized the need for attention to be given to all aspects of the organizational structure of the school, to its climate, to ensure that its total effect is as morally educative as it can be made, and, perhaps especially, to avoid those many influences whose effect is to retard and inhibit rather than to promote the personal, social and moral development of pupils.

This brought us to a recognition of the central role of the individual teacher in this process. We stressed again that the quality of the moral education every child receives will depend crucially on the quality of his or her teachers. And we noted the kind of harm that teachers can do in this sphere and emphasized in particular the need for teachers themselves to be morally educated.

For, in the last analysis, personal, social and moral education depends on the recognition by every teacher of the responsibility to see that his or her own contribution to the processes is such as to assist, or at least not to hinder, the child in his or her progress towards a proper personal, social, moral and, indeed, human autonomy. And that, as we said at the beginning of this chapter, is also the goal of education itself.

CHAPTER 7

THE CURRICULUM

We drew attention in our Foreword to the fact that it is this chapter on the curriculum which has had to be almost totally rewritten for this third edition, as was the case for the second. For this is the area in which there has been the most rapid change and development — not only in the ten years since this book was first published in 1975, but also in the six years which have elapsed since the second edition in 1979.

It may be interesting, therefore, to begin by offering a brief outline of what we took to be the main preoccupations of teachers in this area in 1979 in order to compare these with what we feel are the major concerns now. In 1979 we gave a good deal of attention to the debate over the use of objectives in curriculum planning; it is our belief that most teachers have moved some way beyond the simplicities of that issue and are now concerned with the more complex and sophisticated issues of the choice of curriculum models and the implications of adopting alternative approaches to curriculum planning — even if the thinking of politicians and the inspectorate, as displayed in official publications on the curriculum, continues to trail some way behind in this area. In both earlier editions, we spent much time exploring the philosophical questions raised by the debate over the content of the curriculum, questions about the status of human knowledge and the implications of that debate for curriculum planning; in this edition, although the importance of that problem has by no means diminished, our focus has switched, like that of the national debate, to the several political dimensions of those questions. Much time too was devoted in 1979, as in 1975, to a discussion of curriculum integration, since at that time the claim made by Paul Hirst (1965) that knowledge must be seen in several, logically distinct 'forms', of a kind which precluded their integration, was still regarded as having some significance for curriculum planning; now integrated studies of many kinds can be seen on the timetables of most secondary schools and the undifferentiated approach to the curriculum in the primary school is challenged only from the subject-based perspective of those same official publications on the curriculum, and even there the challenge is often somewhat half-hearted and always ill thought out. It also seemed important in 1979 to say something about the notion of 'enquiry learning' or 'learning by discovery', if only to attempt to clear up some of the misunderstandings which have marred discussions of that approach to teaching and to the curriculum, and we also looked at the related issues of interest-based and needs-based learning; much of that debate has now merged into the rather more sophisticated discussion of curriculum models we mentioned just now. Finally, we explored in 1979 the related issues of curriculum evaluation and the proposals for a centrally determined common curriculum in schools in the United Kingdom; these are matters which, along with the associated issues of school and teacher accountability and appraisal, have increased in importance, although at the same time changing significantly in tone, in the intervening years; and they will thus continue to form a major focus of this new chapter.

In general, the intervening years have seen the curriculum become a battle-ground no longer of educational ideologies — disciplines v. interdisciplinary studies, tradition v. 'progressivism', content v. procedures — but of competing political ideologies — academicism v. egalitarianism, vocationalism/ instrumentalism v. liberalism — and especially of agencies vying with each other for control of the curriculum, the advocates of external, political control pressing their claims more forcibly and vociferously than ever, in spite of the experience of the last two decades which has seemed to suggest that the only effective curriculum is that which is permitted to develop from the responses of the pupils to what they are offered and thus from the day-to-day decisions and judgements of the teachers themselves.

The main concerns of this new chapter, therefore, will be, first, to outline the developing debate over the different possible models of curriculum planning, encapsulating, as this debate does, the age-old issue of what the curriculum is; second, to trace briefly the growth of direct political intervention in the planning of the curriculum in the United Kingdom, especially as it is revealed through the massive output of literature from official sources which the last seven or eight years have seen, and to identify its salient features; and, third, to look at two particular manifestations of that movement, the continuing demands for the increased accountability of schools and teachers, for their evaluation and appraisal, and those for the institution of a common core curriculum. These final points will bring us to the crux of the debate, whether it is by this kind of remote control or by offering the teachers themselves increased responsibility for and control over curricular decisions that the quality of education we offer to our children can best be maintained and, indeed, improved.

Curriculum models

We suggested just now that the question of which model of the curriculum we should adopt, especially in planning a fully educational programme, had recently become an important one for most teachers, and, furthermore, that it had superseded that question which attracted so much attention in the early years of the curriculum debate, the question of what the curriculum is.

That question has elicited over the years a number of answers, a number of different definitions. All of these, however, have tended to focus on the content of the curriculum, what the curriculum is to be seen as containing. It has, for example, been claimed, and quite rightly, that the curriculum is more than a list of subjects or a collection of syllabuses, that it is 'all the learning which is planned and guided by the school, whether it is carried on... inside or outside the school' (Kerr, 1968, p.16), in other words that it must be seen as including all the work that teachers plan and do with their pupils, 'extra-curricular' activities as well as those on the syllabus. It has further been argued that we must not lose sight of the 'hidden curriculum', that learning which goes on as a kind of by-product of what is planned, that we should recognize the important distinction between the formal and the actual curriculum, that which really is learned as opposed to that which is outlined in statements of syllabuses or in curriculum guidelines.

All of these are important contributions to the debate. All of them, however, concentrate on *what* the curriculum should be taken as containing, on its content. It is now much clearer that the real question is not what content should be included in our definition of curriculum, but whether content should be the main concern at all. For recent contributions to the debate have suggested that what is of first importance in curriculum planning is not necessarily that we ask ourselves *what* is to be learned or even *what* is likely to be learned, but rather *why* these things are to be learned. It has further been suggested that the question of why certain things are to be learned can be interpreted in two ways, as implying either that we should have as our first priority the aims and objectives of our teaching, ultimate purposes extrinsic to it translated into immediate objectives through which they are to be achieved, or that we should begin from a concern with the processes of development our teaching is intended to promote, educational principles which must be seen as intrinsic to that teaching.

Thus the real issue of definition is not merely that of what aspects of knowledge or value transmission or acquisition the curriculum should be regarded as embracing, but of what our approach to teaching and learning is to be — whether our concern is to be with the transmission of certain knowledge-content or skills, with the attainment of certain goals or objectives, or the promotion of certain processes of development. In other words, it is not a matter of identifying one definition of curriculum; we must recognize that there are several and, what is more, that the definition we adopt will lead to a particular kind of approach to curriculum planning, that each definition will generate its own, quite distinct planning model.

The best-known advocate of the objectives approach to, or model of, curriculum planning was Ralph Tyler (1949). He suggested a sequence of questions that should be answered by the curriculum planner: first, 'What educational purposes should the school seek to attain?', (p.1), second, 'What educational experiences can be provided that are likely to attain these purposes?' (*ibid.*), thirdly, 'How can these educational experiences be effectively organised?' (*ibid.*) and, lastly, 'How can we determine whether these purposes are being attained?' (*ibid.*). This sequence has, perhaps unfairly but nevertheless influentially, often been summarized in the form — objectives, content, procedures, evaluation.

Adopting a similar view, Paul Hirst (1969) criticized the approaches to curriculum planning he felt he could discern in the schools of the United Kingdom. He suggested that traditionally the secondary schools had been overconcerned with content, with *what* pupils should learn, with the bodies of knowledge or subjects to be taught or transmitted, and that primary schools had given too much attention to procedures, concerning themselves with *how* children are to learn, with such things as 'learning by discovery' and 'interest-based learning'. Both of these approaches, he argued, are inadequate because they ignore the logically prior question of the objectives this learning is intended to attain.

Under the influence of these and similar arguments, much attention has been given in recent years to the 'aims and objectives' of the curriculum, and it has been accepted — too often and too readily — that the sequence suggested by Tyler and reiterated by Hirst is the only possible sequence for effective curriculum planning, and that statements of aims and objectives must precede all else. Thus we find this often treated not as *a* curriculum planning model but as *the* only possible model. This view has even reached the ears and the consciousness of the authors of many of those official documents on the curriculum we mentioned earlier, so that much that we read there is based on (and thus urges on teachers) an uncritical acceptance of this approach, and fails to acknowledge, or even to recognize, that it is highly problematic and should itself be part of the curriculum debate.

It is a view which has also attracted much criticism (Stenhouse, 1970, 1975; Pring, 1971, 1973; Sockett, 1976; Blenkin and Kelly, 1981; Kelly, 1982a). It has been argued that to plan a curriculum by stating its ultimate goals and then devising a step-by-step series of objectives which will lead us to those goals is educationally self-defeating. It makes no allowance for the essential developing autonomy of the educand; and it sees the process of education as an instrumental process, directed at objectives extrinsic to itself rather than concerned with processes intrinsic to it. It thus adopts views of education, of knowledge and even of humanity, which have to be recognized as, at the very least, problematic, as perhaps unacceptable and, even, some would claim, untenable.

What is more important here, however, is to recognize that some recent contributions to this debate have suggested that, rather than seeing Tyler's questions as necessarily following a rigid and supposedly logical sequence, we should see them as offering a choice of starting-points for our curriculum planning (Blenkin and Kelly, 1981; Kelly, 1982a). In particular, it is important that we recognize that the decision over where we start our curriculum planning is a matter of choice and one which thus requires justification. It is neither acceptable nor intellectually honest to treat it as if it were self-evident.

For it is possible, and not in every case reprehensible, to begin one's planning by asking about *what* is to be transmitted, about the knowledge we wish to pass on or the skills we wish to help people to develop. Teaching someone to sail and/or to navigate would seem to be a good example of this. It is also quite acceptable in certain contexts (and probably not incompatible with the approach just described), as in teaching someone to drive a car, to begin with a statement of aims and objectives and to place them in what appears to be a sensible sequence, from both the logical and the psychological points of view — the pupil will learn how to bring the car to a halt before learning how to propel it forward — or backwards — at 30 mph, and so on. Equally, it is possible to start one's planning by setting out the processes of development one wishes the experiences being offered to pupils to promote, by listing the principles which it is intended should underlie all subsequent decisions made about the learning process, principles which are not aims extrinsic to the process and to be attained later but which will inform the process and the decisions we make at every stage.

All of these may have their place in the planning of certain forms of teaching. The crux of the question we must face, however, is which, if any, of them offer a suitable basis for the planning of experiences and of learning which can be regarded as fully educational. And to answer that question we need to decide first what we believe education to be.

It is not the intention to claim, or pretend, here that there is one, simple, clear-cut answer to the question of what is education. It is important to acknowledge that it means different things to different people. It is also important to recognize, however, that the view taken of it will crucially determine the view one takes of the curriculum and of the most appropriate model to adopt for the planning of one's curriculum. Conversely, we must also note that the planning model we adopt or advocate will also imply a particular view of the purposes and principles of education and schooling.

The most we can or should do here, then, is to make plain, in case we have not already done so in earlier chapters, what is the view of education that we take. For this will be necessary for an understanding of the view we take of the curriculum and of how it should be planned. It is also a view, incidentally, which we believe we share with many teachers, although we would be less confident in attributing it to our political masters or to their immediate advisers. This, as we shall see later in this chapter, is a major source of the current conflict.

The view taken of education here is fundamentally that it is the process by which individuals are helped to achieve greater control over their lives, over their environment, over the circumstances of their lives, and to develop the capacities which will give them such control. This is not merely, then, a process of acquiring knowledge but of acquiring what A.N. Whitehead once called 'the art of the utilisation of knowledge' (1932, p.6), acquiring knowledge whose value is recognized and acknowledged by the recipient and whose acquisition is accompanied by developing powers of understanding. It is thus that process of cognitive growth which we saw in Chapter 3 is analysed and advocated by recent work in developmental psychology, such as that of Jerome Bruner, and it must also be seen, as in the very recent work in this field (for example, Donaldson, 1978), as going beyond the cognitive and embracing all dimensions of development. It is a process too by which the individual's horizons will be extended, his or her vision opened up to all kinds of possibilities and experiences beyond those offered by the immediate environment, but always with that emphasis on utilization, on recognition of significance, relevance and value, and a developing understanding. Another way of looking at it is to see it as a process through which one learns to think for oneself, to evaluate sensibly, critically, and again with understanding, all that is presented to one's view, to reach informed and thoughtful decisions, to be autonomous in the full sense. It is thus a quite different kind of process from that which we saw in Chapter 3 was advocated by Skinner (1968) and encapsulated in the advocacy of programmed learning. Hence, nothing but confusion has followed from the assumption that that view could be considered as a theory of education.

If we now return to a consideration of our possible curriculum models from this kind of perspective, it will quickly be clear that such a process will not be enhanced (except perhaps accidentally), and may even be inhibited, by a curriculum which is planned in such a way that the prime consideration is the knowledge-content to be transmitted without reference to the mode of its reception, whether this is advocated on the basis of some epistemological view of the intrinsic value of certain kinds of knowledge (Peters, 1965, 1966; Hirst and Peters, 1970; Dearden, 1968, 1976; White, 1973), or in terms of its technological and economic usefulness. For such knowledge-content will not *of itself* help us to bring about those processes of development (except again by accident and in very few cases), and to plan a curriculum in this light will prevent, and probably impede and inhibit, planning for the achievement of those processes. What is crucial to the attainment of education in our sense of the term is the selection of content on an individual basis and in the light of a clear view of the processes it is being selected to assist.

Nor will such processes necessarily be promoted by a curriculum planned by reference to extrinsic goals, such as the economic or other needs of society, translated into a detailed series of step-by-step objectives — the essence of the 'aims and objectives' approach to curriculum planning and of Skinner's programmed learning techniques. For, in the first place, those steps, like the knowledge-content, will need to vary according to individual circumstances; they will, secondly, need to be chosen in the light of the processes we are concerned to promote, so that, again like knowledge-content, they become secondary rather than prime considerations; and, most crucially, those processes and the principles which they generate must be omni-present, since the capacities we are endeavouring to promote are not things which we attain at the end of a long chain or hierarchy of lesser objectives, we become autonomous by behaving autonomously (to paraphrase what we saw in the last chapter Aristotle said of moral behaviour), so that, if autonomous thinking and behaviour are our concern, then, along with all our other principles, these must be ever-present considerations in our planning and in our practice.

In fact, these principles must be our first concern. And the only route to the achievement of this kind of education is by beginning the planning of our curriculum by a clear statement of the processes it is concerned to promote and the principles upon which it must thus be founded. By all means, these may be called our 'aims', provided that the use of that term, with its connotations of external targeting, does not encourage us to slip into seeing them as extrinsic to what we are doing here and now, and viewing and planning education as a hierarchical series of steps, like those of the teaching machines. The reason why the term 'principle' is advocated is that it has no such connotations, and in fact brings with it the essential notion that these processes should be constantly before our minds — not only in our preplanning of curriculum activities but, perhaps more importantly, in our translating these into practice.

This kind of view underlies several recent sets of general recommendations for the planning of school curricula. One of the earliest documents which emanated from Her Majesty's Inspectorate in the United Kingdom, for example, suggested that we should view and plan the curriculum in terms of eight 'areas of experience', which it designated by its now well-known 'eight adjectives' — 'aesthetic/creative, ethical, linguistic, mathematical, physical, scientific, social/political and spiritual' (DES, 1977a). The use of adjectives here is significant, since it suggests that we view the curriculum not in terms of *subjects* but rather in terms of the *kinds* of experience it offers, and thus it points us towards planning which begins with processes and principles rather than with aims and objectives or content.

It is unfortunate, however, although one can understand the reasons for it, that such suggestions are quickly translated, sometimes even by their authors, into subject-content terms. The logic of the initial stance is not followed through and (leaving aside the confusions of the occasional simultaneous adoption and advocacy of an objectives model) the primacy of processes over content is not maintained, nor is the corollary of that accepted, that such an approach must tolerate significant differences of content, and must, therefore, militate against the establishment of any kind of nationally agreed and/or determined curriculum. This was, for example, the reason for the failure of that experimental attempt to translate that 'eight adjectives' approach into what was called the 'entitlement curriculum' (DES, 1983b). For, in the regions selected, the attempt to provide pupils all with the same balanced diet, consisting of a broad range of experiences in the eight areas delineated, foundered on the inability of teachers and others to relate these experiences to subject specialisms, to enable pupils to enjoy appropriate educational experiences *through* those subjects rather than offering them the often uneducational (and, sadly, too often anti-educational) experiences of the learning *of* the subjects.

It is at this point, then, that we see a major focus of the conflict between what has been emerging from our growing understanding of curriculum and curriculum development, on the one hand, and, on the other, the increased political intervention in curriculum which recent years have witnessed in the United Kingdom. In part, the conflict arises because of a lack of clarity in most of the political pronouncements on curriculum of those subtle differences of approach or of model we have tried to describe. In part too, as we suggested earlier, it stems from a fundamental difference in the view taken of education and schooling. In either case, the distinctions we are attempting to identify must be clearly noted. It is also apparent that there is a major clash, resulting from these differences of perspective, between the individualization which must be a necessary ingredient of the kind of educational process we are concerned with and the demand for increased external control of schools and teachers.

Against this backcloth, then, we must now consider the major features of the recent moves towards increased political intervention in the curriculum.

The political context of curriculum planning

The recent increase of direct political interest in the curriculum in the United Kingdom serves first to remind us that curriculum planning does not and cannot go on in a vacuum. We cannot choose our model and plan our curriculum with complete disregard for the context in which we are working. Before we look in greater detail at the recent manifestations of political intervention, then, it may be as well to remind ourselves that, although it is clearly important that we do give careful thought to the planning of the curriculum, it is not possible to free ourselves from the influences and constraints of other factors, and that we must not lose sight of the fact that any curriculum planning we may engage in must go on in the context of many pressures from both within and without the school itself. (Kelly, 1980)

To begin with, the curriculum must evolve from what is already there. Curriculum innovation must not be totally revolutionary. If it attempts to be, then, for a variety of reasons, not the least among which is the inability of many teachers to adapt to completely new approaches to education, such innovation will not 'take'. Evolution is preferable to revolution and the curriculum must be seen as in part the product of its own history. It is also the product of the history of the society in which it is to be found and, in particular, its cultural history (Williams, 1958). The historical, social and cultural influences on the curriculum offer a fascinating subject for study and must not be ignored by those who plan curriculum change.

Secondly, we must recognize the economic and administrative influences on the curriculum. It is not possible for the education system not to respond to the demands made on it by the economic needs of society. Indeed, one major reason for the upsurge of interest in the curriculum that we have already referred to is that rapid technological development and resultant economic change has led to different demands being made on schools. Such demands make themselves most readily felt in schools through the exigencies of the public examination system and the constraints that these impose on curriculum change and development. They also reveal themselves in the overt demands and pressures that are increasingly generated by politicians and industrialists. They cannot be ignored by anyone who wishes to engage in any kind of curriculum planning.

Lastly, we must note that technological change leads to social change and thus to changes of ideology. Such changes will also have their impact on the curriculum. More than this, however, we must acknowledge that a major feature of advanced industrial societies is the presence within them of many competing ideologies, that, in short, they are pluralist societies, containing, tolerating, even welcoming a variety of value systems. This also has implications for education, especially for the manner in which we approach it, since it will be clear that in planning the curriculum we must not only be aware of the constraints that derive from this source but also of the need to prepare children to play their full part in such a society.

The attempts at increased external control of curriculum development, then, which the last decade or so has witnessed in the United Kingdom, must be seen not as introducing a new set of influences on curriculum planning but rather as trying to create the kind of machinery which will convert these influences into a more direct and overt form of control. The significance of this, as we shall see, is that its general effect is to replace influences which teachers and curriculum planners can take account of in their planning with direct, and far more inflexible, demands. It is thus a potential source of conflict when, as is often the case, there are major differences of ideology, and even of levels of understanding, particularly over such fundamental issues as what education is and how the curriculum should consequently be planned and organized, between the teachers in the classrooms and those whose view of schooling is inevitably taken from the outside.

At this point, however, it may be helpful to trace the development of this movement towards increased external control of the school curriculum in order to then be able to pick out its main features and characteristics and to identify some of the points of such conflict.

It must first be noted that teachers in the United Kingdom have for a long time enjoyed a degree of control over the curriculum, a level of professional autonomy, far beyond that of teachers in most other countries, in many of which the idea of a centrally determined common curriculum, or at least a common core to the curriculum, is regarded as a *sine qua non* of educational planning. It might be argued, somewhat cynically perhaps, that this relative autonomy was accorded to teachers in the United Kingdom only when curriculum development was not seen as a burning issue, or, even more cynically, only when they did not use it to do anything which might be regarded as unusual.

For it is the case that the first real challenge to that autonomy came in the late 1950s and early 1960s when two developments had occurred. The first of these was an awareness of the rapidity of technological progress, as evinced especially in space technology (and specifically in the launching by the USSR of the first space satellite in 1957), and of the need to look closely at the school curriculum in order to ensure that it was keeping pace with this kind of technological development and that the education system would continue to provide that range of experts who could keep our society well to the fore in the technological race. This is the major explanation of the sudden increase in public interest in the curriculum both in the United States and in the United Kingdom at that time.

The second development which attracted public interest in the curriculum was an awareness that some teachers were in fact introducing unusual activities into the curriculum. Children were being permitted, even encouraged, to 'play' in their primary schools, for example, and in the secondary modern schools, many of them newly created, new and strange subjects were appearing on the timetables. Unaccustomed things were also to be seen happening in those comprehensive schools which had been established in some areas.

Both of these developments continue to be important factors in the struggle for control over the curriculum which has been a feature of subsequent years, as we shall see. The first stage in that struggle came in the early 1960s in the United Kingdom when it was decided to establish a national body for the development of the curriculum. The proposal of the government of the day was for a Curriculum Study Group, of the kind which has recently actually been created. Action by the teachers, however, led to the establishment of the Schools Council for Curriculum and Examinations, a body whose control was largely in the hands of the teachers, and which continued to exist until 1983 when it was replaced by the politically controlled School Curriculum Development Committee.

Several milestones can be identified in that intervening period and it may be worthwhile briefly listing these. First, we must note the publication of a series of 'Black Papers' on education (Cox and Dyson, 1969a, b), which heavily attacked and criticized much that was going on in schools and in the education system — in particular, informal methods of teaching in the primary schools, the reorganization of secondary education on comprehensive principles, with the associated closure of selective grammar schools, and the introduction of mixed-ability groupings at all levels. Next, we must note the William Tyndale 'affair' (ILEA, 1976), a crisis over the curriculum of one particular primary school which seemed to many to reflect a more widespread problem and certainly was taken by some as evidence of what the authors of the Black Papers had been claiming. Again it is worth reminding ourselves of the two underlying factors — the interrelated concerns with whether schools were keeping up with technological advance and with what teachers were using their autonomy to bring about.

These concerns were next aggravated by the economic problems which followed on from the crisis over the world's oil supplies in the mid-1970s. Suddenly it became especially important to look very closely at public expenditure, and, in particular, to know not only what schools and teachers were doing but, more specifically, how they were spending increasingly scarce resources.

There thus followed a number of events which can clearly be seen as an accelerating movement towards increased external control over the curriculum, or at least a much closer external monitoring of what schools and teachers are doing. In 1974, the Assessment of Performance Unit (APU) was established to monitor standards of attainment nationally in what are seen as the major areas of the curriculum. In 1977, there was published the Taylor Report on the government of schools (DES, 1977b) with firm recommendations to increase the power of governing bodies of schools, especially in relation to the curriculum. In 1976 James Callaghan, as Prime Minister, in a speech at Ruskin College severely attacked schools for what he saw as several serious failures in the area of curriculum, and thus launched the so-called 'Great Debate'. This in turn was fuelled by a massive output of publications from the Department of Education and Science — major surveys (DES, 1978, 1979, 1982, 1983a), discussion documents prepared by HMI (DES, 1977a, 1980a, 1981a) and resultant sets of proposals or recommendations for change (DES, 1977c, 1980b, 1981b, 1983b, 1985). Two new Education Acts have been passed — in 1980 and 1981 — strengthening external control over the school curriculum. And finally, as we noted above, the Schools Council suffered, first, a major change of constitution and, second, a complete withdrawal of public funding, and has now been replaced by the School Curriculum Development Committee, a body very much like that which the government had first attempted to establish in 1961.

The main thrust of these developments has of course been towards an increase of external control over the work of teachers and the curriculum offered in our schools. Three major aspects of this can be identified — a concern for the monitoring of standards, proposals for the institution of some form of common curriculum or common core to the curriculum and demands for the increased accountability of teachers and schools. All of these raise issues of a general educational or curricular kind as well as of a political kind and these issues we will explore more fully shortly.

Before doing so, however, it might be worth picking out some general features of these developments and the proposals resulting from them, particularly in so far as these relate to our earlier discussion of definitions of education and resulting approaches to curriculum planning.

It is clear, to begin with, that there has been a major emphasis on subject-content throughout this debate, and particularly in the official publications which have supported it. We mentioned earlier that even those documents which have encouraged us to view education in terms of its processes have quickly moved into subject-based discussion. And it is now apparent that subsequent publications, for example those in the 'Curriculum Matters' series, are to be devoted largely to specific subject areas. Subject studies are now being advocated and, indeed, being urged upon our primary schools, and it is clear that the newly established 16+ examinations are to be not only subject-based but also very clearly content-based.

This concern with the content of the curriculum, while in itself constituting a perfectly reasonable approach to the planning of the curriculum, nevertheless, as we suggested earlier, presupposes many things which are problematic and may well be counter-productive to education in the full sense, and thus necessitates some explanation and, indeed, justification. For it is only one of several possible approaches, as we have seen. It is thus highly unsatisfactory that teachers should have thrust upon them an approach which, first, is offered without any justificatory or supporting arguments and, second, is at odds with the view of education which many of them hold. It is even more unsatisfactory to find that these views are confused within the very documents which are purporting to advise teachers on the planning of their curricula.

Much the same can be said about the second major flavour of these developments — their emphasis on the instrumental or the utilitarian, on that which is economically or vocationally useful. This is most clearly noticeable in the passing of responsibility for much of the curriculum at secondary and post-secondary levels to the Department of Industry, through the work of the Manpower Services Commission, in such projects as have been devised under the Technical, Vocational and Educational Initiative scheme (TVEI) and in the establishment of the Certificate of Pre-Vocational Education (CPVE). Again this is an approach which can well be justified. Again, however, as we saw earlier it is an approach which is difficult to reconcile with the principles of education in the full sense, and it is not compatible with other views teachers — and others too — may have about what is of *educational* value. Again too, therefore, one's concern derives from the muddle, the failure to distinguish that whose purpose is educational from that which is utilitarian, the lack of any clearly thought-through concept of education, and the consequent absence of any attempted justification.

The conflict and the tensions thus created can be seen reflected in the major aspects of this recent move towards increased external control of education — the increased accountability of schools and teachers, along with the use of techniques of evaluation and appraisal for that purpose, and the proposals to establish a common core curriculum, with the associated concern with the monitoring of standards. Both of these we must now consider in some detail.

Accountability, evaluation and appraisal

There is nothing intrinsically unacceptable in the notions that teachers should be accountable for their work, that there should be some kind of evaluation of that work and of the curriculum generally, or that some attempt should be made to appraise the quality of the work of individual teachers. Indeed, it might be argued that one of the main disadvantages of that period of relative autonomy to which we referred earlier was the lack of all of these, the absence of any requirement that schools or teachers should give an account of what they are doing, and the consequent failure to make any kind of evaluation or appraisal of their work either collectively or individually. For without these there is no sound base for development or improvement either of individual teachers or of the curriculum. Furthermore, no one should expect to pursue any kind of work or profession in a democratic society, especially in the public sector of such a society, and remain free of the necessity to explain or account for that work to his or her fellows. Indeed, it is the lack of accountability of many of those who currently have the power to control education which is one of the most disturbing features of the present educational scene.

What is crucial, as so often, is the form and the procedures devised for meeting this perfectly justifiable need. And it is here that we see the same kind of tension and conflict we have identified elsewhere. For the forms and procedures used for accountability, evaluation or appraisal will inevitably act as a major influence on the work of the teachers itself. If they are called to account for extrinsic objectives attained (the employment record of graduates, for example, is currently being used as a major 'performance indicator' for the financing of institutions in the Higher Education sector in the United Kingdom), or for the content of their teaching, the success with which their pupils have assimilated the knowledge-content they are held to be responsible for transmitting (one of the 'performance indicators' currently being used to evaluate the work of secondary schools, for example, is the number and level of GCE and CSE passes achieved by pupils), then clearly they will be pressed towards adopting that kind or those kinds of curriculum model and, as a result, away from planning the curriculum in terms of those developmental processes we outlined earlier and suggested were central to education in the full sense. Similarly, if curricula are evaluated in those terms or if the work of individual teachers is to be appraised in those terms, then the same effects will follow.

Fundamentally, the issue is one of the purposes for which these procedures are instituted and operated. If their central concern is with accountability for pre-set objectives attained, with evaluation as a means towards such accountability and with the appraisal of teachers directed to the same ends, and if they are even, additionally, to be used for the disciplining and, in extreme cases, the dismissal of individuals, then their impact on education and the curriculum is unlikely to be supportive of change or development, since their effect will be to inhibit teachers, to discourage them from making those individual judgements which we have claimed are crucial to educational success, and to impose upon them a limiting, and often also limited, conception of what education is essentially about, a simplistic and restricting model of curriculum planning.

On the other hand, there is no reason why procedures for accountability, evaluation or appraisal should necessarily take this form or have this kind of effect. They can be used to provide essential feedback to the teachers themselves as a basis for continuous development both of the curriculum and of their own individual professional skills and competence. They can enhance and improve the quality of the educational experiences offered to pupils.

There is clearly an important tension here and it must be borne in mind throughout the discussions which follow, not only those of accountability, evaluation and appraisal but also those of the idea of a centrally determined common curriculum. It is a tension between the attempt at controlling education from the outside and a recognition that educational experiences in the full sense come only from the day-to-day professional judgements of those on the inside, the teachers themselves. All the evidence of over twenty years of research into curriculum development supports the second view; current political intervention is trending towards the first (Holt, 1978, 1980; Kelly, 1982a). Both David Hamilton (1976, p.128) and Maurice Holt (1978, p.94) quote Stake's experience in the United States:

> Most state accountability proposals call for more uniform standards across the state, greater prespecification of objectives, more careful analysis of learning sequences, and better testing of student performances... What they bring is more bureaucracy, more subterfuge, and more constraint on student opportunities to learn.

David Hamilton goes on to express succinctly what we have been outlining here when he says (*op.cit.*, p.128), 'To produce achievement tests would almost certainly focus too much attention on particular items of knowledge at the expense of more general processes of learning'. It is this problem we must keep constantly in mind when we consider the rival forms of accountability, evaluation and appraisal.

It is to these that we now turn and, in doing so, in the interests of brevity, we shall concentrate largely on issues of evaluation, since these are central to all three of these processes and it is in that area that most work has been done and most research undertaken. In particular, we shall confine ourselves to a discussion of four issues. We shall consider some of the problems that arise from these differences in the demands made on curriculum evaluation, some of the types of evaluation that have been identified or have evolved in response to these different demands and purposes, the important question of whether evaluation is or is not linked to the prespecification of curriculum objectives and, lastly, the question of who can or should be responsible for the evaluation of the curriculum.

There is no doubt that the difficulties that abound in this area of curriculum theory derive in the main from, or are at least compounded by, the variety of purposes that one can have in making any kind of evaluation and the resultant impossibility of achieving any one definition of curriculum evaluation. The great diversity of curriculum projects that recent years have seen has led to a corresponding diversity of evaluation procedures (Schools Council, 1973; Tawney, 1975; Hamilton, 1976). Furthermore, every one of these projects has offered a definition of evaluation that represents a commitment to one or more particular views of evaluation (Harris, 1963; Cronbach 1963; Wiley, 1970; Stenhouse, 1975), and it is only quite recently that attempts have been made to look at the issue of evaluation in its own right.

When we do this, we quickly realize that the procedures we adopt for evaluation and even the definition of it that we accept must vary according to the area of the curriculum we are dealing with, the curriculum model we have chosen and, especially, the purposes we have in mind when we set up the evaluation procedures. The most important task, then, for the evaluator is to be clear about what those purposes are. For there are a number of purposes we might have in undertaking curriculum evaluation. We might, for example, be attempting to do no more than to ascertain that the particular innovation we are concerned with is actually taking place, since there is often a wide gap between the plans of the curriculum developer and the practice of the teachers responsible for implementing those plans. We might be concerned merely to discover whether the programme is acceptable to teachers and/or pupils (Schools Council, 1974). We might, on the other hand, be engaged in a comparative study of the effectiveness of a particular programme in relation to other programmes or methods in the same area. Or again, we might be trying to establish whether our objectives are being attained or whether our chosen procedures or content are right for the attainment of them or, if we are operating without prespecified objectives, we might be concerned to discover just what has been achieved. There are, thus, many different purposes that any process of evaluation might have and it is vital that we be clear about the purpose or purposes of any particular programme of evaluation before we begin.

One especially important distinction must be noted. The questions to be asked in any process of evaluation are of at least two logically distinct kinds (White, 1971). Some of them are empirical questions which explore a project in terms of its effectiveness, its costs, its merits in comparison with other projects, and so on. Such questions are similar to those asked by organizations such as the Consumers' Association of the brands and products they investigate. These are questions about means and it is relevant empirical data that we must gather in order to answer them. Sometimes, however, we are also interested in questions about the desirability of a particular project in itself and these raise those difficult problems of value that can never be far away in any discussion of education. These are questions about ends rather than means, since they ask not whether we are achieving our aims but whether those aims themselves are the right aims, whether they are worth striving after, whether the principles underlying our practice are sound, whether the experience we are endeavouring to offer pupils is of educational value. Here we are attempting, therefore, to evaluate the fundamental principles or the goals of the curriculum itself and not only the effectiveness of its procedures. These are questions, then, that cannot be answered merely by appeal to empirical data. This is a distinction that must be kept clearly in mind, not least because it draws our attention to an important kind of question which the more simplistic forms of evaluation, such as those being used as a central mechanism for political accountability, cannot cope with or even recognize.

Because processes of curriculum evaluation can have this variety of purposes, some of them displaying a difference as fundamental as the one we have just discussed, a number of different types of evaluation procedure have evolved to meet these, several of which have been identified. In all cases too, as we suggested earlier, the type of evaluation used will be closely linked to the curriculum model that has been adopted, as has become clear from the procedures employed by a number of different Schools Council projects (Tawney, 1973).

The simple classical linear model of objectives, content, procedures and evaluation that we referred to at the beginning of this chapter has generated a process of evaluation that has been described as 'summative', since it asks questions at the end of a project which are largely concerned with the extent to which the objectives that were prespecified have been attained. It is a form of post-course evaluation and sums up the experience of the project after it is over; it thus provides data that can be used to modify the project only if it is to be implemented again. It may, of course, be concerned to assess the objectives of the project themselves with a view to subsequent modifications, but its main concern it likely to be with empirical questions about the effectiveness of the procedures adopted.

Contrasted to this is a form of evaluation that has been called 'formative'. This is the kind of evaluation that is necessary when we adopt a more sophisticated model of curriculum planning, recognize that all the four elements we have identified are closely interrelated, and thus regard evaluation as a continuous process that will lead to and make possible in-course modifications. This form of evaluation will involve a number of dimensions. It will be attempting both to assess the extent of the attainment of the objectives of the project and to discover and analyse barriers to the achievement of these goals (Stenhouse, 1975); but it will also be directly concerned to evaluate the goals themselves, in short, to ask those value questions we mentioned earlier.

Both of these forms of evaluation assume to a large extent that the curriculum model adopted will begin with some prespecification of objectives and many people have assumed that such prespecification is necessary if any kind of evaluation is to be possible. Recent experience, however, has demonstrated that this is not so. We do not need to state our objectives in advance in order to make a proper evaluation of the curriculum. We do need, however, to adopt a different approach to the task of evaluation if we wish to plan a curriculum without objectives. This has become clear from the experience of two particular Schools Council projects, the Keele Integrated Studies Project and the Humanities Curriculum Project.

The team associated with the former of these projects adopted a 'horizontal' curriculum model 'in which aims, learning experiences and material were developed concurrently' (Tawney, 1973, p.9). In that kind of context, evaluation was seen not as a process of measuring the results of an experiment but as a device for continuously monitoring the project as it developed. The approach adopted in the evaluation of the Humanities

Curriculum Project, which deliberately eschewed the prespecification of objectives, was 'holistic'. 'The aim was simply to describe the work of the project in a form that would make it accessible to public and professional judgement' (MacDonald, 1973, p.83). The intention was to provide information for consumers, to describe what was happening for the benefit of those who might be concerned to make decisions about the curriculum in these particular areas.

The same kind of approach is adopted by those who have seen evaluation as 'portrayal' (Stake, 1972) and as 'illuminative' (Parlett and Hamilton, 1975). The former attempts to offer a comprehensive portrayal of a curriculum programme which views it as a whole and tries to reveal its total substance. The latter is primarily concerned 'with description and interpretation rather than measurement and prediction' (Parlett and Hamilton, 1975, p.88).

It will be clear that these recent developments in techniques of and approaches to curriculum evaluation have begun to raise the process to a level of sophistication well above that of simple devices for the measurement of pupil progress. They have also begun to reveal more clearly the role of evaluation in curriculum research and development generally. For the data they offer usually have relevance far beyond the particular project they are concerned to evaluate, so that from attempts to approach curriculum evaluation in this way we have learned a good deal both about curriculum innovation itself and about processes of evaluation. In short, they have recognized that evaluation is part of a continuous process of curriculum research and development, that the curriculum is a dynamic and continuously evolving entity, and that, since it is such, both its ends and its means must be under constant review.

One important issue that these approaches to evaluation have also raised is that of who should undertake the task of evaluation, and we must finally turn to a brief discussion of that. Again, of course, the answer that we give to this question will depend on the particular purposes or form of evaluation we have adopted. However, it is almost certainly always the case that our procedures will be designed to meet several purposes and will be an amalgam of several forms. It will also be the case that different people will have different perceptions and conceptions of the project (Shipman, 1972), even if its objectives have been quite clearly stated, so that everyone will have different purposes and expectations and will be looking for different kinds of data.

However, in the end this issue boils down to one of whether the evaluator should be external or internal to the project. The strongest argument for external evaluation, of course, is that of objectivity. An evaluator coming fresh to a project from outside might be expected to have few preconceptions or expectations and a more open mind than a teacher or other member of the project team. On the other hand, curriculum projects are highly complex entities with an intricate interlinking of theoretical and practical elements of a kind that it is difficult for an outsider to get fully to grips with. There is thus a danger that external evaluation will lead to an oversimplification of the project and perhaps to an undesirable pressure on the curriculum developers or the teachers themselves to simplify their work, especially by a clear statement of their objectives, to the point where they feel an external evaluator can understand it or, worse, to put all their efforts into those aspects of it that are most likely to show up in an external evaluation. This, as we suggested earlier, is a major problem with attempts at political accountability. One way around this problem that has been used is to make the evaluator a member of the project team, sometimes from the very beginning of the project. This has many advantages but it does seem to exclude the teacher from the process and for many reasons, not the least among which is the fact that the involvement of teachers in and their commitment to a project is probably the essential ingredient for its success, this would seem to be undesirable.

The teacher must be involved in some way with curriculum evaluation since, in the last analysis, he is the one who possesses most of the data that are needed for a proper evaluation. However, it would also seem that he has a contribution to make beyond that of merely providing these data in an inevitably simplified form by filling in elaborate questionnaires. The relationship between the teacher and the evaluator must be a two-way relationship, since it is important not only that evaluators should have access to the insights of teachers but also that teachers should begin to understand the problems of evaluation and should be directly privy to the evaluation findings. Clearly, there are problems for teachers in attaining the level of objectivity and the capacity for self-criticism that this requires of them. The work of those associated with the Ford Teaching Project has revealed in detail what these problems are. However, their experience has also led them to be 'optimistic about the capacity of the majority of teachers for self-criticism' (Elliott and Adelman, 1974, p.23) and to believe that these problems are merely practical difficulties which can be overcome. One method they have devised for overcoming them they have called 'triangulation', since it involves a three-way process of evaluation by teachers, pupils and independent external observers.

It would seem that this might be the most productive approach to adopt to the question of who should make an evaluation of the curriculum. For it leads to a style of evaluation that is 'democratic' rather than 'autocratic' or 'bureaucratic' (MacDonald, 1975), since its concern is not to evaluate from outside in accordance with the values of those who control the purse-strings of curriculum development but to provide information for teachers and others in the interests of forwarding curriculum development.

In this kind of evaluation the teacher himself or herself is a key figure. Furthermore, his or her place here is justified not only in terms of a right he or she might be considered to have to be involved in curriculum evaluation, but also because of the central role he or she must play in curriculum development. It is this that has led to the emergence of notions of school-based curriculum evaluation, of self-evaluation by teachers and schools and of self-appraisal — the involvement of the teachers themselves directly in the process of evaluation of the school curriculum and appraisal of their own individual performance. It is at this point too, then, that we return to that tension which we noted at the beginning of this section. For it is here that we must note, first, that this is the direction in which both the theory and the practice of curriculum development have been moving, with what one might perhaps call inexorable logic, while, secondly, this is a direction which is the diametric opposite of that of most of the more simplistic demands for public accountability, evaluation and teacher appraisal, since for the most part these have been attempts to establish external procedures for assessing the work of schools and teachers — increased powers for the inspectorate, at both local and national levels, for governing bodies, for parents, even for educational administrators and for others whose position is essentially external to the school and thus to the process of education itself.

This is an issue which perhaps comes into even greater prominence in relation to the idea of monitoring standards and the proposals for the institution of a common core curriculum, so that this may be the right point at which to turn to a consideration of some aspects of those recent developments.

A common curriculum

The question of whether there should be a common curriculum or at least a common core to the curriculum is one that brings together all or most of the threads that have run through our previous discussion of the curriculum, since it has relevance to most aspects of curriculum theory. It is thus a topic that will lead us naturally into a summary of what we have tried to cover in this chapter.

It is also an issue that is currently of great interest in the United Kingdom both inside and outside the teaching profession. The recent public and so-called 'Great Debate' on education has concentrated on the problems associated with this issue in response to demands from politicians, industrialists, and others, and it is worth noting that there has been a similar trend towards this kind of approach to the planning of education in most countries of the world, while some of them have long regarded the need for central control of the curriculum as almost self-evident.

It is important to be clear from the outset about what is involved here, particularly since there are two different, although interrelated, dimensions to the problem. At the most obvious level, demands for a common curriculum constitute claims concerning the content of education, statements of what all pupils should be introduced to and why they should be given this particular educational diet. At a second, less readily apparent but probably more significant, level, they also represent demands for a monitoring of the standards of attainment being achieved by pupils in schools and thus for an increased measure of external control over the work of teachers in an attempt to ensure that standards in certain areas of the curriculum be maintained. And so this is an issue that is of importance at all stages of schooling, primary as well as secondary, and it is salutary to remember in this connection that it was certain public reactions to the work of one particular primary school, the William Tyndale school, that was largely responsible for sparking off these demands for greater public control of educational practice.

The arguments for the establishment of a common curriculum are of four major kinds: philosophical, sociological, ideological, and politico-economic. The first three of these derive from those arguments that have been mounted by philosophers throughout the ages for the intrinsic value of certain kinds of human activity and the corresponding claim that it is these activities that should form the core of any education worthy of the name (Peters, 1965; 1966). They adopt a view of knowledge and values as God-given, transcending the subjective opinions of individual men or even of mankind in general so that they must lead to a view of education as essentially concerned to transmit this knowledge and these values (Kelly, 1980). This approach is also the result of seeing knowledge as irrevocably organized into several 'forms of thought' (Hirst, 1965) or 'realms of meaning' (Phenix, 1964), since the consequence of that kind of theory of knowledge must be that pupils should be given access to all of those forms of experience.

The sociological argument for a common curriculum may well be incompatible with this kind of epistemology since its claim is not for the God-given status of certain kinds of knowledge so much as for the necessity of including in the curriculum that knowledge which is regarded as valuable within the culture of any particular society. However, inconsistent as this may be, it does depend on the same kind of belief in the intrinsic value of certain activities, not only suggesting that the curriculum should consist of a selection of what is valuable in that culture (Lawton, 1973; 1975), and that pupils should be initiated into the culture of their society but also implying the intrinsic value and, indeed, superiority, of major aspects of that culture (Kelly, 1980). Such arguments are never really clear about whether they are pressing these claims for utilitarian reasons or on grounds of the intrinsic value of what society finds or deems valuable. One suspects that they would not be happy to admit the former but, if it is the latter that is their claim, their case is no different from and thus no more cogent than that of the philosophers. At all events, it is time they explained more clearly what their position is.

The ideological case for a common curriculum takes this argument a step further. For, starting from a commitment to the idea of equality of educational opportunity, it argues that, without some kind of common core to the curriculum, we cannot safeguard the right of every child to access to the best or at least to all aspects of the culture of his society, that to provide him or her with an education in some way tailored to his or her needs and existing interests may be to trap him or her in the particular subculture from which he or she hails and thus to limit the range of choices open to him or her. In particular, as we shall see in Chapter 8, this argument has been applied to the education of pupils from lower socio-economic and ethnic minority backgrounds and has been used to oppose the generation of two or three different forms of curricula designed to meet the needs of pupils of differing abilities or of curricula specifically tailored to particular racial groups.

The politico-economic arguments are the most recent additions to this discussion and they are of two unequivocal and basic forms. The first of these starts from the belief that schools exist to serve the needs of the community, that public money is invested in them for this purpose, and that the prime needs of an advanced industrial society are for citizens who have attained minimal standards of literacy and numeracy and for those who are capable of it to have attained the highest possible level of achievement in science and technological studies so that they can meet the continuing needs of an ever-developing technology. A major feature of that speech by the Prime Minister James Callaghan which sparked off the great debate in the United Kingdom was his complaint that too few sixth-formers were choosing to study the sciences and, conversely, too many the arts. The second and associated aspect of this case is the demand for greater control over the activities of teachers, for a higher level of public accountability than has hitherto been required of them.

We have already suggested that there are many difficulties in those arguments that are based on the notion that certain kinds of knowledge or certain aspects of the culture have a self-evidently superior value. And we must note that there is no general agreement about what these are nor, indeed, about the theory of knowledge upon which this kind of claim is based. There are other difficulties, however, with the arguments for a common curriculum and these we must briefly consider here.

In the first place, because of this lack of agreement over what is intrinsically valuable or worthwhile, problems arise as soon as we try to list the things that a common curriculum or its core should contain. One of two things will happen when we begin to do this. For either we offer a statement at such a level of generality that it ceases to have any significance or we immediately start up petty squabbles over what should go into such a core curriculum and what should be left out. The first of these traps is apparent in the definition of a core curriculum we are offered by such writers as Denis Lawton (1973; 1975), since the broad areas he suggests a common core curriculum should consist of are so wide as, on the one hand, to constitute no kind of help to curriculum planners and, on the other hand, to do no more than to describe what all schools are currently engaged in doing anyway. For there can be no school in the United Kingdom, nor anywhere else in the world, that does not in some way try to introduce its pupils to literacy, numeracy, some kind of social awareness, and to offer them a moral and aesthetic education. Indeed, it would be difficult to imagine what else schools and teachers could do.

However, if, in order to avoid being trivial in our claims, we try to be more detailed than this in our definition of the common elements of a core curriculum, we immediately discover the impossibility of reaching agreement at any level. For, while few would disagree with the claim that all schools should concern themselves with literacy and numeracy, there will be a complete lack of consensus over precisely what these claims imply for educational practice. Few too would oppose the need for some kind of social education but it will be difficult, as we saw in Chapter 6, to find any real agreement on what that should be. Some people still want the teaching of religion, currently the only compulsory element in the curriculum of schools in England and Wales, to continue to be a requirement of all schools; others would and do take quite the opposite stance, as is clear from the embargo placed on such teaching in certain other countries, notable among which is the United States of America. Thus, the question of who is to have the right to resolve these disagreements and make the final decisions on these matters also becomes crucial.

We must further recognize the difficulties that arise when we face up to the problem of deciding where such central direction should stop. For even if agreement could be reached over essential subject areas, we must ask whether all schools should be required to pursue a common content within these areas. In short, should there be common syllabuses too? For if there are not, how common will a common curriculum be? This would certainly seem to be the view of those whose demands for a common curriculum are based on the need to cater for the increased mobility of schoolchildren, to ensure that the child whose home is moved from one part of the country to another will find the same things being taught in the same way when he or she gets there. Furthermore, if this is to be so, every teacher will know that it is not enough for syllabuses to be common; there will need to be greater control over methods too, and even the textbooks used, in order to ensure that what each child gets from each individual teacher does not vary unduly, as is clear from the most cursory survey of the many different activities that go under the heading of religious education in our schools at present.

This leads us naturally to a discussion of the monitoring of teachers' work and of the standards attained by their pupils. This question is beset by the same kinds of problem, not least because it is equally difficult to state precisely what is meant by 'standards' or to reach agreement on what standards we should be aiming for. It is a good, emotive word for the politician to use, but it has little place in serious debate because it is a very difficult notion for anyone to explain or define. Such definitions as are offered tend to be couched in highly simplistic terms and the problems of evaluation that we have already discussed, when combined with such definitions, are likely to encourage teachers to accept the short-term goals they set, to work to simple prespecified objectives, to concentrate, for example, on the more easily recognized and measurable 'skills' aspects of reading or number work, to promote reading and computational performance rather than the wider educational aspects of these activities and thus to deprive pupils of what we have tried to argue are the essential components of an education in the full sense.

It is also argued that this kind of central control of the curriculum will lead to a loss of freedom for the child, since it will no longer be easy for teachers to base their work on children's interests or on their existing knowledge. At one level, it is felt that this will lead to pupils' being offered the kind of meaningless and irrelevant material that leads to their becoming in many cases alienated from their schools, their teachers and, ultimately, their society. At a further level, it is even argued that to adopt this approach is to use knowledge as a form of social control, since it makes certain kinds of 'educational' knowledge the key to success within the system and denies the validity of the 'common sense' knowledge that the child brings with him from his own subculture (Young, 1971). Thus an ideological argument against the establishment of a common curriculum strongly emerges from the same kind of ideological and egalitarian position we saw earlier being used to support it.

A further point must be made here which brings these issues of the monitoring of standards, the potential alienation of pupils and the use of the distribution of knowledge as a form of social control, together. The meaning currently being given to the term 'standards' in most official pronouncements on the curriculum is one that is derived from a certain concept of academic excellence or value and is thus linked to that emphasis on subjects and on the content of the curriculum to which we have referred on several occasions. It is also linked to a particular, and by no means nonproblematic, view of knowledge (Kelly, 1986). For it is academic attainment in areas traditionally regarded as 'high-status' subjects which is the central concern not only of the official proposals with which teachers are being bombarded but also, and more importantly because more surreptitiously, of the procedures which are being introduced in many places for accountability, evaluation and teacher appraisal. Pupil attainment as revealed through tests, and especially through the public examination system, is a major criterion of educational success. We have already noted the potential effects of this on the work of teachers, the inhibiting of their professional judgement and the pressing on them of models of education and curriculum which may well be in conflict with their own.

We must note now further the effect of the use of academic criteria of this kind in evaluating educational success on the large proportion of pupils who either cannot, because of intellectual limitations, attain the standards set in these areas or, more importantly and more significantly, lack the interest and/or the motivation, not because of academic inability but because of their social and/or ethnic origins. For pupils of this kind quickly become alienated from a form of education with which they have little sympathy, a form of education which is framed in terms of the transmission of knowledge which others regard as of value rather than in terms of what is likely to assist in the development of their own capacities, and whose implicit values they reject as being at odds with the values of their social and/or racial background. Thus they gain nothing from their sojourn at school except a sense of dissatisfaction and of opportunities missed because they were not offered. It is here that we see the full significance of those claims that the education system is being used by those who control it to impose their own values and their own culture on large sections of the community, including especially those from underprivileged backgrounds, and thus to bring them under their control. This is an issue to which we must return in our discussion of equality of educational opportunity in the next chapter.

Finally, we must briefly consider those arguments against the establishment of a common curriculum that are based on the claim that it limits the freedom and autonomy of the teacher and that this militates against effective education in the full sense. There is no denying the central role that the individual teacher must play in the education of his or her pupils. To play that role he or she must be free to exercise professional judgement. Teachers cannot be operated by remote control. It is for this reason that, as we have come to realize in recent years, it is not possible to control the curriculum from the outside with any degree of efficiency. Attempts at curriculum innovation that have employed what has come to be called the centre-periphery model of dissemination, that is, to plan a programme at some central place and then endeavour to disseminate it to schools, have generally been unsuccessful (Schon, 1971). One reason for this is that teachers need to understand and, perhaps more importantly, to be committed to what is required of them if they are to make it work (Barker-Lunn, 1970) or, worse, if they are not to sabotage it (Kelly, 1975). In other words, central planning cannot work since no amount of monitoring of standards can ensure that teachers will make it work (Kelly, 1982a).

We need to go further than this, however, and recognize the implications of this for the development of the curriculum itself. One essential feature of schools in a changing society, as we have noted before, is that their curricula must also change. Such change, however, can only be successful if it is in every sense a process of development and, if it is to be so, it must be in the hands of the teacher (Stenhouse, 1975). It may be possible to change the curriculum from outside the school but, if such change is to be development in the full sense of the word, it must be school-based and it must be in the hands of the teacher. For the notion of development implies organic growth rather than the grafting on of foreign matter. The teacher is the central figure in such development and he or she needs a high level of freedom and autonomy to fulfil that role.

It has been suggested, therefore, that 'the process to which the term "dissemination" is conventionally applied would be more accurately described by the term "curriculum negotiation"' (MacDonald and Walker, 1976, p.43), that teachers need to be involved in continuing discussion of the curriculum if the right kind of curriculum change is to take place, and this process would seem to be put at risk by suggestions that anything but the most general and loose directions should be imposed from the outside.

The arguments against the detailed specification of what schools should be teaching seem to be strong. On the other hand, looser and more generalized direction seems to be unnecessary, since, as we saw earlier, the constraints, both hidden and overt, placed on schools by the many demands that are made on them make it impossible for them to diverge too much from what would be the content of any such broad directions. At this level of generality, we have a common curriculum already. At the more detailed level, it would seem to be not only undesirable but also impossible to introduce one. In many respects, therefore, it might be argued that, the 'Great Debate' notwithstanding, this is a non-issue.

Two final points might be made, however, that emerge from such a discussion if we can get beyond a superficial concern with statements of curriculum content. The first of these is that there is a strong case to be made for a commonality of educational goals or principles. Whatever debate there might be over definitions of literacy, over what we mean by 'standards' or over the place of religion on the curriculum, it is possible to argue, as we have suggested on several occasions, that what is distinctive about education is that it is a process that is concerned with developing qualities of mind such as the ability to make critical judgements, to respect truth, to distinguish understanding from dogma and to think for oneself. In short, in educational terms a 'process' model of curriculum development is likely to be more productive than an 'objectives' model (Stenhouse, 1975) and it might not be difficult to define a common curriculum in these terms (Kelly, 1982a).

Lastly, it need not be assumed that, if we give teachers the kind of freedom that this approach necessitates, albeit limited by many existing constraints, they must inevitably remain unaccountable. The logic of the term 'accountability', however, would seem to suggest that it should occur *post eventum*. Teachers must be permitted to exercise their professional judgement in an area in which they possess an expertise that others lack but, like all other professionals, they can and should be required to render an account of and a justification for the judgements they have made. It was this rather than the making of collective decisions in advance that was the keystone of that form of democracy that was devised by the Athenians in ancient Greece. Such accounts, however, must be rendered, at least in part, to others who understand the complexities of the teacher's task, that is, to fellow professionals. Furthermore, as we saw in our discussion of evaluation, they themselves must be, indeed have a right to be, involved in the processes of monitoring and evaluating their work. If the demand for public accountability is founded on democratic premises, the involvement of teachers in that process is required by those same premises. Only in this way, then, can we achieve a form of accountability that is both professional and democratic. If it is to be undertaken entirely from outside, its effect must be to inhibit rather than to promote education in the full sense.

Summary and conclusions

We suggested at the beginning of our discussion of the notion of a common curriculum that that discussion would in itself act as a summary to this chapter. This has in fact proved to be the case, since it has taken us back to important issues of curriculum models, objectives, content, processes and to those issues of political intervention, especially accountability, evaluation and appraisal. It has also, however, highlighted two points that we should note here in concluding this chapter on the curriculum.

The first of these is that difficult question of values that must constantly appear in any discussion of education. We have seen that it is this that is the source of most of the difficulties we have examined not only in this chapter but throughout the book. It is this question that we unearth when we dig deeply into the problems of curriculum models, of the context of the curriculum, of accountability and evaluation, of a common curriculum or, indeed, of any other issue that is of such a kind as ultimately to hinge on what we believe to be good, valuable or worthwhile. The notion of value is fundamental to education but at the same time and for this very reason every educational dispute is in the last analysis impossible to resolve. Value questions cannot be answered in any hard and fast or final way. What is important, however, is for us to be able to recognize such questions when we see them. It is the failure to do that rather than the failure to come up with final answers to such questions that is at the root of so many unsatisfactory discussions of education, among teachers and educationists, let it be said, no less than among those outside the profession. Too many issues of this kind are treated as non-problematic and it is this more than merely differences of opinion which has vitiated much of the recent debate.

The second major theme that has emerged from our discussion in this chapter is the central role that the teacher must play in education. It is a truism, but one that cannot be repeated too often, that the quality of the education received by children depends on the quality of their teachers. If pupils are to receive an adequate education and if, as we have argued here, the teacher must carry the major responsibility for the development of the curriculum and thus of education itself, it is vital that we raise the quality of teachers to the highest possible level and maintain that level by continuous support and in-service education. If it is the case, as so many now believe, that curriculum development is essentially teacher development, we would do better to direct our attention, and indeed our financial backing, to what that requires, so as to ensure that our teachers are capable of doing the job we require of them, than to attempt to manipulate them like puppets from somewhere above and beyond the real educational stage.

CHAPTER 8

EQUALITY

All that we have said so far in this book, and particularly what we have said about the curriculum in the last chapter, illustrates how dramatically both the theory and the practice of education have changed in the last twenty or thirty years. One reason for that change has been the increase in our knowledge and understanding of many of the facets of education that we have been discussing. Another, and perhaps more cogent reason, however, has been those changes in society which we discussed in Chapter 5. A prominent feature of these is their egalitarianism and the desire to promote educational equality has been a major theme in those changes that have been made and are being made in the content, the method, and the organization of education both in the United Kingdom and elsewhere in the world. The work of every teacher, therefore, has been affected by this development so that no discussion of the theory and practice of education in present times would be complete without a careful examination of the implications that a commitment to this kind of egalitarian philosophy holds for educational practice.

Much has been done in the name of equality not only in education but also in other sectors of society. It can be argued that recent developments in the providing of state education have been prompted by the central desire to promote equality of educational opportunity and few would be prepared to admit openly that they were opposed to it. Yet very different and sometimes conflicting views are expressed on how it is to be achieved in practice and the practical provisions that have been advocated and implemented have varied enormously, from those that involve careful streaming and selection of pupils to those that would open the doors of all kinds of institution to any pupil who wished to enter them without applying any selection procedures.

The main reason for this discrepancy and confusion is that the notion of equality in education, and even the apparently more precise notion of equality of educational opportunity, are too general and vague to provide any clear directives as to how education should be organized to achieve them. A system can be said to provide equality of opportunity if all pupils have the same chance to compete for a place in a grammar school or a university; it is not necessary that they should all actually gain such places. Indeed, equality of opportunity would exist in a sense even if it amounted to no more than an equal opportunity for every child to take a test at 5+ to decide whether he or she should be admitted to the school system or excluded from it altogether. For this reason, a distinction has been drawn between the 'strong' or 'meritocratic' interpretation of equality, which would provide educational opportunities for all who are capable of taking advantage of them, and the 'weak' or 'democratic' interpretation, which demands suitable provision for everyone (Crosland, 1961).

The notion of equality is an imprecise one, therefore, and not one upon which any practical proposals can be based without a great deal of further clarification and definition of what is to be taken as its meaning. Until we have achieved this, it will not be possible to make a proper evaluation of the extent to which it has been achieved within the education system and, more importantly, some of the areas in which it has not.

A historical view of equality

It is important not to start from an assumption that the notion of social equality is a relatively new one or that it is a product of the twentieth century. It may be that this century has seen mankind come nearer to the achievement of something like the ideals implicit in the notion, although many would want to dispute even that, but as an idea it is almost as old as mankind itself; certainly it dates back to the beginnings of organized thought in the Western world.

From the very beginning, however, the confusion and the tensions between different interpretations of the notion that we have already referred to are apparent. For while there is distinct evidence, particularly in the works of the Greek dramatist, Euripides, that from the beginning for some people equality implied impartial treatment of all human beings, an egalitarianism in the full sense, both Plato and Aristotle accepted the idea of equality as operative only within categories of human being. Thus Plato's 'ideal state', as he described it in the *Republic*, contained three types of citizen — the prototype for many subsequent tripartite systems — and each of these groups had a different role, different responsibilities and, therefore, different rights within the state, 'equality' and 'justice' being achieved by basing membership of each group on talent and suitability rather than on the accident of birth. Plato has also been charged with deliberately opposing egalitarianism in the fuller sense by refusing to discuss it seriously in the arguments he produces to support his view of the ideal state (Popper, 1945). Aristotle too believed that there existed quite distinct categories of being and that, as he is so often quoted as saying, injustice arises as much from treating unequals equally as from treating equals unequally. Each person has his own place; the husband is superior to the wife, the father to his children, the master to his slaves (so long as these are 'barbarians' and not Greeks); to step beyond this place is unjust. 'The only stable principle of government is equality according to proportion.'

However, the other view also took hold, if at a less influential level philosophically. The stoic view of the brotherhood of all men, so well expressed in the words of Pope's *Essay on Man*, 'All are but parts of one stupendous whole, Whose body nature is and God the soul', allied to the Christian doctrine of the equality of all men in the eyes of God, ensured that the idea of human equality without regard to categories should also flourish; and so influential was the Church on man's thinking that when, at the time of the Renaissance, philosophers began for the first time, almost since the time of Plato and Aristotle, to examine philosophical questions independently of theology, the idea of human equality was accepted by most of them as if it were a self-evident truth and was used by them in a largely uncritical manner. John Locke tells us, for example, that the state of nature is 'a state also of equality ... there being nothing more evident than that creatures of the same species and rank, promiscuously born to all the same advantages of Nature, and the use of the same faculties, should also be equal one amongst another, without subordination or subjection' and also that 'the State of Nature has a law of Nature to govern it, which obliges everyone. And Reason, which is that law, teaches all mankind, who will but consult it, that being all Equal and Independent, no one ought to harm another in his Life, Health, Liberty or Possessions'. This is a view that is clearly reflected in the assertions of the American Declaration of Independence of 1789 that 'all men are created equal' and that 'men are born and live free and equal in their rights' (we shall comment later on the significance of the omission of women from these statements), not to mention the 1948 declaration that 'all human beings are born free and equal in dignity and rights'. This was the view that took hold, therefore, and was further developed in the later doctrine of Utilitarianism and in the socialist political philosophy that emerged and grew in the nineteenth and twentieth centuries.

However, we must not lose sight of the fact that, in spite of this, the continued influence of Plato and Aristotle on the thinking of the Western world has been enormous, so that the view of equality within categories has never been far away. Furthermore, the egalitarian movement has always had its opponents, particularly after it seemed to have led to the excesses of the French Revolution. For example, the anti-egalitarian view was put strongly in the second half of the last century by the German philosopher Nietzsche, whose theory that equality led to mediocrity, to the suppression of outstanding individuals who ought to be given their heads and encouraged to be 'unequal' if human evolution was not to be held back, was taken up, albeit in the context of a nationalism that Nietzsche himself would have rejected outright, as one of the basic tenets of the Nazi version of fascism that led to the Second World War. It is a form of argument that, in a somewhat weakened and disguised form, is still put forward by certain opponents of such innovations in education as comprehensive secondary schools and mixed-ability classes.

The tension, then, is still there and its continued presence is due in part to the failure of those who advocate egalitarianism to be clear about what this means. We must now turn, therefore, to a consideration of some of the sources of this confusion in the notion of equality itself, the lack of clarity over the logical grammar of the word 'equal'.

The concept of equality

That all men, or even all people, are equal is clearly not true in any descriptive sense. It is not even true in a qualified sense — except perhaps at the trivial level of bodily functioning — since there are no respects in which all people can be said to be the same. Some of the confusion that bedevils disussions of equality derives from the fact that some philosophers, such as Locke, and some politicians, such as those who framed the American Declaration, have used it as if its meaning were, at least in part, descriptive. We must distinguish the use of 'equal' in mathematical contexts where it clearly signifies that certain things are descriptively 'the same' and its use in political and social contexts where it asserts an ideal, a demand for certain kinds of behaviour in our treatment of other people. In other words, in this kind of context its main force is prescriptive and moral rather than descriptive and mathematical. A confusion of these uses of the term is one source of many of the difficulties associated with it.

The confusion does not end there, however. For, once having accepted that the notion of social equality constitutes a moral demand for something, we still have the problem of discovering exactly what is being demanded. Again confusion results from a failure to answer this question with precision. Again too the mathematical and descriptive connotations of the word compound the confusion. For many people accept that all people are not in any respect the same, but seem to regard the demand for social equality as a demand that in certain respects they be made the same or be made 'equal'. There are at least two good reasons why such a view is untenable.

One difficulty with this interpretation of equality is that it involves a conflict with other social ideals that many people — even among the egalitarians themselves — hold equally dear. In particular, it has been suggested that the demand for equality, if understood in this way, leads to direct conflict with the demand for freedom (Lucas, 1965). It is clear that to try to make people equal will involve considerable interference with their personal liberties. A redistribution of wealth, for example, which many have regarded as a desirable step towards social equality, can only be effected with a great loss of freedom for individuals. This tension is very much apparent in the arguments for and against the continued existence of private schools. To say this is not to say, of course, that such a position is untenable; it is merely to draw attention to one of its implications.

A more serious objection to this view, however, and one which, if true, does render it untenable is the claim that it is not possible to make everyone equal in any sense of the term. One of the fundamental difficulties with the social philosophy of Karl Marx was that it had as a central concept the notion of the classless society and such a society is unattainable. The kind of redistribution of wealth, for example, which we have just discussed, could only result in a crude form of financial equality and would in any case be only temporary, since the differences in people's attitudes to wealth and uses of it, in part responsible for the original inequality, would very soon lead to new inequalities very like the old. One would have to redistribute wealth so regularly — at least daily as far as most punters and bookmakers are concerned — that the whole process would become meaningless.

This is one example of a more general point that must be stressed here, that inequalities are an inevitable part of any kind of society. It has been argued by Ralf Dahrendorf (1962), for example, that, since every human society is a moral society in which behaviour is regulated according to certain norms, there will always be inequalities that will result from the differing degrees to which the behaviour of each individual measures up to these norms. To use one of Dahrendorf's examples, in a society of people that is held together by the desire to exchange news of intrigue, scandal and general gossip, individual members will be distinguished according to the quality of the stories they produce and their manner of recounting them, so that inequalities of rank will result. It is not difficult to see how the same principle will apply in larger and perhaps more serious social groupings. 'The origin of inequality is thus to be found in the existence in all human societies of norms of behaviour to which sanctions are attached' (Dahrendorf, 1962). These sanctions will take many forms but they will all lead to inescapable inequalities of rank. The demand for social equality cannot, therefore, be a demand that all should be made equal.

It has been suggested, therefore, that talk about social equality is a demand not for all to be made equal but for all to be treated equally. Again, however, the descriptive connotations of the term bring confusion. For it looks as though this is a demand that all should be given the same treatment, whereas a moment's thought will reveal that such a practice would seldom lead in any context to equality in the moral sense of justice and fairness (Benn and Peters, 1959; Peters, 1966). It is clearly not just or fair or even desirable, for example, that all patients should be given the same medical treatment or all offenders the same punishment or all children the same educational diet. Clearly there are differences between people that require differences of treatment and only confusion can result if we allow the words we use when we wish to talk about fairness and justice to obscure this important requirement. Some have suggested that social equality is a demand for equality of respect for all people but it has also been pointed out that in this phrase it is the word 'respect' that is doing all the work, the word 'equality' being entirely otiose (Lucas, 1965). Furthermore, this idea in itself gives us no help with the problem of deciding what kinds of treatment of others this equality of respect should lead to nor how we can make decisions about the appropriateness or inappropriateness of adopting different practices in relation to different individuals.

What this seems to point to is that equality is not a demand for similarity of treatment at all but for a justification for differential treatment, a justification which must take the form of demonstrating that our reasons for discriminating between people in certain contexts are relevant reasons and, therefore, arguably, fair, just and impartial reasons. Thus differential treatment of patients is justified if they are shown to have different diseases or different constitutions; differences in our treatment of offenders are to be justified by reference to differences in the nature of their offences or the circumstances under which they were committed; and differences of educational provision are to be justified by appealing to differences exhibited by pupils in their ability to profit from education or what appear to be differences in their educational needs.

Major difficulties in attaining equality in education, however, derive from the problems of defining 'need' and of deciding what shall count as relevant differences of educational need or ability. We have already referred to Aristotle's often quoted dictum that injustice comes as much from treating unequals equally as from treating equals unequally. We are now saying that this is the only reasonable interpretation that one can give to the notion of social equality. However, we must as a consequence face the problem of how one decides on who is to count as unequal, the grounds on which such decisions can be taken and justified, and the different kinds of provision that then become appropriate. In education this means an acceptance of the necessity of making differential provision but at the same time an awareness of the difficulty of deciding what these differences of provision shall be and on what basis discriminations between pupils are to be made. Two main points must be made about this.

In the first place, a difficulty immediately arises if we interpret this as meaning that we must try to place people into a limited number of categories. We have already distinguished the notion of equality within categories from more thorough-going versions of egalitarianism. The main weakness of this approach is that it does not provide us with the subtle instrument we need to make decisions about differential treatment or provision; it offers only the rather blunt instrument of a limited number of discrete categories — masters and slaves, husbands and wives, fathers and children, bright and backward, grammar, technical, and modern, A, B and C, and so on. What is wrong with Aristotle's analysis of social equality is not his identification of the need to treat people differently but the lack of subtlety in his interpretation of the practicalities of this. It is the same lack of subtlety that has bedevilled many of our attempts to secure equality in education. We would not regard as just and, therefore, we would not countenance a judicial system which operated by meting out to all offenders one of two or three kinds of sentence, nor would we have much confidence in a doctor who presented one of three or four types of pill to every patient. The corollary of the assertion that men are not descriptively equal in any way and that justice requires treatment of them in accordance with the differences between them is that our approach to them must be always an individual approach, so that the educational provision we make for each pupil must be based on what seems to be appropriate for him as an individual and not on the allocation of him to one of two or three broad categories. This was a point we noted in our discussion of curricular provision in Chapter 7.

This kind of consideration also draws our attention to the irrelevance of the claims we noted in Chapters 2 and 3 of certain contemporary psychologists, such as Jensen (1969) and Eysenck (1971), concerning the general intellectual capacities of different racial groups. Even if their assertions have any justification or basis, they are meaningless in relation to any practical provision we may want to make, since in practice we will always be dealing with individuals or groups of individuals and never with one racial group as a whole. They merely reveal the fundamental weakness and illogicality of any racist position. Indeed, any comparison of groups, whether offered as a basis for an egalitarian or an elitist system, makes little sense in the context of the individual differences we know to exist between all human beings.

Once we accept this we are nearer to an understanding of what is entailed by demands for equality in education. However, we still have the problems of deciding what are to count as relevant differences between individuals and what differences of provision they should give rise to. The notion of equality itself gives us no help in establishing such criteria of relevance. This, then, is the second point that must be made about this interpretation of social equality in the context of educational provision. We need some criteria by which both of these questions can be answered if we are to be clear about the kinds of educational practice that will lead to the achievement of this kind of equality.

Unfortunately, such criteria are not easy to find. One point must be made, however, and it is a point that has at least two facets that are important to anyone undertaking a search for such criteria. If a difference that can be detected between people is to be regarded as a basis for differential treatment, it must, as we have seen, have some relevance to the context in which we are operating, there must be some connection between the factor we are taking account of and the nature of whatever it is we are trying to distribute justly. Thus in making differential provision of education the only differences we should recognize as relevant to this, if we wish to achieve a fair and just system, are those that can be shown to have a connection with education itself.

To say this is not, of course, to solve the practical problem in any way; it is, however, to point to the direction in which a solution is to be sought. For clearly there are different views of what education is and each will give rise to a different solution to this problem. This has been another source of the confusion that has surrounded the notion of equality in education. For if one sees education as largely or entirely a matter of intellectual growth, this will give rise to one kind of view as to how it should be organized, although for the reasons we gave above it will not suffice to offer only two or three broad types of provision even then. Similarly, views of education as a national investment or as the right of every child regardless of intellectual ability will result in other kinds of answer to questions about relevant differences and kinds of provision (Crowther Report, 1959). All that is entailed by the notion of equality itself is that we should be able to produce relevant reasons for differences of provision; it does not in itself provide us with the criteria on which these differences are to be based.

However, a further point can be made and a second, very important facet of this general feature of equality highlighted. Whatever view we take of education and, therefore, of what criteria shall be relevant to differential educational provision, the notion of equality itself does require those who accept it to repudiate any suggestion that irrelevant factors can be allowed to take a hand. To some extent all discussions about equality that take place in any practical context are negative pleas against what are regarded as unjustifiable inequalities. In other words, it is usually some form of inequality we are talking about and much of what has been said and written about equality in education has been concerned not so much with its promotion in a positive sense as with the need to put right certain inequalities that were felt to be acting as barriers to its achievement, to remove or to remedy certain factors seen to be giving rise to differences both of treatment and of attainment, which were felt to be unconnected with education itself and were, therefore, regarded as irrelevant, unjust, and unequal.

We must now consider in greater detail some of these factors unconnected with education in any sense of the term that have nevertheless been affecting the educational achievement of many pupils. For it is on these that recent discussions of equality have focused, so that no examination of the realities of educational equality in contemporary society is possible without a full awareness of the social factors which have given rise to such impassioned demands for it and the changes in the education system which some have felt would lead to the achievement of it.

Some sources of educational inequality

The 1944 Education Act established in England and Wales the concept of education for all 'according to age, aptitude and ability' and thus a view of equality which required that adequate educational provision be made for all children. In particular, it was intended that such provision would be ensured by making secondary education in some form available to all pupils. It quickly became apparent, however, that these ideals were very far from realization and it is unfortunately the case that even now, over forty years since the passing of that Act, we have made little real progress towards their attainment.

Three major reasons have been identified for the continued inequalities of the education system, or rather three main sources of disadvantage and underachievement — social class, race and gender. Many of the explanations of this are common to all three categories and we will concentrate our attention on these, at least in the first instance. In particular, those factors which have been identified as the major sources of disadvantage for pupils from 'working-class' homes have also been recognized as major reasons for those inequalities which have resulted from racial differences, especially in the USA where the issue of the education of ethnic minority groups was recognized long before it became a matter of concern in the United Kingdom. Some factors, however, are specific to some of these categories, especially to those inequalities arising from gender differences, and we will also consider these briefly as this becomes appropriate.

Within a very short time after the implementation of the 1944 Act in the United Kingdom it became alarmingly clear that the realities of a system offering education for all were very different from the ideals that had led to its institution. For it became apparent that many pupils were not finding it possible to take advantage of the opportunities thus offered. The Report on Early Leaving published in 1954 revealed some very disturbing statistics concerning the wastage from the education system of a high proportion of pupils and, most surprisingly, of those pupils whose intellectual capacities, as measured by intelligence tests, appeared to be of a very high order. Such a situation was clearly very worrying not only in the light of what the new deal of the 1944 Act had hoped to achieve but also in the context of an industrial society dependent on its human resources for economic survival. The same depressing picture emerged from the researches of the Crowther Committee in 1959. Nor was Britain alone in this; a similar situation was found to exist elsewhere, not least in the USA (Riessman, 1962). Equality of educational opportunity existed apparently in name only; in practice many inequalities persisted.

For it was clear that many irrelevant factors were coming into play to decide what profit individuals were able to gain from the educational provision that was made, and it was equally clear that these factors were irrelevant whatever view one took of the aims and purposes of education, since even if one took a very narrow view of education as primarily concerned to develop the highest intellects it was apparent that many pupils of high ability were being excluded from educational success by factors that had little or nothing to do with intellectual potential.

In general, the reasons for this wastage appeared from the first to be closely linked with the social class origins of the pupils. For the figures of the Early Leaving and Crowther Reports themselves revealed that the situation was at its most serious among those children who came from families of low socio-economic status and in the USA a similar situation was seen to exist, particularly in relation to black pupils — a problem that subsequently became significant in the United Kingdom after the large-scale immigrations of the 1950s and early 1960s.

A great deal of attention was immediately directed, therefore, towards these families in an attempt to identify the particular sources of the problem so that appropriate steps might be taken to eradicate them, and this has been a source of concern and of continued attention ever since. A number of studies were undertaken from which it quickly became apparent that there were many such factors and that the situation was a highly complex one. Some of the reasons for this failure of pupils to take advantage of the educational opportunities supposedly made available to them were to be found, as one would expect, in the cultural background of the homes in which they were growing up but, more disturbingly, it soon began to emerge not only that the school system was failing to compensate for these disadvantages but that in many ways it was itself aggravating them and introducing additional factors into the situation that worked to the further disadvantage of the 'culturally deprived' child.

The elements in the home background of certain pupils that make it difficult for them to profit from the educational opportunities opened to them were not hard to find. In many cases a straightforward desire on the part of parents for an extra wage-packet to supplement the family income or on the part of the young person himself for a steady wage and the independence that goes with it have led to departure from school at the earliest date on which it was legally permissible. This has been an especially important factor in the case of girls from such families, since it has been aggravated by a conviction that girls, even more than boys, have no need of anything beyond the minimum of educational provision. Indeed, it might be argued that in relation to the education of girls this is not an attitude which is confined to one social class, since there are more than enough 'middle-class' parents who are inclined to take much the same kind of view of the education of their daughters. One of the strongest arguments for the raising of the school leaving age to sixteen was thus the need to keep pupils from this kind of background at school at least until they have had the opportunity to take some kind of public examination — for their own ultimate benefit and advantage as much as for that of society as a whole.

The desire to leave school, or the pressure to leave school, for reasons of pure family economy, then, accompanied sometimes, although not always, by a reluctance to be 'educated out of one's class' (or even, indeed, one's race and culture), was a prime factor in the situation we have been describing. This one would expect. It is more surprising, however, to find this pattern of behaviour persisting in spite of the current levels of unemployment.

It had become apparent, however, that this was not the only reason why such youngsters were leaving school early. It was also due in some cases to the fact that neither they nor their parents knew what the opportunities open to them were, nor what facilities existed to enable them to take advantage of them. Many were unaware, for example, of the existence of student grants that would enable them to go on to some form of higher education. Sheer ignorance, then, was a major factor in discouraging many from continuing their education beyond the statutory leaving age.

It seemed further, however, that many lacked not only a knowledge of but also any real interest in the educational opportunities that were being offered them. One study suggested that only certain identifiable kinds of family in this sector of society could be seen to be really interested in education and, therefore, prepared to support their children, their sons at least if not their daughters, and to encourage them to take full advantage of it (Jackson and Marsden, 1962). Among these families the study identified the 'sunken middle-class' family, the family which had, say, once owned a shop or other small business and had fallen on bad times or which was a branch of a largely 'middle-class' family and wished to regain that kind of status by way of the education of the children; secondly, the families of foremen or others whose work brought them into contact with the more highly educated and gave them thus some inkling of the advantages of this kind of position; and, thirdly, other families, such as those where the mother had herself been educated in a grammar school but had 'married beneath her' and where there was a frustration and a consequent excitement about the possibilities of social advancement through the education of the children. For the rest, a certain apathy was apparent as a result of which there was no encouragement for the children to do well at school and no desire for them to stay there longer than was required by law.

Furthermore, the whole ambience of this kind of home seemed to lead to a different view of education from that normally taken by teachers and others who were concerned with its provision and also, it has been claimed, to certain personality traits that made success in the system more difficult for children growing up in such homes. It has been suggested, for example (Riessman, 1962), that in many such families, if education is valued at all, it is valued only as instrumental towards vocational inprovement or the avoidance of exploitation in a competitive and fast-moving world, whereas to some extent at least the ethos of most schools is based on a commitment to the idea of education for its own sake or for the development of self-expression. Such a fundamental conflict of attitudes and values must lead to difficulties. One illustration of this is the interest shown by many pupils in apprenticeships and other courses of vocational training, the point of which is more readily appreciated than the need to learn French irregular verbs or abstruse Latin grammatical constructions. It is also one explanation of the interest shown in recent vocational developments within the curriculum in the United Kingdom such as those sponsored by the Manpower Services Commission.

So far the reasons we have produced to explain why children from certain kinds of family do not get on at school have been those that derive from a fundamental lack of interest in or understanding of what is involved in this. Attention has also been drawn, however, to certain elements in the upbringing of these children that make it difficult for them to cope with the demands of the system even when they are motivated to do so. It has been claimed, for example, that the child-rearing practices usually associated with families of this kind lead to the development of certain character traits that are not conducive to educational success, that the granting of food to babies on demand or giving them comforters and even the quick and immediate smack for any kind of misdemeanour creates a need in children for immediate gratification in all spheres and makes it difficult, if not impossible, for them to direct their energies towards any activity the point of which is to be appreciated only by reference to certain long-term goals, such as examination successes or later career prospects. It has also been suggested that the pace of life is often slower in families of this kind, that, as a result, children from them do not reveal that quickness in their approach to learning that teachers tend to associate with potential educational success, so that they come to be regarded not merely as slow learners but also as poor learners and thus do not succeed in a situation where speed of working seems so often to be at a premium. It has even been argued that the patriarchal ethos of such families makes it difficult for their offspring to accept what is felt to be the largely matriarchal ethos of most primary schools.

The most important single factor, however, that has been identified as contributing to this failure of pupils from such backgrounds to cope successfully with the demands of the school system is, as we saw in Chapter 4, the nature of the language that they have acquired through their preschool experiences. The child who has initially acquired his spoken language in a home where a 'restricted' code of language is used will have difficulty in using the formal or 'elaborated' code of the school and thus will not find it easy to learn to read, to extend his vocabulary, to acquire the conceptual understanding necessary for educational progress especially at an abstract level, in short to attain all of those skills that are fundamental to educational achievement (Bernstein, 1961). Indeed, Bernstein suggested further that this problem of language is the most important single factor in educational disadvantage, leading not only to verbal difficulties but also to a certain rigidity of thinking, a reduced span of attention, a limiting of curiosity, impulsive behaviour in which the interval between feeling and acting is short, an inability to tolerate ambiguity, a preference for the concrete and, in general, a distaste for, not to say a positive suspicion of, education as traditionally conceived. As we have seen, there has subsequently been a certain retraction from this extreme position to one which, while maintaining that the language code of such pupils is different, no longer claims that it is inferior or lacking in any way (Bernstein, 1964; Labov, 1969), but, so long as the content of education is couched in a formal 'elaborated' code of language, the pupil whose own language is of a 'restricted' or 'public' kind will be at a disadvantage.

This brief discussion of language, which was developed more fully in Chapter 4, introduces the suggestion that there are factors in the school itself, as well as in the home, that need to be looked at if we want to discover what contributes to the difficulties experienced by pupils of the kind we are here concerned with. For it has become increasingly clear not only that schools have not been doing enough to help these pupils but also that there are many ways in which they have been aggravating the problem and themselves creating further barriers to success. We must now consider some of these in more detail.

To begin with, it should be clear that most of these homes will be in poorer districts and in inner city areas, especially in the large cities, and that the schools these children attend will also be in these poorer areas. It is almost certainly not the case now, as it once was, that these schools are badly equipped or less generously provided for than those in wealthier neighbourhoods, but in terms of human resources they are often less well endowed since they are not attractive places of work for most teachers and the turnover of staff in them has tended to be very high. Certainly most teachers will not be keen to live in such areas themselves so that they will have to be prepared to travel quite long distances to teach in them. Too frequent changes of teacher and too much time spent with supply teachers or well-meaning but inexperienced probationer teachers do not create conditions conducive to educational success.

Furthermore, the attitudes of the teachers themselves often do not help to alleviate these difficulties. Whatever their own origins, teachers by their long education and training have usually developed values very different from those of these pupils and are sometimes less than sympathetic towards those pupils who do not share these values. We considered in some detail in Chapter 2, the evidence of the influence of teachers' attitudes on the achievement of both black pupils and girls and, indeed, we must not ignore the evidence of actual racism on the part of some teachers. Furthermore, we have already referred to the problem of confusing slowness in learning with low ability. When this is done, teachers come to expect a low level of performance from such pupils and, again as we saw in Chapter 2, the demands made by teachers of their pupils and the expectations they have of them seem to be quite crucial in determining the levels of achievement reached (Pidgeon, 1970). Teachers can also be put off, as we all can, by appearance and dress and will often not expect much from children who are not very well turned out and will not give them as much attention as they need or are entitled to. Difference of language will also lead to difficulties of communication and will thus seriously reduce the efficiency of both the teaching and the learning.

Finally, even teachers who are aware of these difficulties and take positive steps to avoid them may unwittingly contribute to the disadvantage. They may quite reasonably fail to answer those important questions that remain unasked, questions like those about grants, career and other possibilities which we mentioned earlier. Furthermore, in their efforts to do what seems to be best for these pupils they may sometimes talk down to them, lower their standards or take the lack of interest for granted (Riessman, 1962). Teachers in the USA, for example, have been known to advise black children against aiming too high, doing this honestly in what they see as the best interests of the pupils. This kind of patronization can be in itself a form of discrimination, 'discrimination without prejudice', as Riessman calls it. The attitudes of teachers, then, constitute one major factor within the school that can aggravate the disadvantages that some pupils experience.

It has become increasingly apparent over the last twenty years or so that many elements in the organization of the school system also contribute to this wastage and the inequality of opportunity. In particular, the existence of selective procedures at various stages in the individual's school life have appeared to result in grave disadvantages for many children, but particularly for those who come to school already disadvantaged in the ways we have indicated. Streaming, the practice of grouping children according to measured ability, is one device that creates difficulties of this kind at whatever stage it is used, although clearly the earlier it is introduced the more influential it will be. There are quite clear indications too that it works particularly to the detriment of the child whose home background is not educationally supportive (Jackson, 1964). Similarly, a selective form of secondary education which necessitates some kind of allocation of pupils to different schools or different forms of education at 11+ or at some other equally early stage of a child's school career will result in inefficiencies and errors which will particularly affect such children. In part this is due to all the factors we have mentioned above, the barriers to achievement created by the home background, teachers' attitudes and expectations, language difficulties and so on, but they all culminate in the difficulties created by the testing procedures used and especially those that involve some attempt to measure intelligence.

The difficulties of doing this have been fully discussed in Chapter 3 and attempts to base differential educational provision on tests of this kind must for a variety of reasons lead to the misallocation of large numbers of children (Yates and Pidgeon, 1957). It is particularly detrimental to the progress of the socially disadvantaged child for a number of reasons. In the case of verbal tests, language differences will clearly play an important part. In all tests the need for speed, often a crucial factor in measuring intelligence, will militate against a high score by the child who sees no particular merit in doing things quickly. A lack of interest or motivation is also unlikely to help a child to show up well in these situations and, where an interview forms part of the testing procedure, the resultant social situation, the relationship with the examiner, will be an added problem for the child who lacks some of the social graces. For all of these reasons children from underprivileged homes can be seen to do themselves less than justice in tests of this kind, so that wherever selection procedures of this type are in use they lead to inequalities of opportunity for such children. The same factors are even resulting in a large proportion of black pupils in the United Kingdom, particularly those of West Indian nationality, being allocated to institutions for the educationally subnormal, having been 'dubbed' or 'made' ESN (Coard, 1971).

It is perhaps worth noting at this point that many other irrelevant factors come into play when this kind of testing and allocation of pupils to different kinds of school or streamed class are employed, factors which affect the progress not only of pupils from underprivileged backgrounds but many others too. We have heard a lot about the effects of 'nerves' in test situations and interviews and also about the advantages of those who possess 'good examination technique', but these are minor factors when compared with others which are less obvious but equally, and perhaps even more, irrelevant and often far more significant. Gender is one such factor; educational advancement at all levels has always been much more difficult for girls than for boys since, in addition to the greater reluctance of parents to support girls through the system, there have been fewer places for them in all selective institutions. Furthermore, it can hardly be maintained that the month of one's birth is relevant to one's educational provision. Yet it has been shown (Jackson, 1964) that this can and does affect the allocation of pupils to streamed classes in junior schools and thus to different types of secondary school, for the very good reason that the month of one's birth governs the date at which one is admitted to the infant school and consequently the length of time one has spent in full-time education up to the time at which the selection is made. Childhood illnesses and the absences that they involve also play their part in this process. The place of one's birth or at least the part of the country in which one has one's education is another crucial factor in determining the kind of education one has, since provision varies dramatically in both quantity and type from one organizing authority to another. Yet this too would seem to be an irrelevant consideration in the decision about what kind of education an individual can best profit from.

It will be clear, then, that equality of opportunity in education is far from a reality whatever interpretation one puts on the term. Even the most confirmed elitist, committed to nothing more than the education of the intelligent, can hardly believe in the face of this kind of evidence to the contrary that even this hard-line kind of equality is being achieved by the system as it has been organized. Only an elitism based on the advancement of the privileged could leave one satisfied with the situation that the enquiries of the last twenty years or so have revealed and few would want to maintain such an extremist position as that.

It has been clear for a long time, therefore, to those with any real understanding of the situation that changes needed to be made and steps taken to rectify the position. Consequently, recent years have seen the introduction of a number of schemes aimed at putting right these deficiencies in the system and at combating the disadvantages of the underprivileged, in order to promote something that could more appropriately be called educational equality. Such schemes, however, have more often than not brought their own form of inequality as we shall see if we briefly explore the idea of compensatory education.

Compensatory education

One major kind of solution that has been suggested to deal with some of the problems we have listed is that of what the Plowden Report (1967) called 'positive discrimination'. This amounts to a suggestion that equality does not require that we give all schools and all pupils an equal share of the educational cake but that it is more likely to be attained if we give larger, and therefore unequal, shares to those with greater needs, if we allocate a larger share of resources of all kinds to certain pupils in order to compensate for the disadvantages under which they labour. Certain children must be given unequal treatment if they are to have equal opportunities. This kind of view has led to a number of different forms of 'compensatory education', each designed to make good the cultural deficiencies we have referred to and to try to compensate for and to put right those factors that have been hindering the educational success of such pupils. This is an idea that had appeared earlier in the USA in answer to the problem of the education of black children.

One of the solutions offered by the Plowden Report itself, although it had other reasons also for making this particular recommendation, was an expansion of the provision of preschool, nursery education. One of the arguments adduced in favour of this recommendation was the need to provide early opportunities for children to receive some kind of formal educational provision that might make up for various forms of social deprivation. Certain children, it argued, suffer later in the system because of poverty of language and 'even amongst children below compulsory school age, the growth of measured intelligence is associated with socio-economic features' (para. 302) so that educational provision from the age of three years onwards may offset this.

The importance of nursery education in this and other respects is now recognized and the British Government affirmed its intention to expand it on a large scale. Furthermore, although this appeared likely to be one of the first casualties in educational provision that have been necessitated by the economic difficulties that have recently been encountered, public demand and the recognition of its value seems to have ensured some continued expansion of provision in this area. In the USA too, attempts have been made to introduce compensatory education programmes at the preschool stage in order to try to ensure that the child from the culturally impoverished background might start his formal school career on a par with his more fortunate colleagues. The 'Headstart' programme was just such an attempt to bring children from poorer homes, especially black children, up to the starting line level with their fellows.

This, then, has been one form of positive discrimination. Where it has been tried, however, it has not been entirely successful. In part this is due to the fact that when nursery schools or nursery classes are created, unless the local authority adopts a deliberate policy of establishing them in areas of social priority, they are used more by children from 'privileged' than those from 'underprivileged' homes. There is little that can be done about this. One cannot make attendance compulsory at this age nor can one exclude the 'privileged' from it, since the arguments for the provision of education at this age for all pupils are strong. One can only recommend, as the Plowden Report does, that all possible means of persuasion should be used by health visitors and other social workers to encourage mothers of children who seem to be in particular need of nursery education to make greater use of the facilities available.

The attitude that is implied towards the culture of these homes has been another factor in the lack of success of this kind of venture. To regard children from poor homes or from non-white families as culturally deprived is to imply that these homes and families are fundamentally inferior. This is a point we will explore more fully shortly. We must note here, however, that it leads to the continuation of a form of education that is linked to a different kind of culture and consequently creates a gap that is difficult to bridge and which does not make any easier the task of convincing the parents, especially the mothers, of these children of the value of what is offered in nursery education. They are unlikely to see it as more than a useful child-minding service which they will use only if they have no more convenient service, such as a resident granny.

This latter point draws our attention also to a third difficulty that is being experienced in this area, the problem of establishing nursery education in a form that has more substance to it than a mere child-minding service, the provision of suitable accommodation and resources and the training of suitable teachers for this kind of work, teachers who understand what is needed and have the expertise to provide it. The conversion of accommodation, resources, and especially teachers who were originally prepared for teaching older pupils is more important than has often been realized. It is also, at least in the case of the teachers, a long process, so that the only suitable form of preparation is the concurrent course of three or four years leading to a first degree in education itself. If nursery education is to be established properly, it will be a long and expensive task. Only if it is done properly, however, can we hope that it might contribute something towards the solution of the problems we have been discussing.

A second kind of approach that has been adopted in the attempt to provide compensatory education has been directed not at preschool children but at all of the school population. It has taken the form of putting extra resources into schools in deprived areas, providing extra payments to teachers, larger allowances for materials and other recurrent expenditure, favourable building grants and financial assistance of this kind in all relevant fields. In suggesting this remedy, the Plowden Report tells us that 'the principle, already accepted, that special need calls for special help, should be given a new cutting edge. We ask for "positive discrimination" in favour of such schools and the children in them, going well beyond an attempt to equalize resources.... The first step must be to raise the schools with low standards to the national average; the second, quite deliberately to make them better. The justification is that the homes and neighbourhoods from which many of their children come provide little support and stimulus for learning' (para. 151).

As a result of this recommendation, many areas in Britain have been officially designated as Educational or, more recently, Social Priority Areas and the schools in them have been given the kind of preferential treatment suggested. Teachers in these schools have been paid more in an attempt to secure a stability of staffing and to halt the rapid staff turnover that we suggested earlier was a significant factor in the lack of success of the pupils in these schools. Additional money has also been made available in order to make possible the establishment of special programmes either in the schools themselves or in outside centres to remedy the deficiencies in experience, language, and other cognitive skills of the children in them. At the same time the back-up services have been strengthened both by increased provision of social services of all kinds and by the appointment of social workers or counsellors to the schools themselves.

While one would not want to deny that this kind of approach has done much to improve the educational lot of certain pupils and to put right some of the inequalities of the system, there are difficulties with it of which we ought to take note.

The first of these arises from the difficulty of establishing adequate criteria for designating an area as an area of priority. The Plowden Report suggested a number of criteria that should be used, the proportions of unskilled and semi-skilled manual workers in the area, the size of families, the extent of the entitlement to supplementary benefits of all kinds, the amount of overcrowding and sharing of houses, the incidence of truancy, the proportions of retarded, disturbed or handicapped pupils, the number of incomplete families, and the proportion of 'children unable to speak English'. Many of these are criteria that can be measured with a high degree of exactitude; others are less easy to determine. Not all of those who are entitled to supplementary benefits actually avail themselves of them, for example, as the Report points out, so that it is not easy to apply this kind of criterion accurately. Furthermore, criteria such as the incidence of truancy are based not on objectively identifiable conditions in the home background of the pupils but on the way in which they react to their schools. Some cynics have claimed, therefore, that this and other criteria that have been used, such as that of a high staff turn-over, create a situation in which an inefficient or incompetent school is 'rewarded' by additional resources and payments to staff, while a school that successfully tackles problems of this kind as they are presented to it is, in a sense, 'penalized'. A certain amount of tension and dissatisfaction has consequently resulted among teachers from this kind of scheme.

This is one aspect of a wider problem. Whatever criteria are used, they will inevitably be rather rough and ready. A line will be drawn somewhere which must be somewhat arbitrary. This is another example of the problem of establishing categories that we referred to earlier. It will also always be the case that wherever that line is drawn there will be many pupils in these areas of priority whose home background is such that they will not need compensatory educational provision and there will always be those outside these areas whose need for it will be every bit as great as that of any of those who are within them, and for the very same reasons. The Plowden Report itself was aware of this and spoke of special groups, such as gypsies and canal boat children whose difficulties would not be met by any such scheme. The problem, however, is not only one of special groups; again we find ourselves dealing with categories, the main need is to provide for individual pupils. Attempts have, therefore, been made to identify pupils rather than areas with special needs and to use the additional resources to develop and provide special programmes for them. It is almost certainly true that a judicious combination of these approaches is the only route that is likely to lead to any kind of solution for all such pupils.

A further point that must be stressed is that, to quote the Plowden Report yet again, 'improved education alone cannot solve the problem of these children' (para. 157). Education cannot compensate for society (Bernstein, 1970). To put extra resources only into the education of such children is to attempt to deal with the symptoms without getting at the root causes of their difficulties. The process of equalizing the life-chances of children must begin outside the school and, unless it does, there is little that the school alone can do. Again to quote from the Plowden Report, 'simultaneous action is needed by the authorities responsible for employment, industrial training, housing and planning' (para. 151). Indeed, it may well be the case that the failure to mount successful attacks simultaneously on these areas has been one factor in the lack of success achieved by some attempts to improve the educational provision of these pupils. This draws attention to the need of a total approach to this problem and this has emerged very clearly from the practical experiences of many of those who have been involved in compensatory schemes of this kind. In many areas of priority it has quickly become apparent that little can be achieved by improving the facilities within the schools if no attempt is made to integrate the schools more fully with their communities. Thus compensatory education has appeared to be possible only if the parents themselves can be brought into the picture and only if one can relate what is being provided for and required of pupils in schools to the realities of the environment of the community in which they live for the other seven-eighths of their young lives.

This brings us directly to the major problem of the concept of compensatory education. The schemes we have been discussing have all started out as attempts to make people equal, and we suggested earlier that such an approach is fundamentally mistaken. The notion of compensation implies the existence of a deficiency and, while there is no doubt that on any definition of deficiency real deficiencies do exist in many families, the considerations behind programmes of compensatory education have too often assumed that these deficiencies are always cultural deficiencies, and that they are an inevitable part of the social background of all children from certain socio-economic or racial groups. It implies that the language and culture of 'working-class' or West Indian families, for example, are inferior to the language and the culture that the school is concerned to promote, that pupils from these kinds of background are 'deficit systems' and that they must be 'cured' of their linguistic and cultural deficiencies if they are to be brought to a 'proper' standard of educational achievement. The problem with this attitude is that at root it perpetuates and reinforces a conflict which, as we have already seen, is itself a major contributory factor in the educational failure of these pupils. It attempts to do no more than to discover new and more effective ways of imposing an 'alien' culture on them, and thus does nothing to overcome the alienation and the conflict of values that we suggested earlier is a major obstacle to the educational achievement of these pupils.

This problem thus directs our attention to the role of the curriculum in the creation of educational inequality and raises again some of the issues of curriculum we discussed in Chapter 7. It may be worthwhile, therefore, if we conclude our exploration of educational equality with some comments on the curricular implications of what has been said so far.

Equality and the curriculum

There is no doubt that the curriculum offered by many schools and, associated with this, the view taken of the curriculum by many schools and many teachers have contributed a good deal to those inequalities we have described. For, as we saw in Chapter 7, behind the curricular provision made, whether by central government fiat, local authority initiatives, the timetabling and curriculum planning of individual schools, or even the day-to-day judgements and decisions of individual teachers, lie certain assumptions — about education, about knowledge, about society and, even, about human nature. Those assumptions will reflect the values of the planners and decision-makers; they will not necessarily reflect the values or the interests of the recipients of the curriculum. Where they do not, conflict will result and inequalities will also follow. It is also important to note that these assumptions are as often implicit as they are explicit. They are seldom fully thought out; and often they come to light only when we explore the 'hidden curriculum', that which is being transmitted as a by-product of the explicitly stated syllabus.

There are several such assumptions which it is important for our present discussion that we note in a little detail. First, there are, or have been, some quite crucial assumptions about sex-roles which have been reflected in the curriculum offered to both boys and girls from the earliest possible age (Delamont, 1980). With very young children, these assumptions have been most apparent in the selection of reading material, toys and activities of all kinds, and have taken the form of discouraging pupils from reading certain books, playing with certain kinds of toys or engaging in certain kinds of activity deemed not to fit the assumed sex-role — boys being discouraged from 'dressing up', for example, or from cooking, girls from the more boisterous activities such as playing football or even from using the microcomputer. They can also be seen in the attitudes of some teachers to the pupils, as reflected, for example, in their response to misbehaviour, and, as we saw in Chapter 1, in the disproportionate amount of time and attention given by some teachers to boys of all ages (Stanworth, 1980). By the time the secondary school is reached, and especially the choice of options at 14+, this has been formalized into Home Economics for girls and CDT for boys, or natural sciences for girls and physics and/or chemistry for boys. Where this is not made explicit, it is often an inevitable effect of the way in which the timetable is organized.

If one adds to this the implicit, 'hidden' effects of similar values built into much of the literature and reading material which have been offered to children from an early age — Janet helping mother in the kitchen, while John helps father in the garage — one can see how the curriculum in many ways, both explicit and implicit, promotes certain attitudes and values, those encapsulated in the assumptions behind it, the principles upon which it is based. And one can further see how these result in inequalities of opportunity for both girls and boys, but especially, in a highly technological society, inequalities of opportunity for girls if they are discouraged in so many ways, both overt and covert, from developing the skills needed to contribute effectively to technological development.

Thus the curriculum offered to the vast majority of girls in our schools, reflecting the values and the assumptions of many teachers and other curriculum planners, has reinforced the attitudes to the education of girls of many parents, of all classes and ethnic origins, but especially of working-class and West Indian background, to create major inequalities of opportunity for girls in the British educational system. It has thus been claimed, with some force as well as pathos, that the most underprivileged members of any school community are the West Indian girls of 'working-class' background, and especially those whose position in the family and/or whose date or place of birth adds to their burden of disadvantage.

The growing awareness of the effects of curricular decisions of this kind, and the assumptions upon which they are based, on the education of girls has led in recent years to a number of initiatives to counter these effects. Several organizations have sprung into existence, such as Women into Science Education (WISE) and the Girls and Mathematics Association (GAMA), whose expressed purpose is to break down these assumptions and to open up the route to complete sexual equality in education. The effects of such movements can already be seen in the opening up of the curriculum in many areas to pupils of both sexes, and in some quite significant changes of attitude by both pupils and teachers (and even by some parents too) to issues in which sexual stereotyping was once remarkably rigid. There has even been some encouragement to such developments in recent official publications on the curriculum. And some local education authorities have issued their own guidelines to teachers on issues of gender in schools. Much still remains to be done, perhaps especially in changing the attitudes of society at large — not least in the implicit sexism of day-to-day language — but enough has already been achieved to suggest that on this question at least things are moving in the right direction, albeit, perhaps, too slowly for some people.

We can be less sanguine, however, about the effects of the curriculum on those inequalities engendered by social class and ethnic differences. For here the issues are far more complex and the solution necessitates a much more sweeping rethinking of attitudes. For here it is not enough to open up subject areas to a wider range of pupils; we need to reconsider and reassess the validity of those subject areas themselves. We need to ask quite searching questions about the justification for including certain subjects in the curriculum, and, indeed, as we saw in Chapter 7, about the wisdom of and justification for planning the curriculum in terms of subjects at all, for adopting a content-based approach to curriculum planning.

For, as we saw earlier, a good deal of educational inequality can be attributed to the alienation which results when we attempt to impose a curriculum framed in terms of white middle-class culture on pupils whose background is non-white or working-class or both. It is clearly unsatisfactory, in educational terms, when pupils, such as those black girls in Mary Fuller's study (1981) to which we referred in Chapter 1, value what the school has to offer for utilitarian reasons only. We need, therefore, to ask some far-reaching questions about the validity of that white middle-class culture if we are to justify not only imposing it on others but also, in order to do so, devaluing their own culture and attempting to 'compensate' them for it.

For this reason, as we saw again when discussing the curriculum in Chapter 7, questions are being asked about the content of education. It is being asserted that human knowledge does not have the kind of objective status often claimed for it and that there is little real foundation for the claim that certain kinds of knowledge, or certain forms of culture, have a value that is superior to that of other kinds in such a way as to justify the insistence that all pupils acquire such knowledge or such a culture and accept the values implicit in them. Work that has been done, for example, on the origin of school subjects suggests that their place on the curriculum is invariably better explained in political than in academic or philosophical terms (Goodson, 1981, 1983, 1984, 1985). Views have been expressed too about the 'stratification of knowledge' (Young 1971), suggesting that decisions about the value of certain kinds of knowledge are linked to the class structure of society and that by such decisions the dominant class attempts to impose its own culture, its own values, on society as a whole. This, it might be argued, is a process which can be seen at work at present in the emphasis being placed by the existing government in the United Kingdom on the maintaining of 'academic standards' in schools and the development of certain kinds of curriculum subject. Such a policy must aggravate rather than alleviate the problems of inequality we have been describing.

If there is any truth in this kind of assertion, to engage in forms of compensatory education such as those we have discussed is to do no more than to attempt to ease and to make more efficient this imposition of values by the dominant class on society as a whole. As a result, it is being suggested that we look again at the content of educational provision and try to relate this to the existing knowledge and culture of the pupil, that we try to base our educational provision on the 'common sense' knowledge of the pupils themselves rather than on the 'educational' knowledge of the teacher. If we do this, some of the barriers to the education of these children will disappear — deferred gratification, for example, need create no problem if there is immediate satisfaction in the subject matter of education here and now — and there might be some hope that a relevant education might be provided for pupils from 'working-class' and black homes, so that they will not become alienated by their experiences at school, at a serious disadvantage in relation to their own personal development and subsequently perhaps delinquent and anti-social. In short, it is being claimed that we should not be attempting to convert such pupils to a new language or a new culture, but that rather attempts should be made to bridge the gap between the cultures if education is to cease to play the divisive role it has hitherto played in society.

The same sort of conclusion is being reached by many of those who have been engaged at a practical level in attempts to deal with the problems of the EPAs. As we have seen, they have come to realize that the problem of the gap between the culture of the home and that of the school requires more than merely building a bridge from one to the other; the gap itself needs to be closed by a rapprochement of school and community, an integration of the school into the community. In order to achieve this, major changes must be made in what the school regards as its role and function and what it considers to be the essential content of education.

A different way of looking at this is to see the curriculum in terms not of its content but rather of the processes of education it is concerned to promote, a distinction we explored in some detail in Chapter 7. For if we see education as essentially concerned not with the transmission of certain bodies of knowledge-content but with the development of certain capacities within the pupils — in particular, those capacities for autonomous thought we discussed earlier — then we can recognize that the content of the educational programme through which these processes of development are promoted can vary in accordance with a number of factors, including the background, social, ethnic or whatever, of the individual pupil. All pupils need not be exposed to precisely the same kinds of curriculum-content, and thus to the values implicit in that content. Equality of educational opportunity implies not that but rather that they should all have access to whatever experiences will help them towards the kinds and forms of development which it might be claimed constitute what it means to be educated. What is essential is that educational provision should give all pupils enhanced control over their lives and the circumstances of those lives, whatever these may be.

Thus, for example, it has been argued that we should reconsider what we mean by 'education', especially in relation to such pupils (Keddie, 1971). The view that is now taken of what has been called the 'restricted' language code of children from certain kinds of home background is no longer, as we pointed out earlier, that such a code is inferior to that of the schools but merely that it is different. It is no longer felt that it need necessarily hinder or limit the development of rationality, since it can be shown itself to be capable of sustaining the most abstract and abstruse relationships (Labov, 1969). If the development of rationality in such pupils is inhibited, it is because the language of the teachers and of education is different and no concessions are made to them nor attempts to bridge the gap between the codes, other than to try to push them into using the different, and largely alien, code of the school, and that the view taken of knowledge and culture is similarly inflexible.

The problem, therefore, becomes one of introducing modifications to the curriculum of the school in order to achieve these purposes and we have already noted in Chapter 7 some of the difficulties of doing this. In particular, we must not lose sight of the dangers of imprisoning pupils in their own culture and of failing to broaden their horizons by not offering them adequate opportunities for experiencing many things they may come to value that are beyond their immediate environment and experience (White, 1968, 1973). Among the prime examples of this kind of over-reaction were the introduction of various forms of 'social education' for pupils from largely working-class backgrounds in the late 1960s and early 1970s, the inadequacies of which we explored in Chapter 6, the establishment of courses in 'black studies' for pupils from ethnic minority groups and the making of special arrangements for mother-tongue teaching to which we referred in Chapter 4. Merely to offer different kinds of content in this way without any fundamental rethinking of the underlying principles is equally disadvantageous to such pupils. But it would be equally unfortunate if we were to lose sight of the rich possibilities offered by the linguistic and cultural diversity which characterizes most present-day schools and classrooms.

On the other hand, it is clear that many of the current difficulties we are experiencing in our schools arise from a failure to question the validity of much of what we are offering, and in particular to do this in the light of the background of many of the pupils we are supposed to be catering for. As we have said a *rapprochement* is needed if we are to achieve a form of education which is relevant, and therefore acceptable, to pupils from all kinds of background. It is being suggested here that such a *rapprochement* may best be brought about if we cease to view the curriculum in terms of its content and to regard education as the transmission of that content, and begin to plan our educational provision in terms rather of the processes of development we are concerned to promote. For until we do that, the curriculum will itself continue to be a major source of educational inequalities.

The only really effective route to the overcoming of educational inequalities, then, is through a complete review of the curriculum and of what we mean and understand by the term 'curriculum'. In particular, we need to move away from the traditional view of the curriculum as a collection of subjects deemed to be in some sense intrinsically worthwhile, and of education as the transmission of these subjects to the next generation. It is for this reason that one must see the policy of the present government in the United Kingdom, which consists not only of seeing the curriculum in subject terms but also of making a major educational priority of maintaining academic standards in those subject areas it values, as likely to aggravate rather than to alleviate the inequalities we have outlined in this chapter.

Much has been attempted at the organizational level in recent years to resolve these problems — the establishment of comprehensive forms of secondary education, for example, and the introduction of mixed-ability classes, both of which devices were designed to overcome in particular those inequalities arising from selective procedures which we noted earlier. It has been a major error, however, to believe that such organizational changes can in themselves resolve these problems. They can achieve little unless they are accompanied by a complete rethinking of the purposes and principles of education, and especially of the forms of curriculum through which those purposes and principles are to be attained or fulfilled. It is the failure to do this that has resulted in little change in the pattern of educational inequalities in the twenty years since the comprehensivization of secondary schooling was first officially required and legally demanded in the United Kingdom.

Summary and conclusions

We have in this chapter considered some of the difficulties, both theoretical and practical, that attend attempts to attain equality of educational opportunity. In doing so, we have suggested that failure to achieve it in practice is in part a result of the lack of a clear conception of what in essence we are seeking. We, therefore, began the chapter by attempting to attain a clearer notion of the concept of equality and we were immediately made aware of some of the difficulties that process is fraught with. We were forced to conclude that educational equality is an ideal which, like all ideals, is unattainable in its pure form but that it does, nevertheless, provide us with certain criteria by which we can evaluate the practical provision we make and, in particular, by reference to which we can recognize when we are failing to attain it. Like many of those concepts which derive from political or social philosophy, equality is what some philosophers have called a 'trouser' word; it is something that is interesting and worth talking about only, or primarily, when it is not there. We were thus led to suggest that a more productive approach to this issue might lie in identifying some of the sources of educational inequality so that we might work to find ways of eradicating them.

For this reason, we went on to examine some possible sources of educational inequalities in the home, in the school system, and in the individual school and classroom. These inequalities we found to be particularly associated with class, race and gender. We then considered the curriculum as a source of inequality in education and concluded that this is the crux of the problem and that little progress is likely to be made towards overcoming inequality in education until we are prepared to engage in a complete rethinking of what we mean by the curriculum and thus of what we see as being the central purposes and principles of education itself. In particular, it was suggested that education should be seen as a process, or a series of processes, of development and the curriculum as the means by which this development is promoted, so that the processes of education rather than its content become the central concerns of educational planning, and educational equality comes to be regarded as equality of access to whatever will promote those forms of development rather than to preplanned and predetermined bodies of knowledge. The equal right to control over one's own life, whatever its context and circumstances, is what is crucial.

In fact, throughout this discussion, two themes seem to have emerged clearly and vividly, two factors that appear to lie at the heart of the issue. These are the related problems, firstly, of establishing appropriate categories for the making of differentiated educational provision and, secondly, of achieving adequate and fair selection procedures for the allocation of pupils to these categories. These are problems which, we have seen, dog all attempts to achieve equality. They can only be avoided if we cease to look for categories and recognize that every individual is different and entitled to be catered for on his own merits. To say this is not to suggest, of course, that it is an easy process; it is to suggest, however, that it may be a more fruitful way of working towards equality than the provision of two or three or any number of types of curriculum or school or class or any other kind of educational offering.

For this kind of approach may make more readily possible the adaptation of the content of education to the individual's needs, interests, and requirements. We have seen some of the inequalities that can result from attempts to fit 'off-the-peg' curricula or programmes to all pupils and we have considered some of the demands that pupils should not have an 'alien' culture imposed upon them. All of this would seem to point to the desirability of individually tailored provision. The paradox of equality in education is that it is only when the educational diet of every child is different from that of every other that we can really hope we are near to achieving it.

CHAPTER 9

IN CONCLUSION — EDUCATION THEORY AND THE TEACHER

The processes we have described and the complex issues we have debated in this book can leave no one in any doubt that the shift that has taken place in educational theory and practice has led to a vast increase in the demands made on the expertise of the teacher, on his or her professional skills and, above all, on his or her professional understanding. We are still a long way from establishing, or even recognizing the need for forms of initial and continuing education of teachers which will ensure that they can develop and maintain both those skills and that understanding. Indeed, current developments in the control of teacher education in the United Kingdom are trending in the opposite direction and taking us further away from the establishment of such forms (DES, 1983c). The need for teaching skills most people can readily recognize; the need for understanding, although in many ways far more vital, is less commonly acknowledged. However, the open school, as we described it earlier, will require 'open' teachers, teachers who have learned to think for themselves and have recognized the importance of doing so in many areas of education beyond the immediate concerns of their own classrooms, teachers who have come to realize that in any case their work in their own classrooms will be enhanced by the wider understanding that a familiarity with educational theory can give them, since only that will enable them to make effectively those day-to-day professional judgements upon which the education of their pupils crucially depends.

We need, then, a more sophisticated concept of educational theory than that view of it as something to be learned in college and applied in schools, and a more subtle model of educational research, if these are to play a productive and supportive role in the work of schools and teachers. It is to a discussion of the inadequacies of much of what has hitherto been offered to teachers under both these headings and to an exploration of what might constitute a more helpful approach to educational theory and research that we turn in this concluding chapter.

Research in education

'For as long as anyone cares to remember, teachers have complained that educational research is an incomprehensible jargon-ridden activity that has little to do with their everyday problems and practices' (Carr, 1982, p.206). Much of it can in fact be described as 'stratospheric', in that there has been a dense layer of clouds above which 'academics' have talked to one another about their theoretical concepts of education and below which teachers have, in almost total isolation, carried on with the practice of it. It has been more like Aristophanes' caricature of Socratic philosophy than philosophy itself, and one is tempted to adapt Herbert Feigl's comment on philosophical activity and say that 'educational research has been the disease of which it should be the cure'.

As a result, teachers have either ignored the results of this kind of research or, worse, have selected and adopted from it those features which reinforced their already held views or prejudices. Since to some extent the latter is what the researchers have been doing anyway, this is probably a very reasonable form of response to the activity. Hence, most major developments in education have been based not on research 'findings' but on one form or other of ideology — whether political or educational.

Thus, major developments like the introduction of comprehensive secondary education, of mixed-ability groupings or of 'informal', progressive methods have been the result of ideological pressure of one kind or another, and the role of research in such developments has been merely to trail behind describing what has already happened and is already there, and offering very little justification of its existence except perhaps at the 'nuts and bolts' level of means and methodology (Kelly, 1982b). Major theories have been developed from political ideologies or from the work of practitioners like A.S. Neill, seldom from anything which might be described as educational research.

Furthermore, some of this research has actually inhibited educational development (Kelly, 1981), in particular by operating with uncritically assumed models of curriculum design and views of education which teachers lack the sophistication to recognize and disentangle and which have often led to the assertion of 'findings' which, although of questionable validity, have nonetheless had a discouraging impact on the work of those many teachers who find it difficult to articulate, or even to clarify for themselves, an appropriate response to them. This kind of situation is, of course, exacerbated when the popular press seizes on such 'findings' as a useful stick with which to engage in the national sport of beating teachers. One need look no further than the work of Bennett on *Teaching Styles and Pupil Progress* (1976) for a classic example of the point which is being made.

Finally, the use of such 'findings' by administrators, who have always taken such research far more seriously than the teachers themselves, has also resulted often in the creation of administrative structures which have inhibited rather than promoted educational development. The creation of a tripartite system of secondary education which we are still a long way from unscrambling is a prime example of this phenomenon. It is perhaps worth noting here that this reflects a view of education essentially taken from an external perspective and it will emerge as a factor of some significance in this chapter that it is only to the outsider that such research has appeared to be important.

It is the contention here that the inadequacies of educational research just listed, and its almost total lack of productive influence on the development of education, have been due in the main to a fundamental, even a monumental, misconception of the nature of both activities — that of education and that of educational research. It is not enough to argue (Verma and Beard, 1981) that it is due to a language or communication gap between researcher and teacher and that all we need to do to put matters right is to close that gap. It is not the jargon of research which is primarily responsible, it is the research models adopted, and Wilfred Carr (1982, p.208) is surely right in saying that 'closing the gap between research and practice depends, not on teachers taking the language of research more seriously, but on researchers taking the language of teachers more seriously'.

This chapter sets out, then, first to expose some of the deficiencies of research models which have been used in attempts to explore educational practice in the past; second, to identify certain fundamental problems which may explain these inadequacies; thirdly, to review certain developments which have occurred in the attempt to improve the effectiveness of educational research; and, finally, to suggest, albeit tentatively, a direction in which to seek a more appropriate and more productive model.

The inadequacies of earlier models

To some extent to criticize traditional models is to cover already well trodden ground, so that it may not be necessary to devote too much space to this. However, some mention needs to be made of the main feature of these approaches for two reasons. First, it is in part an appreciation of the inadequacies of early attempts at research in education which will reveal the principles upon which a more suitable model must be based. And, second, there are still more than residual traces of those traditional models. For they are still to be found in full use, notably, for example, in the obsession of the NFER and other bodies, both within and outside the profession, with performance testing as a major source of data for educational planning and development. Indeed, we have already noted that this concept of educational research continues to be defended by two notable contemporary exponents of it (Verma and Beard, 1981).

There are four major kinds of inadequacy in this approach to research in education to which this chapter will later return but which it will be helpful to signal now as a major theme. The first of these is the inability of such research to cope with questions of *ends*, issues of *value*. The second is the questionable validity of those general 'truths', which seem to be a major preoccupation of such research. The third is a consequence of this, the lack of predictive validity of such research 'findings'. And, fourthly, such research has been, and must be, essentially external to the process of education itself, treating teachers as subjects, or objects, of the research activity rather than as legitimate participants in it.

All of these features are clearly apparent in the earliest and most primitive versions of educational research and of educational theory — that which sees both as parasitic on other disciplines and that which attempts to adopt the hypothetico-deductive positivist approaches of early sociological method.

For the first of these approaches completely fails to recognize the issues it is attempting to explore as educational issues. Instead, they are seen as psychological or sociological issues — again a viewing of educational practice from the outside. Thus, most early research was not educational research at all but was entirely psychological in its orientation. The study of education was equated with the study of psychology and, indeed, education itself was seen as a kind of applied psychology. One needs to look no further than behaviourist psychology and all the 'educational' theory which that has spawned to acknowledge the truth of this. Nor does one need to look further than the current scene in the field of Special Education to recognize that this is not yet a phenomenon of the past. Yet such an approach to education is clearly one-sided; it lacks any kind of balance of perspectives and any kind of base for such a balance; in particular it fails to embrace the value dimension of educational activity; and, what is least forgivable, it has often got, and continues often to get, things wrong. Yet major administrative decisions have often been made on the basis of this kind of research and the 'theory' it has generated, such as the introduction of tripartism to which reference has already been made, on the basis of research 'findings' on the nature and measurement of intelligence. And — again especially notable in the field of Special Education — such administrative decisions continue to be made on the same kinds of basis. One of the major reasons, then, for the past inadequacies of much educational theory and research has been the insistence on exploring educational practice as if education were a brand of psychology or sociology or philosophy.

The problems of the positivist, hypothetico-deductive model highlight the other two major inadequacies of traditional approaches — the search for generalizations and the desire to use these as a basis for predictions. For that approach was only able to achieve such generalizations by creating an interlinking framework for them — along the lines of what was, mistakenly, assumed to be the methodology of the natural sciences — and that framework was found in history. History became the interconnecting rationale for this kind of positivist assertion about society. The study of the past was seen as leading to the attainment of certain general 'laws', the identification of broad sweeping trends, which would provide a basis for predicting the future — a kind of retrospective futurology. It was this that led to the offering of definitions of sociology as history with the hard work left out and of history as sociology with the brains left out. This kind of 'historicism' was rightly castigated by Popper (1957) as not only politically dangerous but as also methodologically unsound. For unless one can accept that kind of metaphysical approach to history — and there is not, nor could there be, of course any evidence for doing so — the problems of verification for what are essentially *a priori* utterances, assertions not based on experience or evidence of any kind, are insuperable. Furthermore, if one also accepts Popper's view of scientific method as being concerned with falsification rather than verification, the difficulties of this approach to research in the social sciences are further compounded. For there is no general sociological assertion to which exception cannot readily be found. Yet such broad general 'truths' are still sought by some researchers in education.

The use of other models culled from the social sciences also bring problems for the researcher in education. In the first place, different social sciences have different viewpoints and none of these is that of education (Loukes *et al.*, 1983). Secondly, the data produced are quantitative rather than qualitative; the value issues continue to be elusive. Thirdly, even this quantitative material creates difficulties within education. What is the validity of statistical data? 'Statistics', someone once said, 'are like bikinis. What they reveal is suggestive but they conceal what is vital' (I believe it was Marx — Groucho Marx). Their use also implies that the truth is to be found in consensus or majority views. Yet Galileo would not be the only one with good reason to challenge that. They thus have no prescriptive significance and yet they are constantly being offered to us as if they did, as if they constituted exactly those generalized 'laws' from which these desired predictions can be deduced. This is the naturalistic fallacy in its most obvious manifestation — an illicit process, yet one which we can constantly see being used and one which this kind of research pushes us into. For what is the point of collecting such 'information' if we are not to do something with it. It is this which constituted a major feature of the *Aims into Practice in the Primary School* project (Ashton *et al.*, 1975) whose assumption that the way to find out what the aims of primary education *ought* to be was to conduct a survey to find out what they *are* was a perfect example of this erroneous methodology and was rightly castigated by Dearden (1976) on those grounds. At least that team was honest in stating what it was doing. Many other researchers merely offer us the data and invite us to make the illicit process from 'is' to 'ought' for ourselves. What other purpose could they have? Yet, as has been said of the NFER study of mixed-ability teaching (Kelly, 1982b, p.299), 'it may be reassuring to a teacher who is unhappy, for example, about the increased preparation or marking that his mixed-ability class necessitates to know that 32% of his colleagues share his unhappiness: but it is not evident that this will help him to cope with it'.

Lastly, one must also note the converse problem, which may indeed be more serious. To go from the particular to the general is serious enough but when we move on this same kind of basis from the general to the particular we find ourselves at the source of all of those problems of 'labelling' which we discussed in detail in Chapter 2. General assertions about less able pupils, about members of ethnic minorities, about children of one-parent families and so on will lead most of us to particular assumptions about individual representatives of such groups we may find ourselves responsible for.

Thus the issue of what might give validity to general 'truths' asserted on the basis of such forms of research, and, in particular, that of the validity of any prescriptions these might lead us to, continue to be central problems and crucial weaknesses in these approaches to educational research. So too does the fact/value, means/ends problem to which we must now devote some additional attention.

The problem of values

Some attempts to study education — and society — have merely ignored the value issues, but if this is how one attempts to study education one must end up not studying education at all, since the value element is of its essence. Hence others have attempted to deal with the problem by separating the value element out, by distinguishing fact from value, means from ends, for example by researching into the effectiveness of teaching or instruction, and take the values, the goals as already given or as at least outside the research specification. It is this approach which is at the root of the NFER's obsession with performance testing. We might also note here the honesty of those who, like Bloom (1956) have declared themselves and their offerings to be 'value-neutral' and have suggested that, if the 'findings' of all such research were offered in this form, we could take it or leave it, according to whether or not it fitted our ends, our goals, our value positions.

There are, however, two serious difficulties with this approach. The first is that it offers us no help at all with decisions about ends, goals, values. It thus leaves open the questions of how you research them, what kinds of evidence you might offer those who, like teachers, cannot ignore this dimension of education, in other words how you engage in research into education, rather than into teaching or instruction. (To suggest that we should look to the philosopher for guidance over ends and to social science for advice on means is naive in the extreme and misconceives not only the nature of education but also that of philosophy.)

Secondly, this approach fails to recognize that the fact/value distinction is not tenable at any level. Whether you deliberately choose to ignore ends or merely forget them (because they do not fit your scheme or because they complicate your life and work or because they do not interest you or for whatever reason), they will be implicit in your research approach since that must make assumptions about values, ends, aims, principles — assumptions which remain implicit and unquestioned because they are outside the research specification so that the research methodology cannot handle them. There is no doubt, for example, what the NFER view of education is. All researchers approach their task with their own, unexamined and thus unchallenged, assumptions about what education is, about what knowledge is and which bits of it are of most importance, and thus, as we saw in Chapter 7, about what curriculum is. All, then, have their own categories into which all data must be fitted or else rejected as irrelevant. These assumptions, these categories, these underlying values are not only unrecognized and unacknowledged, so that they are consequently unexamined and unquestioned; they are also all-pervasive. For they determine the selection of the subject or focus of the research; they are reflected in the language in which both the questions and the findings are expressed; they underlie decisions about the questions to be asked; they condition the selection of data from the mass available, restricting that selection to those data which fit the categories adopted; they form the basis for the interpretation of those data and the conclusions drawn; and they are, of course, as a result, the ultimate explanation of the prescriptions which are based on, suggested by or implied in such conclusions.

Also the very research itself has an unavoidable prescriptive force, in that not only does it invite responses from the teachers and others who are the objects or subjects of the study framed in terms of the categories and values assumed by the researchers (this being a result not only of the framing and wording of the questions but also of the authority which teachers tend to see as invested in research workers), it also offers those categories and values as desirable and thus encourages a similarly uncritical acceptance of its assumptions. It thus imposes these not only on the teachers who are studied as part of the research but also on all who read its 'findings' with a less than critical eye. Again, this is especially true when they receive those 'findings' in the distorted version offered by the popular press. It is for this reason that this kind of research is not merely unhelpful and unproductive; its effects are often negative and undermining of teachers' work (Kelly, 1981).

The conclusion of this argument would seem to be that that value dimension which is crucial to education must elude and, indeed, delude all attempts to study it 'scientifically'. Teaching and instruction may well be 'scientific' activities which can be studied and researched 'scientifically'. Education, however, can never be an activity of this kind. It can, therefore, never be studied by methods which seek to ignore its value dimension and to produce 'scientific' generalizations as a basis for 'scientific' predictions. Education is not a science; it is an art. And it must be researched and evaluated as such.

The four major features of those attempts at 'scientific' research in education, then, which constitute the main weaknesses of this approach are its failure to take proper account of the value dimension, its search for universal 'truths', its desire to make predictions and its consequent failure to recognize the teacher's role in an activity which thus remains essentially external to the practice of education. These must be major considerations in the attempt to discover a more suitable and more productive model for research in this field.

The move towards qualitative research in education

The reaction to the inadequacies of this traditional approach to research in education, and indeed in the social sciences generally, has been a move away from quantitative studies towards a recognition that no research in education can be productive or helpful at the level of classroom practice unless it attempts also to be qualitative, to make some assessment of the value of what is going on. This has been associated (inevitably in view of the points made earlier in this chapter) with a parallel recognition that the focus of such research must narrow, that broad sweeping generalizations are neither helpful nor valid and that a much more piecemeal approach must be accepted and adopted. It will be the contention of these final sections that this shift has not yet gone far enough.

Several models of such research can be identified in the approaches adopted by researchers in education in recent years, in particular the use of participant-observer techniques, studies of classroom interaction and the production of case studies.

The classic examples of the use of participant-observer techniques are of course the studies of Hargreaves (1967), Lacey (1970) and Keddie (1971), to which we have referred earlier, although some of the recent work of the ORACLE project has used these kinds of technique too (Galton, 1983). Although clearly a step in the right direction, all of the inadequacies we noted earlier are apparent here too. The value positions adopted by the observer continue to be a major feature of the research and have not always been made explicit. And most studies of this kind have been fundamentally external, even though a prime purpose of this kind of approach has been to avoid the difficulties inherent in the role of outsider. For there has been little direct involvement of other teachers in the drawing up of the research specification or the analysis of results, the 'authority' of the researcher has continued to be something of a barrier even in this context and on occasion a result of this has been that, like much of that research which was being criticized earlier, the effects of such research have been negative and even damaging to the teachers involved rather than productive of solutions to problems identified. Finally, such studies have inevitably been descriptive of particular situations, but that has not prevented them either from making or at least from inviting others to make generalizations as a basis for prediction or prescription. A key question, however, must be that of how generalizable such local findings can be.

Similar criticisms can be levelled at most classroom interaction studies, some of which we considered in detail in Chapter 1. Again these cannot cope with the value issues. The use of this model to explore, for example, levels of match and mismatch between teachers' intentions and the actualities of pupils' experiences (Bennett *et al.*, 1984) offers no scope for research into these intentions themselves and thus is focusing on only a part — and that probably the least important part — of the activity. Again the attempt is to be value-neutral, but again the results reinforce the claims made earlier in this chapter that in education such a stance is untenable. The values of the researcher are there, usually again unrecognized, unacknowledged and thus unquestioned, in the implicit assumptions of the research focus, in the underlying views about knowledge, about education, about curriculum (e.g. the linear, objectives-based, subject-specific assumptions of the Bennett studies), in the kinds of question put to the teachers, in the selection of significant data from what is observed and so on. Again too there is little or no involvement of teachers in planning the research strategies or the research specification so that again what emerges is a researcher's external view of what is going on, with the result that the fundamental mismatch is not so much between teachers' intentions and pupils' experiences as between teachers' intentions and the limited understanding of them demonstrated by the researchers. This in turn explains why yet again the results of such research are often largely negative, identifying problems but not offering solutions, discouraging teachers from going beyond the often narrow limits set by the researchers' view of their classroom activity. Finally, such research continues to be in essence positivist, descriptive, 'mechanistic' (Holt, 1982) and again raises questions concerning its generalizability and the propriety of using it as a base for any kind of prescription.

The production of case studies would seem *prima facie* to be a step forward from these techniques. For, to begin with, this approach seems to accept the particularity and the peculiarity of individual situations and to content itself with describing those situations without making any attempt to generalize. Much depends, however, on how case studies are envisaged. Most case studies have hitherto been produced by outside observers and have thus revealed all the problems which have just been identified in participant-observer techniques and classroom interaction studies. Rob Walker's 'three good reasons for not doing case-study research' (1983, p.156) reflect the criticisms just offered but, as we shall hope to show later, they apply only to this external form of case study. For his first criticism is that they represent an intervention, often uncontrolled, into the lives of others and that often there is a resultant conflict of values. This will only happen if there is little or no direct involvement of the teachers themselves in the research design and in its execution. Similarly, his suggestion that, although this approach makes it appear that a lot of power is being handed to the subjects of the research, in fact it is the power of the researcher that is being increased because the subjects are in less of a position to withhold commitment to the research is also one which only applies if this dichotomy between researcher and teacher is accepted. Secondly, he argues that they are essentially conservative in that they 'embalm what is established practice simply by describing it' (*op. cit.*, p.163). This again will only be true if they are produced by outsiders. Case studies produced by the teachers themselves, albeit with help and guidance, can only lead to their own further development, as we hope to show. His final criticism is that they give a distorted view of the world, that they 'tell *a* truth but not *the* truth'. This is surely true, but it can only be seen as a criticism if one's expectations of research in education are that it will give rise to generalizations as a basis for making predictions or prescriptions.

Towards a genuine form of qualitative research

Such attempts, then, at establishing models for qualitative research in education, although they have taken us some way forward, are still either essentially positivist and 'mechanistic' or else they continue to hanker after similar kinds of 'objective findings'. In the light of those earlier discussions, we shall now try to identify what might be the fundamental features of a piece of research we might genuinely describe as qualitative.

The first point that needs to be made is that merely to call a piece of research 'qualitative' does not in itself change its fundamentals. The term has been much misused by researchers in recent times and it is important to be sure it does not lose all meaning. What might be the fundamentals of such meaning?

The first of these must be a serious concern with values. The very notion of quality entails a recognition of the value issues and thus of the need for explicit value specifications, a clear delineation of the value assumptions made — about education, about knowledge, about curriculum. Indeed, it is dishonest of any research in education to conceal these. This suggests in turn that it is time we got back to seeing education as an art rather than as a science — or at least its study as more akin to the Humanities than to the sciences. It was the 'scientific' approach to educational research which smothered the ideas of Dewey in the first half of this century. It will continue to have this effect unless we rid ourselves of it and of all its attendant assumptions.

Next, if we have been right to argue that the lack of teacher involvement in research has been a major source of weakness and a major reason for its lack of validity, then a genuine form of qualitative research must involve teachers in defining the research problems, implementing the research itself and evaluating the data; in fact teachers must be fully and centrally involved at every stage and level. And the logic of that points to the notion of the teacher as researcher, to the development of research communities in schools or of schools as research communities. It also, of course, requires that the teacher develop the kind of theoretical understanding of education which this book has been designed to promote.

This suggests in turn that such research must be school-based and thus largely piecemeal. It will no longer be a search for universal truths. For much research is not about universals; it is about specifics. It is not a search for *the* truth, but a whole series of particular truths. It involves 'a new mode of connection between theory and practice' (Foucault, 1977, p.12; Nixon, 1981, p.31). For 'intellectuals have become accustomed to working not in the character of the "universal", the "exemplary", the "just and true for all", but in specific sectors, at precise points where they are situated either by professional conditions of work or their conditions of life' (ibid.). It is this development that education must come to terms with.

These considerations bring us towards a concept of 'action research' of the kind defined by John Elliott (1981, p.1) as 'the study of a social situation with a view to improving the quality of action within it'. Such a definition is of course or ought to be a truism since that is surely the function that all research would claim to fulfil. It thus in itself highlights the inadequacies of earlier approaches as well as pointing the way towards a more productive model. It also, however, brings us to a concept which looks more and more like evaluation and less and less like research of the traditional kind. For we are essentially speaking of the researching of individual situations by those who are themselves active within them for the purpose of improving the quality of their activity; and we are essentially speaking of piecemeal evaluation for individual development rather than for collective assurance.

Some implications of the view of research as evaluation

A major question which this view raises centres on the role of the researcher, the external evaluator in this kind of process, and indeed on the question of whether there is a role for such a person. (It will be remembered that the late Laurence Stenhouse (1975) felt there was not.) For if all research is personal evaluation, at the level of the individual teacher or the individual school, if this evaluation is to be school-based, if education is to be seen as a creative art rather than as an applied science, what kind of objective data can anyone hope to produce from the outside?

This is certainly the kind of line taken by Michael Armstrong (1983) who offers the word 'enquiry' as a better term for this activity than 'research' and suggests that it must be 'grounded in the experience of teaching, and in particular in that practice of sustained observation which is inseparable from good teaching' (*op.cit.*, p.5). He goes on to argue that 'the method by which we study learning is also the method by which the objects, or rather the subjects, of our study learn ... the quality of observation ... which is required of us as teachers to understand our pupils' learning is in essence the same quality which is displayed by those pupils themselves in the best of their learning' (*ibid.*).

This may, however, suggest the kind of role that exists for the outsider — as a consultant whose relationship with the teacher-researcher is analogous to that of the teacher in relation to his or her pupils — a matter of the timing and the form of suitable and appropriate interventions. For to suggest that all research must be personal and thus totally subjective must be to oversimplify. A more sophisticated answer is needed. As Elliot Eisner (1979, p.12) has said, 'qualitative methods and artistic or humanistic assumptions complement quantitative and scientific ones to the benefit of both'.

There is then a continuing need for some 'factual' or 'mechanistic' research, but, as Maurice Holt (1982) has suggested, we need rather less of it than we have had, we must appreciate that it is not the only kind of research we need and we must recognize the problems which it trails with it. For it can have that inhibiting effect on teachers' work we have already noted if it is misunderstood. It can only be descriptive and cannot *of itself* give rise to prescriptions, although its tendency to encourage these must also be recognized. Its purpose must be seen as to assist individuals towards their own prescriptions and to this end it must endeavour to be 'holistic' and to avoid making its own selection of data according to its own value presuppositions. Some of the recent research in the field of Early Childhood Education has exemplified the possibilities of this kind of approach, since it has attempted merely to describe what is going on in order to provide teachers with information upon which their own judgements might be based. The 'findings' of such research must also be highly tentative. We must 'distinguish in our research between the context of discovery or invention and the context of verification or justification' (Walker, 1973, p.66; Holt, 1982, p.274). This necessitates in turn putting into a proper context all the press publicity given to 'research findings' of the more apparently sensational kind. As Maurice Holt suggests, this might begin with a self-denying ordinance on the part of those responsible for such research, although it would be reassuring first to be convinced that they themselves recognized the tentative nature of such 'findings'.

There is also clearly a need for 'conceptual' research (Holt, 1982). 'What is the nature of this school subject?... What do HMI mean by the term "personal and social development"? What is the significance and value of "pastoral care"? What does the Schools Council mean by "skills" in Working Paper 70?... What do administrators and politicians mean when they talk of encouraging "the link between school and work"?' (op.cit., p.272) and so on. This is what he calls a 'watchdog role' (ibid.) and it is a most important role. For nothing has bedevilled education theory more seriously in recent years than conceptual confusions. And teachers do need help in clarifying the concepts with which they undertake both their planning and their evaluation. However, again, this kind of research must be context-specific rather than the kind of navel-contemplating activity that has hitherto been engaged in by many 'philosophers of education'. For essentially its concern must be with meaning and as G. E. Moore pointed out a long time ago, 'meaning is use', or, to use Wittgenstein's analogy, to consider meaning out of context is like looking at an engine idling.

This has been the point and purpose (if a commercial break may be permitted) of some recent collections of case studies (Kelly, 1975; 1983; 1984). We suggested earlier that the criticisms offered by Rob Walker (1983) of this approach to educational research were valid in relation only to case studies produced by outsiders observing and recording the work of others. They do not apply to case studies written by teachers themselves of their own work. For they then become part of the process of evaluating their own work. They are offered to others with no deliberate sense of prescription, with no attempt at generalization, but as possibly interesting examples of particular approaches to particular problems. It is interesting that every teacher who has written such a case study has found it necessary in doing so to make a clear declaration of his or her value positions. And everyone too has found it necessary to place the description of their work in a clearly delineated theoretical perspective. It is this which constitutes what we believe to be the right kind of relationship between the theory and the practice of education.

It is at this point that the role of the outsider begins to become clear. The outsider is not there to describe nor to evaluate — except possibly in the context of some form of dialogue. The outsider's task becomes one of assisting in the articulation of the work. It is essentially the role of 'midwife' to the birth of the case study. It involves at the simplest level helping with the expression of the ideas. At the other end of the scale, it involves helping the individual to sort out the theoretical perspectives and especially to clarify the concepts involved. It is thus conceptual rather than empirical. It is essentially analogous to the role of teacher in relation to pupil as Michael Armstrong suggests. It is perhaps better expressed as an analogy with the role of teacher-educator to student-teacher. It is thus a role which HMI, local authority inspectors and advisers are assumed to play; it is unfortunately one they cannot always be seen to fulfil.

It is perhaps worth adding that this kind of approach may well generate a number of different research models, each tailored to a particular context. For each area of research should be tackled in relation to its own demands and its own peculiarities. We need some notion of a 'tool-kit' of research instruments along the lines currently being developed by some social scientists. For it will become necessary in each particular case to identify and frame the specific questions to be addressed, to delineate clearly the value specifications, to consider the relation of this specific area of enquiry to more general considerations, both 'conceptual' and 'mechanistic', and then in the light of those considerations to devise a specifically appropriate form of research strategy. Such a process is unlikely to be productive of general 'truths', but it is likely to improve the quality of educational practice and it may lead to the development of all forms of research/evaluation in parallel, in a harmony that has hitherto been conspicuously absent.

Fundamentally, therefore, this approach sets out to assist teachers to evaluate their own work in order to develop it. It is based on the belief that development in education and curriculum comes from a critical evaluation of what is already going on in one's own school and classroom. It is an attempt to improve the quality of education *from the inside*. It argues that school-based curriculum development implies school-based curriculum evaluation and that this in turn implies school-based curriculum research. It involves a new concept of research and a new concept of evaluation. It entails the recognition of the teacher's role as researcher and of that of the outside 'expert' as consultant. It is a process which, if properly handled, will also generate those broader theoretical perspectives which traditional research has sought after in vain. But it will generate such perspectives in a manner complementary to those individual insights which are its main focus and concern. And it is that which will give these broad perspectives any validity they have.

Summary and conclusions

We have tried in this concluding chapter to show some of the inadequacies of traditional approaches to research in education, emphasizing in particular its failure to take proper account of the value dimension, the absence of a proper role for the teacher in the activity, and its futile and mistaken search for 'general truths' which might form the basis of prediction or prescription. We have further tried to show that these fundamental inadequacies are also reflected in many of the recent attempts to establish more sophisticated research models.

We then went on to argue that a logical consequence of those inadequacies is the need for a model of research which is primarily specific rather than universal, individual rather than general, tentative rather than dogmatic, and a task for the teacher rather than the outside/external researcher. The conclusion of this was that it is to evaluation strategies we must look for educational developments rather than to research as such.

Although this is assumed by some to imply that there is no role for the researcher as such in educational development, we went on to suggest that there may be a role but that that role must be seen as essentially subsidiary to that of the teachers themselves — a consultancy rather than a research role, the role of midwife rather than that of parent. Thus a reconceptualization of the role of such research activity in education must be undertaken, one result of which must be a reduction in the scope and sphere of its assumed influence, but, associated with that, a corresponding extension of the scope and sphere of its real influence.

There are clearly implications here for the relationship between theory and practice in education, and, consequently also for the education of teachers, at both initial and in-service levels, indeed for the study of education generally. In particular, there are important implications for the nature of research degrees in Education, the kinds of individual research activity it is appropriate to encourage teachers to undertake. For if these do not enhance and extend their own professional insight, understanding and even performance, then, like some of the traditional courses of Education Theory at the initial level, one must question their point and validity. Conversely, if they become totally personal and anecdotal, they will be equally unsatisfactory. A proper marrying of theory and practice both in teacher education and in educational research is long overdue.

If schooling is seen as a process of instructing pupils in those skills and bodies of knowledge determined by society to be necessary (or, worse, merely assumed by society to be necessary), then not only does external control and external evaluation of such schooling become possible, so too does external research along traditional lines and on the old models. For the value specification is clear, if unchallenged, and the concern is with identifying the most efficient means to the attainment of ends which are not seen as problematic and which remain beyond the scope of the evaluation and the research specifications. This is the explanation of those traditional models we have discussed, and this view of schooling is still prevalent among those who view it from the outside. (If this model of schooling comes to be widely adopted, incidentally, research will soon show that it can be better done by computers, as ultimately the research itself will be.)

If, however, one clings to a concept of education as a form of schooling which goes far beyond this, which embraces other, more subtle forms of development and whose underlying values and ends must always be seen as problematic and as subject to constant review and attention, then such external control, such external evaluation and such external research becomes much more difficult and even impossible to attain. For that form of education will always be much more elusive. It will not only elude the politicians, it will also continue to elude the researcher. It will thus go by default if we permit it consequentially, because of the pressures of the politicians reinforced by the assumptions and the 'findings' of the researchers, to elude us as teachers. We must resist the temptation, simply because it is elusive and even controversial, to opt out of it and settle for more easily identifiable and thus measurable and quantifiable goals.

Research and, indeed, much educational theory have hitherto contributed little to our understanding and less to our practice of this form of education. In fact, in a number of ways they have restricted and inhibited it. Unless we develop a new research model, and a new concept of educational theory, this process will continue. That new model must be something like the individual, context-specific model we have endeavoured to describe. In our attempts to develop it, we will find it more helpful to explore studies of evaluation than research in education.

Education theory, then, is not something to be learned and applied. As we said in our Introduction, we need a far more sophisticated model than that of the relationship between the theory and practice of education. If this book has led teachers and student teachers even one step towards the achievement of, or even an appreciation of the need for, such a model, its major purpose will have been attained.

BIBLIOGRAPHY

Adams, R.S. and Biddle, D.J. (1970) *Realities of Teaching*, Holt, Rinehart & Winston, New York

Adelman, C. and Walker, R. (1975) *Developing pictures for other names*. Action Research and Case Study. In G. Chanan and S. Delamont (eds) *op. cit.*

Adorno, T. W., Frenkel-Brunswik, E., Levinson, D. J. and Sanford, R. N. (1960) *The Authoritarian Personality*, Harper & Row, New York

Allport, G. (1937) *Personality, a Psychological Interpretation*, Holt, New York

Anderson, H. H. and Brewer, H. M. (1945) Studies of Teachers' Classroom Personalities. Applied Psychological Monographs of the American Association for Applied Psychology, Stanford University Press

Archambault, R. D. (ed) (1965) *Philosophical Analysis and Education*, Routledge and Kegan Paul, London

Argyle, M. (1969) *The Psychology of Interpersonal Behaviour*, Penguin, Harmondsworth

Aristotle, *Politics*

Armstrong, M. (1983) The Story of Stories — An Enquiry into Children's Narrative Thought, *Curriculum* 4, 2

Asch, S. E. (1946) Forming impressions of personality, *Journal of Abnormal and Social Psychology*

Ashton, P. (1975) *The Aims of Primary Education: A study of teachers' opinions*, Macmillan, London

Ashton, P. T. (1975) Cross-cultural Piagetian research: an experimental perspective, *Harvard Educational Review*, Vol 45

Ausubel, D. P. (1968) *Educational Psychology — A Cognitive View*, Holt, Rinehart & Winston, New York

Ausubel, D. D. and Robinson, F. G. (1969) *School Learning*, Holt, Rinehart & Winston, New York

Bailey, C. (1975) Knowledge of others and concern for others. In J. Elliott and R. Pring (eds) *op. cit.*

Ball, C. and Ball, M. (1973) *Education for a Change*, Penguin, Harmondsworth

Bandura, A. and Walters, R. H. (1970) *Social Learning and Personality Development*, Holt, Rinehart & Winston, New York

Banks, O. (1976) *The Sociology of Education* (3rd edn), Batsford, London

Bantock, G. H. Towards a theory of popular education. In R. Hooper (ed) *op. cit.*

Barker-Lunn, J. C. (1970) *Streaming in the Primary School,* NFER, Slough

Barnes, D. and Todd, F. (1977) *Communication and Learning in Small Groups,* Routledge and Kegan Paul, London

Barnes, D. *et al* (1971) *Language, the Learner and the School,* Penguin, Harmondsworth

Barnes, D. *et al* (1976) *From Communication to Curriculum,* Penguin, Harmondsworth

Barton, L. and Tomlinson, S. (eds) (1981) *Special Education: policy, practice and social issues,* Harper & Row, London

Becker, H. S. (1971) Social class variations in the teacher-pupil relationship. In B. Cosin *et al.* (eds) *op. cit.*

Becker, H. S. (1971) Personal change in adult life *(Sociometry 1964).* Reprinted in B. Cosin *et al.* (eds) *op. cit.*

Benn, S. I. and Peters, R. S. (1959) *Social Principles and the Democratic State,* Allen & Unwin, London

Bennett, S. N. (1976) *Teaching Styles and Pupil Progress,* Open Books, London

Bennett, N., Desforges, C., Cockburn, A. and Wilkinson, B. (1984) *The Quality of Pupil Learning Experiences,* Lawrence Erlbaum Associates, London

Bereiter, C. and Engelmann, D. (1966) *Teaching Disadvantaged Children in the Pre-School,* Prentice-Hall, New Jersey

Berger, P. L. and Luckman, T. (1967) *The Social Construction of Reality,* Penguin, London

Berlyne, D. E. (1960) *Conflict, Arousal and Curiosity,* McGraw Hill, New York

Bernstein, B. (1967) Open schools, Open society? *New Society,* 14 September, 1967

Bernstein, B. (1971) *Class, Codes and Control,* Vol. 1. Routledge and Kegan Paul, London

Bernstein, B. (1973) *Class, Codes and Control,* Vol. 2. Routledge and Kegan Paul, London

Bernstein, B. (1972) *Education cannot compensate for society.* In S. Cashdan (ed) Routledge and Kegan Paul, London

Bernstein, B. and Henderson, D. (1969) Social class differences in the relevance of language to socialization, *Sociology*

Bierley, M. (1983) The development of a record-keeping system. In G. M. Blenkin and A. V. Kelly (eds), *op. cit.*

Blank, M. and Solomon, F. (1968) A tutorial language programme to develop abstract thinking in socially disadvantaged school children, *Child Development*

Blenkin, G. M. and Kelly, A. V. (1981) *The Primary Curriculum,* Harper & Row, London

Blenkin, G. M. and Kelly, A. V. (eds) (1983) *The Primary Curriculum in Action,* Harper & Row, London

Bloom, B.S. (ed) (1956) *A Taxonomy of Objectives,*Vol. 1. Longman, London

Bloom, B.S. (ed) (1964) *A Taxonomy of Objectives,* Vol. 2. Longman, London

Bloom, B. S. (1971) *Mastery learning and its implications for curriculum development.* In M. Golby *et al* (eds) *op.cit.*

Bloom, B. S. (1976) *Human Characteristics and School Learning,* McGraw Hill, New York

Bloom, B. S. (1978) New views of the learner, *Education for Leadership*

Britton, J. (1970) *Language and Learning,* Penguin, Harmondsworth

Britton, J. N. (1978) *The Development of Writing Abilities 11-18,* Macmillan

Bronfenbrenner, V. (1961) The Changing American Child, *Journal of Social Issues*

Broadfoot, P. (1982) The pros and cons of profiles, *Forum* Vol. 24. No. 3

Brook, M. (1980) The mother tongue issue in Britain, *Journal of Social Education,* Vol. 1

Brown, G. and Desforges, C. (1977) Piagetian psychology and education: time for revision, *British Journal of Educational Psychology*

Brown, G. and Desforges, C. (1979) *Piaget's Theory: A Psychological Critique,* Routledge and Kegan Paul, London

Brown, R. and Bellugi, V. (1964) Three processes in the child's acquisition of syntax, *Harvard Educational Review*

Bruner, J. *et al* (1961) The Act of Discovery, *Harvard Educational Review*

Bruner, J. *et al* (1960) *The Process of Education,* Vintage Books, New York

Bruner, J. *et al* (1966) *Studies in Cognitive Growth,* Wiley, New York

Bruner, J. (1973) Organization of early skilled action, *Child Development,* Vol. 44

Bruner, J. (1975) The ontogenesis of speech acts, *Journal of Child Language,* Vol. 19

Bruner, J. (1979) From communication to language — a psychological perspective *(Cognition,* Vol. 3) Reprinted in V. Lee (ed) *op. cit.*

Bull, N. (1969) *Moral Judgment from Childhood to Adolescence,* Routledge and Kegan Paul, London

Burgess, T. and Adams, E. (1980) *Outcomes of Education,* Macmillan, London

Burns, R. (1982) *Self-Concept Development Education,* Holt, Rinehart & Winston, Eastbourne

Burstall, C. (1967) French in Primary Schools: Research Project, *New Research in Education*

Burt, C. (1955) The evidence for the concept of intelligence, *British Journal of Educational Psychology*

Burt, C. (1966) The genetic determination of differences in intelligence, *British Journal of Psychology*

Carr, W. (1982) What is Educational Research? *Journal of Curriculum Studies*, 14, 2

Cashdan, A. and Grugeon, E. (1972) *Language in Education*, Routledge and Kegan Paul, London

Cashdan, A. and Whitehead, Z. (1971) *Personality Theory and Learning*, Routledge and Kegan Paul, London

Cazden, C. B. (1968) *Environmental assistance to the child's acquisition of grammar*, referred to by D. I. Slobin in N. S. Endler, *et al* (eds) *op. cit.*

Chanan, G. and Delamont, S. (eds) (1975) *Frontiers of Classroom Research*, NFER, Slough

Chazan, M. (1982) *Language and learning: intervention and the child at home.* In A. Davies (ed) *op. cit.*

Cheshire, J. (1982) Dialect features and linguistic conflict in schools, *Educational Review*, Vol. 34.

Cheshire, J. (1984) *Indigenous non-standard English varieties and education.* In P. Trudgill (ed) *op. cit.*

Child, D. (1981) *Psychology and the Teacher* (3rd edn) Holt, Rinehart & Winston, Eastbourne

Chomsky, N. (1959) Review of Skinner's 'Verbal Behaviour', *Language*

Chulliat, R. and Oleron, P. (1968) The role of language in transposition tasks, referred to in D. Lawton (1968b) *op. cit.*

Cicourel, A. V. and Kitsuse, J. (1971) The social organization of the High School and deviant adolescent careers. In B. Cosin *et al* (eds) *op. cit.*

Clark, E. V. (1978) *Awareness of language: some evidence of what children say and do.* In A. Sinclair *et al* (eds) *op. cit.*

Clarricoates, K. (1978) Dinosaurs in the classroom, *Womens Studies International Quarterly*, Vol. 1. No. 4.

Coard, B. (1971) *How the West Indian Child is Made Educationally Subnormal in the British School System.* New Beacon Books

Coopersmith, B. (1967) *The Antecedents of Self-Esteem*, Freemantle

Cosin, B. *et al* (eds) (1971) *School and Society*, Routledge and Kegan Paul, with Oxford University Press

Coulthard, M. (1969) A discussion of restricted and elaborated codes, *Educational Review*

Cronbach, L. (1963) Course improvement through education, *Teachers' College Record*

Cox, C.B. and Dyson, A.E. (eds) (1969a) *Fight For Education: A Black Paper*, Critical Quarterly Society, Manchester

Cox, C.B. and Dyson, A.E. (eds) (1969b) *Black Paper Two: The Crisis in Education*, Critical Quarterly Society, Manchester

Crosland, A. (1961) Some thoughts on English education, *Encounter*

Dahrendorf, R. (1962) On the origin of social inequality. In P. Laslett and W. G. Runciman (eds) Philosophy, Politics and Society, 2nd series, Blackwell, Oxford

Davies, A. (1982) *Language and Learning in Home and School,* SSRC with Heinemann, London

Dearden, R. F. (1968) *Philosophy of Primary Education,* Routledge and Kegan Paul, London

Dearden, R.F. (1976) *Problems in Primary Education,* Routledge and Kegan Paul, London

Degenhardt, M.A. (1976) Creativity. In D. I. Lloyd (ed) Philosophy and the Teachers, Routledge and Kegan Paul, London

Delamont, S. (1976a) *Interaction in the Classroom,* Methuen, London

Delamont, S. (1976b) *Beyond Flanders' fields: the relationship of subject matter and individuality to classroom style.* In M. Stubbs and S. Delamont (eds) *op. cit.*

Delamont, S. (1980) *Sex Roles and the School,* Methuen, London

Deutsch, M. (1949) An experimental study of the effects of cooperation and competition upon group processes, *Human Relations,* Vol. 2.

Dewey, J. (1916) *Democracy and Education,* Macmillan, New York

Donachy, W. (1976) Parent participation in pre-school education, *British Journal of Educational Psychology*

Donaldson, M. (1978) *Children's Minds,* Fontana, London

Donaldson, M. (1982) Conservation: what is the question? *British Journal of Psychology,* Vol. 73

Donaldson, M., Grieve, R. and Pratt, C. (eds) (1983) *Early Childhood Development Education,* Blackwell, Oxford

Downey, M. E. (1977) *Interpersonal Judgments in Education,* Harper & Row, London

Downey, M. E. and Kelly, A. V. (1978) *Moral Education: theory and practice,* Harper & Row, London

Duckworth, E. (1979) Either we're too early and they can't learn it or we're too late and they know it already: the dilemma of applying Piaget, *Harvard Review,* Vol. 49

Dumont, R. V. and Wax, L. M. (1971) Cherokee School Society and the Intercultural Classroom. In B. Cosin *et al* (eds) *op. cit.*

Dunham, J. (1964) Appropriate Leadership Patterns, *Educational Research*

Dweck, C. (1980) Referred to in M. Stanworth *op. cit.*

Edwards, A. D. and Furlong, V. J. (1978) *The Language of Teaching,* Heinemann, London

Edwards, G. (1983) *Processes in the Secondary School: MACOS and Beyond.* In G. M. Blenkin and A. V. Kelly (eds) *op. cit.*

Edwards, V. (1983) *Language in Multicultural Classrooms*, Batsford, London

Egan, K. (1983) Children's path from reality to fantasy: contrary thoughts about curriculum foundations, *Journal of Curriculum Studies*

Eisner, E. (1979) The contribution of painting to children's cognitive development, *Journal of Curriculum Studies*

Eisner, E. (1979) *The Educational Imagination: On the Design and Education of School Programmes*, Macmillan, New York

Eisner, E. (1982) *Curriculum and Cognition*, Longman, New York and London

Elliott, J. (1981) *Action Research: A Framework for Self-Evaluation in Schools*, Institute of Education, Cambridge

Elliott, J. and Adelman, C. (1974) *Innovation in Teaching and Action-research*, Norwich Centre for Applied Research in Education

Elliott, J. and Pring, R.A. (1975) *Social Education and Social Understanding*, University of London Press, London

Elliott, R. K. (1971) The concept of creativity. *Proceedings of the Philosophy of Education Society of Great Britain*

Endler, N. S., Boulter, L. R. and Osser, H. (eds) (1968) *Contemporary Issues in Developmental Psychology*, Holt, Rinehart & Winston, New York

Erlenmeyer-Kimling, L. and Jarvik, L. F. (1963) Genetics and intelligence *Science*

Esland, G. M. (1971) Teaching and Learning as the Organisation of Knowledge. In Young, M. F. D. (ed) *op. cit.*

Etzioni, A. (1961) *A Comparative Analysis of Complex Organisations* Free Press, New York

Evans, K. (1979) Pupil profiles: a rationale, *Secondary Education Journal*, Vol. 9, No. 3.

Eysenck, H. J. (1971) *Race, Intelligence and Education*, Temple Smith, London

Ferri, E. (1972) *Streaming: two years later*, NFER, Slough.

Flanders, N. A. (1970) *Analysing Teacher Behaviour*, Addison-Wesley, New York

Fletcher, R. (1984) *Education in Society: The Promethean Fire*, Penguin, Harmondsworth

Flew, A. (1954) The justification of punishment, *Philosophy*

Fontana, D. (1981) *Psychology for Teachers*, Macmillan, London

Foucault, M. (1977) The political function of the intellectual, *Radical Philosophy*, 17

Fraser, C., Bellugi, V. and Brown, R. (1963) Control of Grammar in Imitation, Comprehension and Production, *Journal of Verbal Learning and Verbal Behaviour*. In Oldfield, R. C. and Marshall, J. C. (eds) (1968) Language, Penguin, Harmondsworth

Frenkel-Brunswik, E. and Sanford, R. N. (1948) The Anti-Semitic Personality: A Research Report. In Simmel, E. (ed) (1948) *Anti-Semitism: A Social Disease*, International Universities Press, New York

Fromm, E. (1942) *The Fear of Freedom*, Routledge & Kegan Paul, London
Fuchs, E. (1968) *How Teachers Learn to Help Children Fail.* In Keddie, N. (1973) Tinker, Tailor . . . The Myth of Cultural Deprivation, Penguin, Harmondsworth
Fuller, M. (1981) *Black Girls in a London Comprehensive.* In James, A. and Jeffcoate, R. (eds) *op. cit.*
Furlong, V. (1976) Interaction Sets in the Classroom: Towards a Study of Pupil Knowledge. In Stubbs, M. and Delamont, S. (eds) *op. cit.*
Gahagan, D. M. and Gahagan, G. A. (1970) *Talk Reform,* Routledge & Kegan Paul, London
Galton, M. J. *et al* (1976) *Processes and Products of Science Teaching,* Macmillan, London
Galton, M. and Simon, B. (eds) (1980) *Progress and Performance in the Primary Classroom,* Routledge & Kegan Paul, London
Galton, M., Simon, B., and Croll, P. (1980) *Inside the Primary Classroom,* Routledge & Kegan Paul, London
Gelman, R. and Gallistrel, C. R. (1983) *The child's understanding of numbers.* In Donaldson, M. *et al* (eds) *op. cit.*
Getzels, J. W. and Jackson, P. W. (1962) *Creativity and Intelligence,* Wiley, New York
Gibbins, K. (1967) Communication aspects of women's clothes and their relation to fashion ability, *British Journal of Social and Clinical Psychology*
Giles, H. (1971) Our reactions to accent, *New Society*
Gleeson, D. and Whitty, G. (1976) *Developments in Social Studies Teaching,* Open Books, London
Goffman, E. (1959) *The Presentation of Self in Everyday Life,* Penguin, Harmondsworth
Golby, M., Greenwald, J. and West, R. (1975) *Curriculum Design* Croom Helm, London
Goldman, R. (1964) Researches in religious thinking, *Educational Research*
Goodacre, E. (1968) *Teachers and Their Pupils' Home Background,* NFER, Slough
Goodson, I. F. (1981) Becoming an Academic Subject: Patterns of Explanation and Evolution, *British Journal of Sociology,* 163-180
Goodson, I. F. (1983) *School Subjects and Curriculum Change,* Croom Helm, Beckenham
Goodson, I. F. (ed) (1984) *Social Histories of the Secondary Curriculum: Subjects for Study,* Falmer, London and Philadelphia
Goodson, I. F. and Ball, S. J. (1985) *Defining the Curriculum: Histories and Ethnographies,* Falmer, Philadelphia and London
Green, L. (1965) Should Parents Report Too? *Where?* No. 20, Spring
Grieve, R. (1980) Language Awareness in Children. In Donaldson, M. *et al* (1983) *op. cit.*

Guilford, J. P. (1968) Traits of Creativity. In Vernon, P. E. (ed) (1970) *Creativity*, Penguin, Harmondsworth

Guilford, J. P. (1950) Creativity, *American Psychologist.* (1950), Reprinted in Cashdan, A. (ed) (1972) *Personality Growth and Learning*, Longman with Oxford University Press, London

Haddon, F. A. and Lytton, H. (1968) Teaching Approach and the Development of Divergent Thinking Abilities in Primary Schools, *British Journal of Educational Psychology*

Haddon, F. A. and Lytton, H. (1971) Teaching Approach and Divergent Thinking Abilities — 4 Years On, *British Journal of Educational Psychology*

Halliday, M. A. K. (1973) *Explorations in the Functions of Language* Arnold, London

Halsey, A. H. (1974) *Government Against Poverty in School and Community.* In Wedderburn, D. Poverty, Inequality and Class Structure, Cambridge University Press, Cambridge

Hamblin, D. (1974) *The Teacher and Counselling* Blackwell, Oxford

Hamel, B. R. (1974) *Children from 5-7* Cerix Press, Rotterdam

Hamilton, D. (1976) *Curriculum Evaluation,* Open Books, London

Hamlyn, D. W. (1972) *Objectivity.* In Dearden, R. F., Hirst, P. H. and Peters, R. S. (eds) (1972) Reason, Routledge and Kegan Paul, London

Hare, R M. (1964) *Adolescents into Adults.* In Hollins , T. H. B. (ed) *op. cit.*

Hargreaves, D.H. (1967) *Social Relations in a Secondary School* Routledge and Kegan Paul, London

Hargreaves, D. H. (1972) *Interpersonal Relations in Education* Routledge and Kegan Paul, London

Harris, A., Lawn, M. and Prescott, W. (eds) (1975) *Curriculum Innovation* Croom Helm, London

Harris, C. N. (1963) Some Issues in Evaluation, *The Speech Teacher*

Hartshorne, H. and May, M. A. (1908-30) *Studies in the nature of character* Macmillan, London

Hasan, P. and Butcher, H. J. (1966) Creativity and Intelligence: a partial replication with Scottish children of Getzels' and Jackson's study, *British Journal of Psychology*

Hebb, D. O. (1949) *The Organisation of Behaviour* Wiley, New York

Hirst, P. H. (1965) *A Liberal Education and the Nature of Knowledge* In Archambault, R. D. (ed) *op. cit.*

Hirst, P. H. (1969) The Logic of the Curriculum, *Journal of Curriculum Studies*

Hirst, P. H. and Peters, R. S. (1970) *The Logic of Education,* Routledge and Kegan Paul, London

Hirst, P. H. (1975) The Curriculum and its Objectives — a defence of piecemeal national planning, in *Studies in Education 2*, The Curriculum — The Doris Lee Lectures, University of London Press, London

Hoghughi, M. (1979) The Aycliffe Token Economy, *British Journal of Criminology*

Hollins, T. H. B. (ed) (1964) *Aims in Education; the Philosophic Approach*, Manchester University Press, Manchester

Holt, J. (1964) *How Children Fail*, Penguin, Harmondsworth

Holt, M. (1978) *The Common Curriculum: Its Structure and Style in the Comprehensive School*, Routledge and Kegan Paul, London

Holt, M. (1980) *Schools and Curriculum Change*, McGraw Hill, Maidenhead

Holt, M. (1982) Whole Curriculum Planning in Schools: Some Research Implications. *Journal of Curriculum Studies*. 14,3.

Hooper, R. (ed)(1971) *The Curriculum: Context, design and development*, Oliver & Boyd, Edinburgh with Oxford University Press

Hudson, L. (1966) *Contrary Imaginations*, Penguin, Harmondsworth

Hunt, J. McV. (1960) *Using intrinsic motivation to teach young children*. In Cashdan, A. and Whitehead, J. (eds) *op. cit.*

Hymes, D. (1970) On Communicative Competence. Reprinted V. Lee, (ed) *op. cit.*

Inhelder, B. and Piaget, J. (1958) *The Growth of Logical Thinking from Childhood to Adolescence*, Basic Books, New York

Jackson, B. (1964) *Streaming: an education system in miniature* Routledge and Kegan Paul, London

Jackson, B. and Marsden, I. (1962) *Education and the working class* Routledge and Kegan Paul, London

Jackson, P. W. and Messick, S. (1965) The Person, The Product and the Response: conceptual problems in the assessment of creativity, *British Journal of Educational Psychology*

Jackson, P. W. (1971) Those bad school reports, *Where?* No. 54 February

Jahoda, G. (1963) The development of children's ideas about country and nationality, *British Journal of Educational Psychology*

James, A. and Jeffcoate, R. (eds)(1981) *The School in the Multicultural Society*, Harper and Row, London

Jeffcoate, R. (1981) *Ethnic minorities and education*, Harper & Row, London

Jensen, A. R. (1969) How much can we boost I. Q. and scholastic achievement? *Harvard Educational Review*. In Eysenck, H. J. (1971) *op. cit.*

Jones, J. (1966) Social class and the under-5s, *New Society*

Jones, R. M. (1972) *Fantasy and feeling in education*, Penguin, Harmondsworth

Kagan, J. (1966) Conceptual impulsivity and inductive reasoning, *Child Development*, Vol. 37

Kagan, J. *et al* (1967) *Child development and personality*, Harper & Row, New York

Kay, W. (1968) *Moral Development*, Allen & Unwin, London

Keddie, N. (1971) *Classroom Knowledge*. In Young, M. F. D. (ed) *op. cit.*

Kelley, H. H. (1950) The warm-cold variable in first impressions of persons, *Journal of Personality*

Kellmer-Pringle, M. L. and Edwards, J. B. (1964) Some moral concepts and judgments of junior school children, *Journal of Social and Clinical Psychology*

Kelly, A. V. (1975) *Case Studies in Mixed Ability Teaching* Harper & Row, London

Kelly, A. V. (1978) *Mixed-Ability Grouping: Theory and Practice,* 2nd edition, Harper & Row, London

Kelly, A. V. (1980) *Curriculum Context* Harper & Row, London

Kelly, A. V. (1981) Research and the primary curriculum, *Journal of Curriculum Studies* 13,3

Kelly, A. V. (1982a) *The Curriculum: Theory and Practice,* Harper & Row, London

Kelly, A. V. (1982b) Mixed Emotions *Journal of Curriculum Studies,* 14,3

Kelly, A. V. (1984) *Microcomputers and the Curriculum,* Harper & Row, London

Kelly, A. V. (1986) *Knowledge and Curriculum Planning,* Harper & Row, London

Kelly, G. A. (1955) *The Psychology of Personal Constructs,* Norton, New York

Kerr, J. F. (ed) (1968) *Changing the Curriculum,* University of London Press, London

Klein, S. S. (1971) Student influence on teacher behaviour, *American Education Research Journal*

Kohlberg, L. M. (1966) Moral education in the schools, *School Review*

Labov, W. (1969) *The logic of non-standard English.* In Cashdan, A. and Grugeon, E. (eds) (1972) *op. cit*

Lacey, C. (1970) *Hightown Grammar: the school as a social system,* Manchester University Press, Manchester

Lawton, D. (1968a) Social science in schools, *New Society,* 25

Lawton, D. (1968b) *Social class, language and education,* Routledge and Kegan Paul, London

Lawton, D. (1973) *Social change, educational theory and curriculum planning,* London University Press, London

Lawton, D. (1975) *Class, culture and the curriculum,* Routledge and Kegan Paul, London

Lee, V. (ed) (1979) *Language development,* Croom Helm with Oxford University Press, London and Oxford

Lewin, K., Lippitt, R. and White, R. K. (1939) Patterns of aggressive behaviour in experimentally cleared social climates, *Journal of Social Psychology*

Linguistic Minorities Project, (1983) *Linguistic minorities in England,* Routledge and Kegan Paul, London

Little, A. and Westergaard, J. (1964) The trend of class differentials in educational opportunity in England and Wales, *British Journal of Sociology*

Lock, A. and Pisher, E. (1984) *Language development,* Croom Helm with Oxford University Press, London and Oxford

Locke, J. *Second treatise on civil government,* paragraph 6

Loukes, H., Wilson, J. and Cowell, B. (1983) *Education: An Introduction* Robertson, Oxford

Lucas, J. R. (1965) Against equality, *Philosophy*

Luchins, A. S. (1959) *Primary-recency in impression formation in order of presentation in persuasion,* Yale University Press, New Haven

Luria, A. R. (1959) The directive function of speech in development and dissolution, *Word.* In Cashdan, A. and Grugeon, E. (eds) (1972) *op. cit.*

Luria, A. R. (1961) *The role of speech in the regulation of normal and abnormal behaviour,* Pergamon Press, Oxford

Macdonald, B. (1973) *Humanities Curriculum Project,* Schools Council, *op. cit.*

MacDonald, B. (1975) *Evaluation and control of education.* In Tawney D. (ed) (1975) *op. cit*

MacDonald, B. and Walker, R. (1976) *Changing the curriculum,* Open Books, London

Macintosh, H. G. (1984) Assessing and examining: policies, practices and alternatives. In Skilbeck, M. (ed) (1984) *Readings in school-based curriculum development,* Harper & Row, London

MacIntyre, A. and Nowell-Smith, P. H. (1970) Purpose and intelligent action, *Proceedings of the Aristotelian Society,* Supplement

Mahon, Y. P. (1983) How Alice's chin really came to be pressed against her foot: sexist processes of interaction in a mixed sex classroom, *Women's Studies International Forum*

Marland, M. (1977) *Language across the curriculum,* Heinemann, London

McClelland, D. C. *et al* (1953) *The achievement motive,* Appleton-Century-Crofts, New York

McClelland, D. C. (1972) What is the effect of achievement motivation training in the schools? *Teachers College Record,* Vol. 74

McClelland, D. C., Atkinson, J. W., Clark, R. A. and Lowell, E. L. (eds) (1976) *The achievement motive,* Irvington Publishers, New York

McGarrigle, J., Grieve, R. and Hughes, M. (1983) Interpreting inclusion: a contribution to the study of the child's cognitive and intellectual development. In Donaldson, M. *et al* (eds) *op. cit.*

McIntyre, D., Morrison, A. and Sutherland, J. (1966) Social and educational variables relating to teachers' assessment of primary school children, *British Journal of Educational Psychology*

McNeill, D. (1966) The creation of language, *Discovery.* Reprinted in Cashdan, A. and Grugeon, E. (eds) (1972) *op. cit.*

McPhail, P., Ungoed-Thomas, J. R. and Chapman, H. (1972) *Moral education in the secondary school*, Longman, London

Mead, G. H. see Blumer, H. (1965) Social implications of the thoughts of G. H. Mead, *American Journal of Sociology*

Merson, W. W. and Campbell, R. J. (1974) Community education: instruction for inequality, *Education for Teaching*

Midwinter, E. (1972) *Priority Education*, Penguin, Harmondsworth

Mill, J. S. *On Liberty*

Miller, J. (1983) *Many Voices*, Routledge & Kegan Paul, London

Miller, N. E. and Dollard, J. (1941) *Social Learning and Imitation*, Yale University Press, New Haven

Milner, D. (1975) *Children and Race*, Penguin, Harmondsworth

Modgil, S. and Modgil, C. (eds) (1981) *Piaget: Controversy and Consensus*, Praeger, Eastbourne

Moreno, J. L. (1934) Who Shall Survive? *Washington, Nervous and Mental Disease Monograph, Series* No. 58

Musgrove, F. (1973) Power and the Integrated Curriculum, *Journal of Curriculum Studies*

Musgrove, F. and Taylor, P. H. (1969) *Society and the Teacher's Role*, Routledge and Kegan Paul, London

Nash, R. (1973) *Classrooms Observed*, Routledge and Kegan Paul, London

Nash, R. (1974) Pupils' Expectations of Their Teachers, *Research in Education*

Natadze, R. G. (1963) The Mastery of Scientific Concepts in School. In Simon, B. and J. (eds) *Educational Psychology in the USSR*, Routledge and Kegan Paul, London

Newsom, J. (1948) *The Education of Girls*, Faber, London

Nixon, J. (1981) Towards a Supportive Framework for Teachers in Research, *Curriculum* 2, 1

Observer, November 5, 1968

O'Connor, D. J. (1957) *An Introduction to the Philosophy of Education*, Routledge and Kegan Paul, London

Open University (1976) *Personality & Learning* E201 Block 5: Cognitive Styles, Floyd, A.; Block 6: Intelligence and Creativity, Lee, V. and Webberley, R.

Opie, I. and Opie, P. (1959) *Languages and the Tone of School Children*, Clarendon Press, Oxford

Owen Cole, W. (1981) World Religions in the Multi-Faith School. In James, A. and Jeffcoate, R. (eds) (1981) *op. cit.*

Palfrey, C. F. (1973) Headteachers' Expectations and Their Pupils' Self Concepts, *Educational Research*

Parlett, M. and Hamilton, D. (1985) *Evaluation and Illumination*. In Tawney, D. (ed) (1975) *op. cit.*

Parry, M. (1975) *Preschool Education*, Macmillan, London

Parry, M. and Archer, H. (1975) *Two to Five*, Macmillan, London

Pask, and Scott (1971) referred to in Goldstein, K. M. and Blackman, S. (1978) *Cognitive Style*, Wiley, New York

Peel, E. A. (1972) Understanding School Material, *Educational Review*

Peters, R. S. (1959) *Authority, Responsibility and Education*, Allen and Unwin, London

Peters, R.S. (1965) *Education as Invitiation*. In Archambault, R.D. (ed) *op.cit.*

Peters, R. S. (1966) *Ethics and Education*, Allen & Unwin, London

Phenix, P. H. (1964) *Realms of Meaning*, McGraw-Hill, New York

Piaget, J. (1960) *The Moral Judgment of the Child* (1932) Routledge and Kegan Paul, London

Piaget, J. (1950) *The Psychology of Intelligence*, Harcourt Brace, New York

Piaget, J. (1952) *The Origins of Intelligence in Children*, International Universities Press, New York

Piaget, J. (1959) *Language and Thought of the Child* 2nd edition, Routledge and Kegan Paul, London

Plato, *Republic*

Pollard, A. (1985) *The Social World of the Primary School*, Holt, Rinehart & Winston, Eastbourne

Popper, K. R. (1945) *The Open Society and Its Enemies*, Routledge and Kegan Paul, London

Popper, K. R. (1957) *The Poverty of Historicism*, Routledge and Kegan Paul, London

Price-Williams, D. R., Gordon, W. and Ramirez, R. M. (1969) Skill and Conservation, *Developmental Psychology*, Vol. 1

Pring, R. A. (1971) Bloom's Taxonomy: A Philosophical Critique, *Cambridge Journal of Education*

Pring, R. A. (1973) Objectives and Innovation: The Irrelevance of Theory, *Education Review*, London

Pring, R. A. (1975) Socialisation as an Aim of Education. In Elliott, J. and Pring, R. A. (1975) *op. cit.*

Quinton, A. M. (1963) On Punishment. In Laslett, P. (ed) (1963) *Philosophy, Politics and Society* 1st Series, Blackwell, Oxford

Raleigh, M. and Miller, J. (1981) *The Languages Book*, ILEA, English Centre

Raven, J. (1982) Language in its Social Context and the Role of Educational Home Visitors. In Davies, A. (ed) (1982) *op. cit.*

Richards, C. (1973) Third thoughts on discovery, *Educational Review*

Richmond, J. (1982) *The Resources of Classroom Language*, Arnold, London

Riessman, F. (1962) *The Culturally Deprived Child*, Harper & Row, New York

Rist, R. C. (1979) Student Social Class and Teacher Expectations: the self-fulfilling prophecy in ghetto education, *Harvard Education Review*

Robertson, I. (1980) *Language Across the Curriculum: Four Case Studies*, Schools Council Working Paper No. 67, Methuen, London

Robinson, W. P. and Rackstraw, S. J. (1967) Variations in Mothers' Answers to Children's Questions as a Function of Social Class, Verbal Intelligence Test Scores and Sex, *Sociology*

Rosen, H. (1967) The Language of Text-Books. In Britton, J. (ed) (1967) *Talking and Writing*, Methuen, London

Rosen, H. (1972) *Language and Class: A Critical Look at the Theories of Basil Bernstein*, Falling Wall Press, Bristol

Rosen, H. (1982) *The Language Monitors*, Bedford Way Papers No. 11, Institute of Education, London

Rosen, H. and Burgess, T. (1980) *Languages and Dialects of London School Children: An Investigation*, Ward Lock, London

Rosen, H. and Rosen, C. (1973) *The Language of Primary School Children*, Penguin, Harmondsworth

Rosenthal, R. and Jacobson, L. (1968) *Pygmalion in the Classroom*, Holt, Rinehart & Winston, New York

Rousseau, J. J. *Emile*

Roussel, G. D. (1973) The Open Report and Its History, *Comprehensive Education* No. 25

Ryan, A. (1965) Freedom, *Philosophy*

Ryle, G. (1960) *Concept of Mind*, Hutchinson, London

Sarah, E. (1980) Teachers and Students in the Classroom: an Examination of Classroom Interaction. In Spender, D. and Sarah, E (eds) (1980) *op. cit.*

Sartre, J. P. (1957) *Being and Nothingness*, Methuen, London

Schaffer, H. R. (ed) (1977) *Studies in Mother-infant Interaction*, Academic Press, London

Schofield, A. J. (1977) *Pastoral Care and the Curriculum of a Comprehensive School*, unpublished MA dissertation, University of London

Schon, D. A. (1971) *Beyond the Stable State*, Temple-Smith, London

Schools Council, (1965) *Raising the School Leaving Age*, Working Paper No. 2, HMSO, London

Schools Council, (1967) *Society and the Young School Leaver*, Working Paper No. 11, HMSO, London

Schools Council, (1970) *Crossed with Adversity*, Working Paper No. 27, Evans/Methuen, London

Schools Council, (1970) *The Humanities Project: An Introduction*, Heinemann, London

Schools Council, (1973) *Education in Curriculum Development: Twelve Case Studies*, Schools Council Research Studies, Macmillan, London

Schools Council, (1974) *Social Education: An Experiment in Four Secondary Schools*, Working Paper No. 51, Evans/Methuen, London

Schools Council, *Talking, Writing and Learning*, Working Paper No. 59, Methuen, London

Schools Council, (1980) *Learning Through Science: Formulating a School Policy*, MacDonald, London

Schools Council, *Learning through Talking 11-16*, Working Paper No. 64, Methuen, London

Schutz, A. (1962) *Collected Papers*, Vol. 1, Nijhoff

Schwebel, M. (1975) Journal Operations in First-Year College Students, *Journal of Psychology*, Vol. 91

Scottish Council for Research in Education, (1977) *Pupils in Profile*, Hodder & Stoughton, London

Secord, B. (1958) *The Role of Facial Features in Interpersonal Perception*. In Taguiri, R. and Petrullo, L. (eds) *Person Perception and Interpersonal Behaviour*, Stanford University Press, Stanford

Shipman, M. (1971) Curriculum for Inequality? In Hooper, R. (ed) (1971) *op. cit.*

Shipman, M. (1972) Contrasting Views of a Curriculum Project, *Journal of Curriculum Studies*

Simon, B. and Willcocks, J. (1981) *Research and Practice in the Primary Classroom*, Routledge and Kegan Paul, London

Sinclair, A., Jarvella, R. J. and Levelt, W. J. M. (eds) (1973) *The Child's Conception of Language*, Springer, Berlin

Skinner, B. F. (1957) *Verbal Behaviour*, Appleton-Century Crofts, New York

Skinner, B. F. (1968) *The Technology of Teaching*, Appleton-Century Crofts

Slobin, D. (1978) *A Case Study of Early Language Awareness*. In Sinclair, A. *et al* (eds) (1973) *op. cit.*

Smith, F. (1982) *Writing and the Writer*, Heinemann, London

Snow, C. E. (1977) The Development of Conversation Between Mother and Babies, *Journal of Child Language*, Vol. 4

Sockett, H. (1975) Aims and Objectives in a Social Education Curriculum. In Elliott, J. and Pring, R. (1975) *op. cit.*

Sockett, H. (1976) *Designing the Curriculum*, Open Books, London

Spender, D. (1978) The facts of life: sex differentiated knowledge in the English classroom. In *English in Education* Vol. 12 no. 3

Spender, D. (1980) Talking In Class. In Spender, D. and Sarah, E. (eds) (1980) *op. cit.*

Spender, D. and Sarah, E. (1980) *Learning to Lose: Sexism in Education*, The Women's Press, London

Stake, R. (1972) *Analysis and Portrayal*. Paper originally written for AERA Annual Meeting Presentation. Republished as Responsive Education (1974)

in *New Trends in Education*, Institute of Education, University of Goteborg, No. 55

Stanworth, M. (1980) *Gender and Schooling: A Study of Sexual Divisions in the Classroom*, WRRC, London

Stendler, C. B., Damrin, D. and Haines, A. C. (1951) Studies in Cooperation and Competition, *Journal of Genetic Psychology* Vol. 21

Stenhouse, L. (1970) Some Limitations of the Use of Objectives in Curriculum Research and Planning, *Pedagogica Europaea*

Stenhouse, L. (1975) *An Introduction to Curriculum Research and Development*, Heinemann, London

Stoch, M. B. (1967) The Effect of Undernutrition During Infancy on Subsequent Brain Growth and Intellectual Development, *South African Medical Journal*

Stone, M. (1981) *The Education of the Black Child in Britain*, Fontana, London

Stones, E. (1979) *Psychopedogogy*, Methuen, London

Stott, D. H. (1966) Commentary on The Genetic Determination of Differences in Intelligence; A Study of Monozygotic Twins Reared Together and Apart, *British Journal of Psychology*

Stott, D. H. and Albin, J. B. (1975) Confirmation of a General Factor of Effectiveness Motivation by Individual Tests, *British Journal of Educational Psychology*

Stott, D. H. and Sharp, J. *Effectiveness Motivation Scale* publication pending

Strivens, J. (1981) The Use of Behaviour Modification in Special Education: A Critique. In Barton, L. and Tomlinson, S. (eds) (1981) *op. cit.*

Strongman, K. T. and Hart, C. J. (1968) Stereotyped Reactions to Body Build, *Psychological Reports*

Stubbs, M. (1975) Teaching and Talking. In Chanan, G and Delamont, S. (eds) *op. cit.*

Stubbs, M. (1976) *Language, Schools and Classrooms*, Methuen, London

Stubbs, M. (1976) Keeping in Touch: Some Functions of Teacher Talk, In Stubbs, M. and Delamont, S. (eds) (1976) *op. cit.*

Stubbs, M. and Delamont, S. (eds) (1976) *Explorations in Classroom Observation*, Wiley, New York

Sugarman, N. (1973) *The School and Moral Development*, Croom Helm, London

Tamburrini, J. (1981) Some educational implications of Piaget's Theory. In S. Modgil and C. Modgil (eds) *op. cit.*

Tawney D. (1973) Evaluation and curriculum development. In Schools Council, (1973) *op. cit.*

Tawney, D. (ed) (1975) *Curriculum Evaluation Today: Trends and Implications*, Schools Council Research Studies, Macmillan, London

Taylor, P. H. (1962) Children's evaluations of the characteristics of the good teacher. *British Journal of Educational Psychology*

Taylor, P. H. (1970) Curriculum Planning for Compensatory Education: A suggested procedure, Schools Council, London

Thibaut, J. W. and Riecken, A. W. (1955) Some determinants and consequences of the perception of social causality, *Journal of Personality*

Tizard, B. and Hughes M. (1984) *Young Children Learning Language*, Fontana, London

Torbe, M. (1976) *Language Across the Curriculum: Guidelines for School*, N.A.T.E. with Ward Lock, London

Torbe, M. (1980) *Language Policies in Action*, Ward Lock, London

Torrance, E. P. (1964) Education and creativity. In O. W. Taylor (ed) *Creativity, progress and potential*, McGraw-Hill, New York

Torrance, E. P. (1967) Give the devil his dues. In J. C. Gowan *et al* (eds) *Creativity: its Educational Implications*, Wiley, New York

Tough, J. (1973) *Focus on Meaning*, Allen & Unwin, London

Tough, J. (1976) *Listening to Children Talking*, Ward Lock, London

Tough, J. (1977) *The Development of Meaning*, Allen & Unwin, London

Tough, J. (1977) *Talking and Learning*, Ward Lock, London

Trevarthen, C. (1977) Descriptive analyses of infant communicative behaviour. In H. G. Schaffer (ed) *op. cit.*

Trudgill, P. (1983) *On Dialect*, Blackwell, Oxford

Trudgill, P. (ed) (1984) *Language in the British Isles*, Cambridge University Press, Cambridge

Tyler, R. W. (1949) *Basic Principles of Curriculum and Instruction*, University of Chicago Press, Chicago

Tyler, V. O. and Brown, G. D. (1968) Token reinforcement of academic performance with institutional delinquent boys, *Journal of Educational Psychology*

Verma, G. K. and Beard, R. M. (1981) *What is Educational Research?* Gower, Aldershot

Vernon, P. E. (1969) *Intelligence and Cultural Environment*, Methuen, London

Vernon, P. E. (1979) *Intelligence — Heredity and Environment*, Freeman, San Francisco

Vetta, A. (1980) Concepts and issues in the I. Q. debate, *Bulletin of the British Psychological Society*, Vol. 33

Vigotsky, L. (1962) *Thought and Language*, M.I.T. Press, Cambridge, Mass.

Walker, D. F. (1973) What Curriculum Research? *Journal of Curriculum Studies*, 5, 1

Walker, R. (1975) *A Guide to Classroom Observation* Methuen, London

Walker, R. (1983) Three Good Reasons for Not Doing Case Studies in Curriculum Research *Journal of Curriculum Studies* 15, 2

Walker, R. and Adelman, C. (1976) *Strawberries.* In Stubbs, M. and Delamont, S. (eds) (1976) *op. cit.*

Walker, R. and Goodson, I. (1977) *Humour in the Classroom.* In Woods, P. and Hammersley, M. (1977) *op. cit.*

Watson, P. (1972) Can Racial Discrimination Affect I.Q? In Richardson, D. *et al* (eds) Race, Culture and Intelligence, Penguin, Harmondsworth

Weber, M. (1947) *Theory of Social and Economic Organisation,* Oxford University Press, London

Wechsler, D. (1944) The Measurement of Adult Intelligence Testing and the Theory of Intelligence, *British Journal of Educational Psychology*

Weldon, T. D. (1953) *The Vocabulary of Politics,* Penguin, Harmondsworth

Wells, G. (1977) Language Use and Educational Succcess: An Empirical Response to Joan Tough's 'The Development of Meaning', *Research in Education* Vol. 17

Wells, G. (1981) Some Antecedents of Early Educational Attainment, *British Journal of Social Education,* Vol. 2

Wells, G. (1982a) Influences of the Home in Language Development. In Davies, A. (ed) (1982) *op. cit.*

Wells, G. (1982b) *Language, learning and education,* Bristol Centre for the Study of Language and Communication

Wells, G. (1982c) Story Reading and the Development of Symbolic Skills, *Australian Journal of Reading*

Wells, G. (1983a) Language, Learning and the Curriculum, *Education 3-13*

Wells, G. (1983b) Talking with Children: The Complementary Voice of Parents and Teachers In Donaldson, M. *et al* (1983) *op. cit.*

Weiner, B. (1977) An Attributional Approach for Educational Psychology. In Schulman, L. (ed) (1977) *Review of Research in Education,* Peacock, Drasca

Wier, G. (1962) *Language in the Crib,* Moulton, The Hague

Werthman, C. (1963) Delinquents in Schools. In Cosin, B. *et al* (eds) (1971) *op. cit.*

West, E. G. (1965) Liberty and Education: John Stuart Mill's Dilemma, *Philosophy*

White, J. P. (1968) Instruction in Obedience, *New Society*

White, J. P. (1973) *Towards A Compulsory Curriculum,* Routledge & Kegan Paul, London

White, J. P. (1971) The Concept of Curriculum Evaluation, *Journal of Curriculum Studies*

White, R. K. and Lippitt, R. (1960) *Autocracy and Democracy: An Experimental Enquiry* Harper & Row, New York

Whitehead, A. N. (1932) *The Aims of Education,* Williams and Norgate

Whitehead, M. (1983) Language Developments in the Primary Curriculum. In Blenkin, G. M. and Kelly, A. V. (eds) (1983) *op. cit.*

Wiley, D. E. (1970) Design and Analysis of Evaluation Studies. In Wittrock, M. C. and Wiley, D. E. (eds) *op. cit.*

Williams, R. (1958) *Culture and Society 1780-1950* Chatto and Windus, London

Williams, W. and Rennie, J. (1972) Social Education. In Rubinstein, D. and Stoneman, C. (eds) *Education for Democracy* 2nd edition, Penguin, Harmondsworth

Wilson, J. (1964) *Education and Indoctrination.* In Hollins, T. H. B. (ed) *op. cit.*

Wilson, J. (1973) *Practical Problems in Moral Education,* Heinemann, London

Wilson, J., Williams, N. and Sugarman, B. (1967) *Introduction to Moral Education,* Penguin, Harmondsworth

Wilson, P. S. (1971) *Interest and Discipline in Education* Routledge & Kegan Paul, London

Wiseman, S. (ed) (1961) *Examinations and English Education,* Manchester University Press, Manchester

Winterbottom, M. R. (1958) The Relating of the Need for Achievement to Learning Experiences in Independence and Mastery. In Atkinson, J. W. (ed) *Motives in Fantasy, Action and Society,* Van Nostrand Reinhold, New York

Wittgenstein, L. (1953) *Philosophical Investigations,* Blackwell, Oxford

Wittrock, M. C. and Wiley D. E. (1970) *The Evaluation of Instruction: Issues and Problems* Holt, Rinehart & Winston, New York

Woods, P. (1975) Showing Them Up in Secondary School. In Chanan, G. and Delamont, S. (eds) (1975) *op. cit.*

Woods, P. (1976) Teaching for Survival. In Woods, P. and Hammersley, M. (eds) *op. cit.*

Woods, P. and Hammersley, M. (eds) (1977) *School Experience,* Croom Helm, London

Wragg, E. C. (1973) A Study of Student Teachers in the Classroom. In Chanan, G. and Delamont, S. (eds) (1975) *op. cit.*

Yates, A. and Pidgeon, D. (1957) *Admission to Grammar Schools,* Newnes

Young, M. F. D. (ed) (1971) *Knowledge and control,* Collier Macmillan, New York

Official publications referred to in the text

Board of Education 1926 Hadow Report *The Education of the Adolescent* HMSO, London

Board of Education 1931 Hadow Report *Primary Education,* HMSO, London

Board of Education 1938 Spens Report *Secondary Education with Special Reference to Grammar Schools* HMSO, London

Board of Education 1943 Norwood Report *Curriculum and Examinations in Secondary Schools,* HMSO, London

Central Advisory Council for Education 1954 *Early Leaving* HMSO, London
Central Advisory Council for Education 1959 Crowther Report *15 to 18*, HMSO, London
Central Advisory Council in Education 1963 Newsom Report *Half Our Future* HMSO, London
Central Advisory Council for Education 1967 Plowden Report *Children and Their Primary Schools*, HMSO, London
Department of Education and Science 1975 Bullock Report *A Language for Life* HMSO, London
Department of Education and Science 1977a *Curriculum 11-16*, HMSO, London
Department of Education and Science 1977b Taylor Report *A New Partnership for Our Schools*, HMSO, London
Department of Education and Science 1978a *Primary Education in England, A Survey by HM Inspectors of Schools*, HMSO, London
Department of Education and Science and the Welsh Office 1977c *Education in Schools: A Consultative Document* HMSO, London
Department of Education and Science 1979 *Aspects of Secondary Education in England: A Survey by HM Inspectors of Schools* HMSO, London
Department of Education and Science 1980a *A View of the Curriculum. HMI Series Matters for Discussion No. 11*, HMSO, London
Department of Education 1980b *A Framework for the School Curriculum*, HMSO, London
Department of Education and Science 1981a *Curriculum 11-16: A Review of Progress*, HMSO, London
Department of Education and Science 1981b *The School Curriculum*, HMSO, London
Department of Education and Science 1982 *Bullock Revisited: A Discussion Document by HMI*, HMSO, London
Department of Education and Science 1982 *Education 5 to 9: An Illustrative Survey of 80 First Schools in England and Wales*, HMSO, London
Department of Education 1983a *9-13 Middle Schools, An illustrative survey*, HMSO, London
Department of Education and Science 1983b *Curriculum 11-16. Towards a Statement of Entitlement. Curricular Reappraisal in Action*, HMSO, London
Department of Education and Science 1983c *Teaching Quality*, Cmnd 8836 HMSO, London
Department of Education and Science 1985 *The Curriculum from 5 to 16, Curriculum Matters 2*, HMSO, London
Inner London Education Committee 1976 *Report of the Public Enquiry into Teaching, Organisation and Management of William Tyndale Junior and Infant Schools*, The Auld Report, Inner London Education Authority, London

INDEX OF NAMES

INDEX OF SUBJECT